Telling Tales About Men

MANCHESTER
1824

Manchester University Press

Telling Tales About Men

Conceptions of Conscientious Objectors to
Military Service During the First World War

LOIS S. BIBBINGS

Manchester
University Press

Manchester and New York

distributed in the United States exclusively by Palgrave Macmillan

The right of Lois S. Bibbings to be identified as the author of this work has been asserted by her in accordance with the Copyright, Designs and Patents Act 1988.

Published by Manchester University Press
Oxford Road, Manchester M13 9NR, UK
and Room 400, 175 Fifth Avenue, New York, NY 10010, USA
www.manchesteruniversitypress.co.uk

Distributed in the United States exclusively by
Palgrave Macmillan, 175 Fifth Avenue, New York,
NY 10010, USA

Distributed in Canada exclusively by
UBC Press, University of British Columbia, 2029 West Mall,
Vancouver, BC, Canada V6T 1Z2

British Library Cataloguing-in-Publication Data
A catalogue record for this book is available from the British Library

Library of Congress Cataloging-in-Publication Data applied for

ISBN 978 0 7190 6922 2   hardback

First published 2009

The publisher has no responsibility for the persistence or accuracy of URLs for any external or third-party internet websites referred to in this book, and does not guarantee that any content on such websites is, or will remain, accurate or appropriate.

Typeset in Sabon
by Servis Filmsetting Ltd, Stockport, Cheshire
Printed in Great Britain
by CPI Antony Rowe, Chippenham, Wiltshire

Contents

Acknowledgements

Given that I first began research on conscientious objection and objectors in the First World War nearly twenty years ago, there are many to thank. Doubtless I have unwittingly omitted to mention some of those who helped along the way, so I begin with a general vote of thanks and apology to those who do not figure here but should.

This work began as a postgraduate thesis in the area of socio-legal studies. It was supervised by Phil Thomas and examined by Chrisje Brants and Phil Fennel, all of whose support has remained invaluable. For the idea to revisit this work through the lens of gender I am, as in so many things, indebted to Simon Flynn, who also helped inspire the approach adopted here. Those who have read and commented upon (the numerous) incarnations this project has taken deserve special acknowledgement: Graham Bibbings, Alastair V. Campbell, Geraldine Hastings, Richard Huxtable, Genevieve Liveley, Morag McDermont, Simon Wilson, Richard Young. And for encouraging me to actually let go of the manuscript special thanks go to Simon Wilson and Petra Wilson.

There are other individual votes of thanks: my parents consented to be interviewed, approved the text and, along with Anne Bibbings and Betty Lee, provided the family photos which appear within these pages; Alastair V. Campbell discussed his recollections about his father, conscientious objector William Campbell, and (with the agreement of his brother) allowed me to use the latter's letter about his feelings towards the war. Similarly, Edward Stanton gave me access to his father Harry E. Stanton's papers. Also, thanks go to Nicholas Hiley for supplying two of the cartoons reproduced here ('THE CONSCIENTIOUS OBJECTOR AT THE FRONT' and 'CONSCIENTIOUS OBJECTORS!' by 'A.E.') and to Roy Light who furnished a copy of the Richardson Report on the behaviour and treatment of objectors in Wandsworth Prison (*Inquiry Held into the Allegations Made Against the Acting Governor of Wandsworth Prison*, Cmd. 131, 1919).

Over the years I have given papers on the topic of conscientious objection at a number of staff seminars and conferences. In particular, I am grateful to those who contributed at events at Bath Spa, Bristol, Cardiff, Kent, Queen's Belfast and Queen Mary Universities. The research that led to this book has been conducted in a variety of libraries and records offices including: the Friends Library (London); the British Library and British Library Newspapers; the Imperial War Museum; the National Archives; as well as a collection of local records offices and university libraries. I should like to thank staff for their assistance and for making the process so enjoyable.

In addition, this project would not have been possible without the support of colleagues, past and present, at the University of Bristol as well as the School of Law's study leave policy. I am also grateful to the anonymous readers who commented on this text along with staff at Manchester University Press for their advice, support and patience.

I owe an immense amount to my friends who have been amazingly supportive despite my tendencies towards obsessive working, continual rewrites and (not least) epistemological angst. Their backing and (seeming) willingness to listen to me wittering on about, amongst other things, objection and gender theory has been hugely appreciated. In particular, and in addition to those mentioned above, the following need to know how great I think they are: Linda and Alex James; Robyn Martin and family; Wambui Mwangi; Christina Pantazis; Caitlin and Ciaran Wilson. I would also like to thank the Widening Participation 'crew' (past and present) at Bristol for their continued faith, commitment and sense of fun (you know who you are). Finally, my family have both supported and been a part of this project. So my thanks go to my parents, Suzanne and Graham, as well as Grace, Ian and Louise. Last but by no means least, John and Lottie also inspired this book and briefly appear within its pages.

The Bunkhouse
Mullaghmore
County Sligo

Illustrations

Part I

About *Telling Tales*

Introduction: telling tales and constructing conscientious objectors

Telling Tales About Men explores the ways in which conscientious objectors to compulsory military service during the First World War were viewed, portrayed and treated in England.[1] It considers these men's experiences, their beliefs, perceptions and actions. In doing so, the book provides a new socio-cultural approach to this area and one which also takes an innovative approach to writing about the past.

Objectors (who were also known as COs or by the often more derogatory soubriquet 'conchies') refused to enlist voluntarily in the military, and subsequently resisted conscription on the grounds of 'conscience'. Thus, these were men who objected to the military on some principled grounds and they usually did so from the outset. Although the distinction is by no means entirely clear, they can, therefore, be contrasted with people like Siegfried Sassoon who protested against the conduct of the war, or those who were shot for desertion or supposed cowardice (sometimes as a result of shell-shock), and others who received treatment from early psychiatry for so-called 'soldier's heart'.[2]

COs were a diverse group with vastly different backgrounds, views and politics. 'Conscience' could cover a whole range of motivations including Christians, who took the commandment prohibiting killing to mean that they could take no part in either the military or the war effort and men who embraced the ideals of international socialism, refusing to fight their fellow workers. Others would not accept the authority of the state to direct their actions, resisting any form of legal compulsion, including conscription. The strategies adopted by objectors in the expression of their beliefs also varied considerably; some practised passive resistance in relation to military service but were keen to be obedient in all other regards, whilst others were determined to cause the maximum amount of trouble for the state.

Not least because of the range of stances and actions taken by objectors, a variety of perspectives relating to these men and their conduct were in evidence both during the war years and after. These drew upon ideas about such things as manliness, nationality, race, sexuality, Christianity and criminality. It is these and other notions which *Telling Tales* focuses upon. Thus, Chapters 1 to 6 below each configure a particular cluster of ideas that were associated with objectors during the war, including their conception as cowardly, unmanly, deviant, conscientious, devout and heroic. At the same time late twentieth- and early twenty-first-century theories, methods and scholarship from pertinent fields assist the analysis.[3] So, for instance, the consideration of objectors in terms of First World War views about manliness is informed by more recent writings about gender, masculinities and sexualities. Similarly, the exploration of the supposed criminality of objectors is based upon attitudes present during the conflict but also utilises subsequent work on law, criminal justice and criminology.

As a consequence of this approach, the book's structure, its use of sources and theory as well as its socio-cultural focus are distinctive – both in terms of other history texts and other writings about COs. In particular, its novel configuration around collections of ideas about objectors[4] results in the production of a number of tales about these men; each of the main chapters, through examining different notions of the objector, effectively represents a version of this narrative, with a discrete thematic focus and tone.

The remainder of this Introduction expands upon the above, concluding with a brief overview of the chapters. Or, to put it another way, the text in this chapter represents one telling of the story of how this book came about, including discussion of why it takes the form it does and how it relates to and is shaped by existing scholarship in relevant fields.

Telling Tales and writing history(ies)

In part, the origins of this book lie in an interest in resistance, protest and campaign movements, along with state and societal responses to them. Over time this coalesced around war resistance and, in particular, conscientious objection to military service, focusing upon the

First World War. Initially this work explored legal and societal reactions to this phenomenon, looking not only at the law and policies adopted to deal with such men but also their treatment in practice. As time passed, the analysis broadened out to include a wider frame, both in terms of the sources considered and the ideas incorporated.[5] Thus, items referenced within this volume include legal material, official documents, anti-conscription organisations' papers, newspapers, literature, cartoons, photographs, diaries, letters, oral history recordings and other autobiographical accounts as well as writings on war, pacifism, military compulsion, soldiering, Englishness, eugenics, deviance, sexual inversion and degeneration.[6] This in turn entailed the consideration of scholarship from a variety of fields.

Once the idea of a book about Great War objectors and objection which took a socio-cultural-legal and multidisciplinary approach began to take shape, however, questions of structure and form came to the fore; exactly what kind of text was *Telling Tales* going to be? The first dilemma in this context was whether the structure would be broadly chronological or in some way thematic. An early decision to opt for the latter raised further questions about the ideas around which to construct chapters. In the end, the form that this text takes was to some degree inspired by the different ways in which 'the objector story' could be and has been told. Consequently, divergent conceptions of objectors and their experiences seemed to suggest a spectrum of possible ways of recounting tales about these men. In addition, thinking about the different ways in which narratives about the past could be written also suggested that perhaps this book could include more than one story about objectors.[7]

Ultimately, the structure embodied in *Telling Tales* settled into the series of seven tales about objectors, including in the Prologue a version of their story cast in more chronological and expositional form. The latter is intended to serve as a sort of map to the subject area and a background to the other chapters (and seeks to avoid repetition elsewhere in the book). The seven narratives are framed by this Introduction along with a Conclusion and Epilogue – all of which explore the nature of *Telling Tales*. Also, the book includes sometimes lengthy endnotes for those not familiar with all the ideas drawn upon within these pages and for the generally curious (these are, of course, optional).[8]

As a consequence of its approach and structure, this book differs greatly from previous work on (First World War) objectors. It is to these CO texts and their relationship to *Telling Tales* that this Introduction now turns.

Telling Tales and writing about objectors

A reasonably large number of authors have directed their attention towards the conscientious objectors of the First World War, whilst others have touched to a greater or lesser degree upon the topic in looking at related subjects such as pacifism and war resistance or in considering COs within a wider timescape. Indeed, upon reviewing the wide range of writing about objectors in different genres (just a very few of which are mentioned here)[9] it might perhaps be thought that this book is situated within a crowded field. However, *Telling Tales* stands apart from those works which precede it in a number of respects – although earlier writings provide a rich seam of material which inform this book and are important sources referenced within its pages.

Most fundamentally, *Telling Tales* differs from other texts on objectors in its presentation of seven narratives about objectors. In comparison, other texts on COs in this period are more singular – in that they are based upon one organising story and an argument which is linear (progressing from a beginning, to a middle and, thence, an ending) and often broadly chronological. For example, David Boulton opens his 1967 book about socialist objectors, *Objection Overruled*, by declaring it to be '*the* story of . . . men who refused to fight' (emphasis added), and explaining that '[w]e look first at the political tradition which produced their objection; then at the events which led to conscription; then at resistance.'[10] In *Conscience and Politics: The British Government and the Conscientious Objector to Military Service 1916–1919*, published in 1970,[11] John Rae's account is encapsulated within a single narrative (with a progression in terms of a developing story and argument) which traces a broadly chronological path through the course of the text. Thus, *Conscience and Politics* opens with a chapter on the move from voluntary enlistment to military conscription. The next two chapters consider the drafting of the legislation which was to introduce compulsion and its passage through Parliament. The text then considers how this shift was implemented, focuses upon the identity of objectors and proceeds to consider their treatment in various spheres, concluding with a chapter detailing what happened to them after the war. Moreover, its tale-telling centres, as the title suggests, upon a (generally pro-state) story (or defence) of how the government dealt with these men.

Similarly, Thomas C. Kennedy's 1981 text *The Hound of Conscience: A History of the No-Conscription Fellowship*[12] gives a description of the key organisation which championed the COs' cause, adopting a straightforwardly chronological and linear approach to the organisation of narrative; starting with the origins of resistance it moves on to the outbreak of war, the period of voluntarism, and follows the Fellowship during the period of conscription, focusing upon the internal politics between different individuals and factions. In a more recent foray into the field of conscience, *Comrades in Conscience: The Story of an English Community's Opposition to the Great War*, Cyril Pearce examines opposition to war in Huddersfield, organising his chapters according to different periods of the war. The overarching story in this excellent book concerns the position of and attitudes towards objection in this locale.[13]

Unsurprisingly, personal descriptions of the experiences of COs, such as James Scott Duckers's 1917 book, tend to be broadly chronological, following a pathway through the war. Duckers records his time as an objector from the beginning of the war, with the text abruptly ending part way through the conflict (at the point at which it was presumably smuggled out of the prison in which he was being held).[14] George Baker's post-war reflections, published in 1930 as *The Soul of a Skunk: The Autobiography of a Conscientious Objector*, beginning with his early family life, move through the course of his war years, although here more space is accorded to explorations of such things as the author's views on life, politics, society and war as well as some amusing anecdotes unconnected to objection.[15] Similarly, those who supported objectors during the conflict tended to opt for a traditional narrative form. Published in 1917, Frank G. Jannaway's *Without the Camp: Being the Story of Why and How the Christadelphians were Exempted from Military Service* presents a chronological tale which foregrounds his own efforts to a gain a special status for COs who were members of this Christian sect.[16]

Despite these differences between this volume and other texts, *Telling Tales*'s presentation of a number of yarns about COs is informed by the range of conceptions of objectors contained within existing writings about these men. As well as recounting a particular narrative about objectors, each of these works takes a specific overarching perspective on COs and their experiences. Indeed, whatever the style and form adopted by these texts and whether written during the war, with the benefit of a few years' or decades' hindsight or much more recently, they each cast the story they tell in particular ways. Of course, these very different conceptions of objectors are also reflected in other sources, such as contemporary newspapers, parliamentary debates, official documents and the propaganda of both the pro-war establishment and those organisations which supported objectors. Similarly, as the pictures contained within these pages demonstrate, visual representations of these men also cast them in particular hues. For example, CO G.P. Micklewright's 1917 cartoon 'WHAT A C.O. FEELS LIKE', reproduced on page 10, depicts a range of images of objectors, from the saintly to the hated outsider.[17]

In terms of texts about COs, Boulton's perspective and depiction of objectors is reflected and utilised at various points in *Telling Tales* but particularly in Chapter 1. His study of socialist objectors is constructed around the notion that these men were almost universally hated. This demonstrates a particular political interest and a construction of the socialist CO as underdog and scapegoat, standing up for what was right in the face of adversity.[18] In contrast, Pearce's focus is the role of anti-conscription organisations and trade unions and their impact upon the experiences of objectors and, in particular, working-class men. Unlike the majority of other texts on the subject, the volume challenges the idea of the unpopularity of COs. Here the construction of the objector is as an insider – one who reflects the views of those around him and is supported by them. These themes figure primarily in Chapters 5 and 6 of *Telling Tales*.

In a very different tone Stanley Bloomfield James's 1917 *The Men Who Dared: The Story of an Adventure* applauds intrepid, dare-devil COs.[19] Adopting a less racy style, Will Ellsworth-Jones's journalistic *We Will Not Fight: The Untold Story of World War One's Conscientious Objectors* (2008), romanticises objectors in a manner not dissimilar to that in which the military men of the First World War are sometimes written and spoken of; indeed, this is framed as a story which valorises COs and celebrates their courage.[20] As such, both Ellsworth-Jones's and James's texts accord most closely with Chapter 6 of the present volume, which centres upon the objector as hero.

The range of styles, tones, genres and textures espoused in existing works on objectors also, to some degree, influenced *Telling Tales*'s unusual multiple narrative structure. More specifically, the fact that there were already so many different ways of writing about COs suggested the idea of thinking creatively about the construction of a new book on the subject. For example, there are conventionally styled histories, overtly partisan accounts of a movement or a particular man, journalistic studies and fast-paced celebrations. Of particular note in this context are James's *The Men Who Dared*, Rose Allatini's 1918 *Despised and Rejected* (published under the pseudonym A.T. Fitzroy[21]) and Felicity Goodall's 1997 *A Question of Conscience: Conscientious Objection in Two World Wars*.[22] James's volume tells of COs in a manner reminiscent of contemporary stories about the exploits of both fictional and real soldiers or adventurers. Here, then, the style is fast paced – yet this is presented as factual work. In contrast, Allatini elects to depict objectors through the medium of the novel. However, despite its apparently fictional status, this book adopts a much more measured tone and form and appears to be founded upon the author's personal association with and knowledge of objectors. Thus, in different ways both works suggest that the boundaries between supposedly fact-based and fictional stories are not only fuzzy but distinctly unstable and indicate that there may be a range of ways of representing objectors and narratives about their experiences. More recently, *A Question of Conscience* also shows that there may be different ways of structuring texts about these men. Goodall's book, which focuses upon a wider timeframe, examines objectors and their experiences by presenting 'a series of snapshots from people's lives, told in their own words' – thus, it gives 'a flavour' of COs' experiences and is not 'intended to be a history of conscientious objection'.[23] Indeed, it takes the form of a collection of excerpts from COs surrounded by explanatory text and, by its nature, is thus a more fragmentary work.

However, having noted the influence of other works upon *Telling Tales*, it remains to highlight a further significant difference between these texts: namely that, unlike previous forays into the sphere of conscience, this book sets out to consider objectors within a socio-cultural context and so explores the way in which they were regarded and dealt with by their families and friends,

1 G.P. Micklewright, 'WHAT A C.O. FEELS LIKE', 1917. Friends Library, London, Picture Collection, 86/A 80.

by communities, employers, government, the legal system and the military, as well as their depiction in the press and in fiction. Few authors have strayed even briefly into this terrain. A notable exception is Kennedy's work. *The Hound of Conscience*, along with a 1973 article, 'Public opinion and the conscientious objector, 1915–1919',[24] goes some way towards a more contextual approach. Whilst the former includes some consideration of wider cultural factors relevant to the treatment of those who claimed conscience (for example, in the first chapter there is some discussion of the origins of the militarism which he sees as existing at the beginning of the war), the latter examines a range of different attitudes towards COs. However, in both cases the socio-cultural elements and their analysis are limited.

This socio-cultural approach also involves the consideration of a wider range of ideas and theories – both contemporary to the First World War and more recent – than have previously been addressed in works on COs. In this regard, not only the variety of sources cited but also the range of academic disciplines drawn upon within these pages lend this book a distinct shape and texture. In particular, *Telling Tales* explores attitudes to war and soldiering, and ideas about nationality (focusing upon Englishness), race, gender, criminality and mainstream Christianity. Of these threads the most significant is gender and, more specifically, masculinity, along with linked notions about sexuality – hence the decision to call this volume *Telling Tales About <u>Men</u>*. Because of its importance this strand receives specific consideration below.

Telling Tales About Men

Whilst there is a considerable body of writing about COs in the First World War, it has been little influenced by gender studies. Nor has it explicitly examined COs *as men*, in the context of contemporary wartime ideas about manliness and more recent scholarship about masculinities.[25] Of course, one of the reasons for this lack is that work on masculinities is relatively new. However, the subject of conscientious objection provides a rich terrain for the study of notions of masculinity. For example, there is the Victorian focus upon 'manliness' as a virtue[26] and the associated well-known fears about the male of the species in the late nineteenth and early twentieth century (including the war years)[27] as well as links between these ideas and the image of the soldier hero.[28] Also significant in this context is the tendency to construct war as being the business of men. More particularly, during these years of conflict pre-existing efforts to affect thinking about manhood became increasingly focused, deliberate and, perhaps, more desperate. Thus, as chapters 1–6 below will illustrate, whilst pronouncements on what it was or should be to be a man were by no means unknown before the war and came from a range of sources, they developed and intensified during the conflict. Consequently, gender seems fundamental to the study of both objection and objectors.

Research on masculinities and men has expanded rapidly over recent years in a variety of disciplines, as has the interest in applying such gendered approaches to specific historical periods or groups of men. The Great War has begun to be considered in some of this work, and *Telling Tales* draws upon such scholarship. For example, Joanna Bourke's *Dismembering the Male: Men's Bodies, Britain and the Great War* looks at the ways in which masculinity was disrupted, constructed and reconstructed during the conflict, focusing upon the war's impact upon the male body. George Mosse's *Fallen Soldiers: Reshaping the Memory of the World Wars* focuses on explorations of masculinity, sexuality and war, examines how men confronted modern war along with the political consequences of that confrontation, and seeks to explore how men and women came to accept warfare as a part of life.[29] More specifically, Ilana R. Bet-El's work on conscript soldiers is an important reference point for the present volume, given its focus upon another group of men affected by conscription – and one that has largely been eclipsed in work on the conflict. Her writing looks at those men who, rather than voluntarily enlisting or resisting compulsion, for various reasons obeyed the call-up. Thus, attitudes to war and the military amongst these soldiers are explored as well as their experiences, and this forms a useful counterpoint to *Telling Tales* and its exploration of conceptions of COs. Significantly also, in common with this text, Bet-El considers these men *as* men.[30]

Scholarly interest in military masculinities in various disciplines also suggests the impulse to look more closely at the objector. For instance, sociologist David Morgan's *'It Will Make a Man of You': Notes on National Service, Masculinity and Autobiography* describes the author's reflections on his own compulsory military training,[31] and elsewhere his paper 'Theatre of war: combat, the military and masculinities' looks at the relationship between militarism and masculinities.[32] The collection of cross-disciplinary essays edited by Paul R. Higate *Military Masculinities: Identity and the State* is also illustrative of the growing trend to study soldier men in terms of their gender.[33] Moreover, such texts suggest frames within which to examine the objector as a man who, in various ways, decides to refuse these (supposed) ways of being a man.

A more cultural and literary work in the area, and thus one which resonates with some of the concerns in *Telling Tales*, is Graham Dawson's *Soldier Heroes: British Adventure, Empire and the Imagining of Masculinities*. It is especially significant given its focus upon images of the male in terms of soldiering and, more particularly, the construction of the soldier hero within adventure stories from the nineteenth century to the late twentieth century. Also, Michael Paris's *Warrior Nation: Images of War in British Popular Culture, 1850–2000* explores the way in which images of battle, both literary and visual, have been constructed in British fiction and popular culture since the mid-nineteenth century.[34] Both these works, broadly speaking, seek to examine ideas about manhood and the military from specific sources in a particular historical period and suggest contexts within which to construct the CO. They are, thus, amongst the texts which shape the socio-cultural turn adopted here.

In addition, there is now a wide range of writings on men, masculinities and manliness, many of which also inform *Telling Tales*. These span different disciplines. Notably, in history there is the work of John Tosh, including his 1994 contribution which considers 'What should historians do with masculinity?'[35] Given the focus upon contemporary First World War ideas about men in *Telling Tales*, his observations about the pervasiveness of conceptions of manliness are especially significant. Indeed, the degree to which some of the Victorian versions of manliness were elite cultural forms that barely touched working-class consciousness has been the subject of some discussion and, thus, his argument that such images did filter through to the working classes helps support much that is contended here.[36] There is also the collection *Manful Assertions: Masculinities in Britain since 1800*, compiled by Michael Roper along with Tosh, which provides a range of approaches to looking at men in different historical contexts and similarly influences the present volume.[37]

Such scholars and works are but the tip of the iceberg when it comes to the flurry of interest in studying masculinities or men *as men* in history, let alone elsewhere in the humanities and beyond. Given the cross- and multidisciplinary nature of gender-related studies, some of this wider scholarship resonates with and impacts upon the present text.[38] However, this book is not a text about gender, sexualities or masculinities *per se* and, thus, such theorising does not play a dominant role here.

How then do masculinities figure in the present volume? The idea of objectors *as men* is the most important of the elements considered in relation to their construction. Thus, the maleness of objectors is an underlying concern throughout the book, whilst at some points it becomes an explicit focus with the text addressing different conceptions of what it is or (apparently) should be to be male and some of the constellations of ideas associated with these paradigms. In so doing *Telling Tales* focuses upon a range of shifting, often contradictory, notions about men, viewing the linked concepts of gender, masculinity, femininity and sexuality as social constructions and, accordingly, as plural, contingent, mutable and relational.

Consequently, the examination of intramasculine oppositions and wartime versions of maledom are a central concern in this project, so that soldiers, along with civilian men and boys, appear within these pages. Women also play a part here, as images of femininity are an important part of the currency in which the deployment of representations of masculinities trade. In the current context, for example, soldiers were sometimes depicted as both the antithesis and the defenders of the female population, while COs tended to be portrayed as feminised men. Moreover, many women were aiding the war effort, labouring in environments such as munitions factories, wearing masculine clothes such as trousers or uniforms and enjoying the new-found freedom which better wages and swift societal change had brought into being. They were, thus, acting and dressing in supposedly male ways both at work and in leisure.

The chapters

Telling Tales is divided into three parts. Part I consists of the present Introduction, with its focus upon the nature, purpose and approach adopted within this text and a mapping of this volume's relationship with other scholarship. Part II forms the main body of the text and is made up of a Prologue along with six chapters. The very brief Part III encompasses two sections: the Conclusion further considers some of the theoretical underpinnings of the book's methodology and structure; in contrast, the Epilogue locates the origins of *Telling Tales* within more personal realms. Thus, whilst Parts I and III are about *Telling Tales* the book, Part II tells tales about conscientious objectors.

In Part II the Prologue offers what is to be the first presentation of a narrative about COs. This provides a guide and reference point in a text organised in terms of thematic conceptions of objector men. In order to serve this purpose, the tale told in this part of the book is organised into a chronological overview narrative.

Each of the next six chapters groups together and examines clusters of wartime ideas about objectors, considering them in the context of different narratives about the conflict. Chapter 1, 'Despised and rejected', explores the notion of the objector as a hated figure and an outcast. This is set against the backdrop of a conception of the war which presents it as a popular endeavour, with men, women, boys and girls supporting the national effort. Consequently, the CO was rejecting the dominant ideas of the time and tended to be detested and ostracised or ridiculed as a figure of fun. In addition, this chapter, with its narratives of initial war enthusiasm, continuing support for the conflict and dislike for the objector, sets the context for the negative portrayals in the following three chapters.

Chapter 2, 'Of cowards, shirkers and unmen', depicts the CO as unmanly and contrasts this image with the idealised notion of the soldier. Thus, it continues the idea of the upbeat national mood towards the war. Here, however, the focus is upon early twentieth-century ideas about men and the objector is cast as the antithesis of the soldier, embodying selfishness, indolence and cowardice rather than altruism, vigour and bravery. Moreover, the objector's failure in terms of his gender is further demonstrated by his un-English/un-British and un-Christian stand.

Again focusing upon less than flattering conceptions of the objector and founded upon the narrative of mass support for the war, the third chapter, 'Deviance: degeneracy, decadence and criminality', examines the idea of COs as deviant from the perspectives of race, gender and, more particularly, criminality. Following on from this a darker, potentially more threatening portrait of the objector is proffered in Chapter 4, 'The national danger'. At this juncture in the text the CO is represented as posing a threat to the very country which others are working to protect. In this construction, far from being perceived of as pathetic and unmanly, objectors were seen as a menace; the peril that they represented might even bring down the nation.

Examining more positive constructions of objectors, Chapter 5, '*Conscientious* objectors', marks a shift in the text. It describes such men as upstanding and honourable citizens who, far from being outcasts, were supported and often admired. At this point the CO compares favourably with the image of men and women, who, for example, failed to share in the enthusiasm for the war, became weary of it or sought to profit from it. Indeed, in this context objectors also fare well when contrasted with men who endeavoured to evade conscription through cowardice and in the interests of self-preservation.

The sixth chapter continues in this more upbeat mode as far as the objector is concerned by picturing him as both a patriot and a hero. At the same time, at this point in the text the soldier is shown as failing, in various ways, to live up to his exemplary image. Thus, 'Patriots and heroes' considers both the CO and the soldier in a vastly different light to their portrayal earlier in this volume.

Part III concludes the volume by further considering the nature and origins of this book. The Conclusion revisits the structure and the approach to writing history embodied within *Telling Tales* and investigates some further influences upon the book's form. Finally, the Epilogue marks a shift in terms of voice. Taking a more autobiographical tone, the narrative traces the origins of the present volume in a more personal manner. Thus, familial stories about war, militarism and pacifism take centre stage at this point in the text.[39] Consequently, the Introduction, the Conclusion and the Epilogue all represent different ways of telling the story of *Telling Tales*.

Notes

1 The text is concerned with England and, consequently, includes some consideration of ideas about Englishness, although overarching notions of Britishness are also sometimes cited. Conscription applied across Britain but the text does not address Scottish or Welsh objectors, as each had their own distinct attitudes towards conscription and, of course, conceptions of Scottishness and Welshness differ both from

each other and from ideas associated with Englishness. For example, as Peter Brock notes, 'Scottish pacifists, whether religious or political, did not merely imitate their anti-war colleagues in England; they developed a personality of their own', *Pacifism Since 1914: An Annotated Reading List* (Toronto: University of Toronto Press, 2000), p. 13. See further William H. Marwick, 'Conscientious objection in Scotland in the First World War', *Scottish Journal of Science*, 1:3 (1972), 157–64.

2 Sassoon was the most well-known soldier who challenged the way the war was run by the military authorities – see further Chapter 6 in this volume. For studies of executions during the war see Julian Putkowski and Julian Sykes, *Shot at Dawn* (Barnsley: Wharncliffe, 1989); Anthony Babington, *For the Sake of Example: Capital Courts-Martial 1914–1920* (London: Leo Cooper in association with Secker & Warburg, 1983). On shell-shock see, for example: Anthony Babington, *Shell Shock: A History of the Changing Attitudes to War Neurosis* (London: Leo Cooper, 1997); Peter Leese, *Shell Shock: Traumatic Neurosis and the British Soldiers of the First World War* (New York: Palgrave, 2002); Tracey Louise Loughran, 'Shell-Shock in First World War Britain: An Intellectual and Medical History' (PhD dissertation, University of London, 2006). See further Chapter 6 below.

3 Of course, every reflection on the past cannot but be influenced by the knowledges of the particular present in which their author is situated.

4 Thus, the main chapters look at some of the ways in which objectors were conceptualised or socially constructed. On social construction see, for example, Peter L. Berger and Thomas Luckmann, *The Social Construction of Reality: A Treatise in the Sociology of Knowledge* (Garden City, NY: Anchor Books, 1966). This approach has had a particular influence in gender, sex and sexuality scholarship. For example, see Judith Butler, *Gender Trouble: Feminism and the Subversion of Identity* (New York: Routledge, 2nd edn, 1999) and *Undoing Gender* (New York: Routledge, 2004). Thus, recent theorists have argued not only that sex, gender and sexuality are overlapping and mutable concepts but also that they are all constructions. For the author's take on this see, in particular, Bibbings 'Heterosexuality as harm: fitting in' in Paddy Hillyard, Christina Pantazis, Steve Tombs and Dave Gordon (eds), *Beyond Criminology: Taking Harm Seriously* (London: Pluto Press, 2005).

5 See, in particular: Lois Bibbings, 'State reaction to conscientious objection' in Loveland (ed.), *The Frontiers of Criminality* (London: Sweet and Maxwell, 1995); 'Conscientious objectors in the Great War: the consequences of rejecting military masculinities' in Paul R. Higate (ed.), *Military Masculinities: Identity and the State* (Westport, CT: Greenwood, 2003); 'Images of manliness: the portrayal of soldiers and

conscientious objectors in the Great War', *Social and Legal Studies*,
12:3 (2003), 335–58.

6 Most of these are contemporary to the period studied, although, as
the inclusion of the last two categories suggests, some are recollections
recorded at a little distance from the events of the war. Such subsequent
descriptions, reflections and retellings are consciously included with
a recognition that, whilst narratives of events, experiences and emotions can change over time for a variety of reasons or motives, be they
conscious or unconscious, contemporary accounts are by no means
necessarily imbued with a greater degree of authenticity, accuracy
or, indeed, 'truth'. The use and usefulness of accounts given at some
remove from the experiences to which they relate has been the subject
of some debate amongst historians, with, for example, Michael Roper's
analysis of Lyndall Urwick's various recountings of a First World War
experience purporting to reveal 'Urwick's memoirs as *not* an accurate
rendering' of the events ('Re-remembering the soldier hero: the psychic
and social construction of memory in personal narratives of the Great
War', *History Workshop Journal*, 50:2 (2000), 181–204). Roper, thus,
distinguishes between the '"truth" of the event' and 'the "truth" of the
memory', seeing a value in each – but in doing so he also foregrounds
the idea of *truth* (200). In contrast, my decision to use sources from
beyond the war again reflects the influence of a variety of disciplines,
in particular the social sciences, upon this book. For example, it is well
recognised in qualitative research with human participants that accounts
of and 'meanings' of the past will change over time and that this does
not mean that one version of events is more or less valid than another –
'each moment of our lives, each thing we say, is equally true and false. It
is true because at the very moment we are saying it that is the only reality
and it is false because the next moment another reality will replace it' (C.
Simic, 'Tragicomic soup', *The New York Review of Books*, 47:9 (2000),
8–11, p. 11). Thus, 'the ability of research to discover truths or to represent the realities of others' has been much and long debated (Jennifer
Mason, *Qualitative Researching* (London: Sage, 2nd edn, 2002), p. 6).

In addition, oral historians, in focusing upon giving voice to the
excluded and writing histories from below, have provided ample justification for their methods and the material that they work with, whilst
being conscious of the fallibility of all attempts to describe experiences (see, for example, Alistair Thomson, 'Unreliable memories? The
use and abuse of oral history', in William Lamont (ed.), *Historical
Controversies and Historians* (London: Routledge, 1998). Also in the
field of history Joanna Bourke, for example, in her work on the 1914–18
war acknowledges (admittedly with some caution) the 'invaluable guide'
that memoirs and oral histories can 'provide . . . to the construction of

gender identities' (*Dismembering the Male: Men's Bodies, Britain and the Great War* (London: Reaktion Books, 1995), p. 15). Similarly, see Angela Woollacott, *On Her Their Lives Depend: Munition Workers in the Great War* (Berkeley: University of California Press, 1994), pp. 206–9. Moreover, the fallibilities of witness testimony (particularly identification evidence), regardless of how closely to the events described it is recorded, is also a familiar topic within legal spheres. Consequently, both its usefulness and the extent to which it should be used or relied upon in court are areas of contention. See, for instance, Brian L. Cutler and Steven Penrod, *Mistaken Identification: The Eye Witness, Psychology and the Law* (Cambridge: Cambridge University Press, 1995).

The postmodern turn of *Telling Tales* also means that the text rejects the 'somewhat forced distinctions . . . between memory and history: history as what happened, memory as that which is remembered of what happened'. Instead, the book adopts the view that 'things happen *and* they get told' and that these are 'two ontologically distinct categories'. This by no means denies that '[t]here is at the ground of history that which happened: facts and events that occurred', although these can be represented in multiple narratives (James E. Young, 'Towards a received history of the Holocaust', *History and Theory*, 36:4 (1997), 21–43, pp. 37, 34).

From a more practical perspective, another reason for utilising reports given some time after the events described is that in a number of instances it was difficult for objectors themselves to create contemporaneous records of their experiences when, for instance, they were being punished in the military or in prison. In addition, many of the official documents relating to COs were destroyed in 1921 as they were 'not considered of sufficient public value to justify preservation' (National Archive, London, MH 47/3), so there is another reason for looking at a wide variety of sources.

7 The result is a book which is influenced by thinking about the 'nature' of history and what it might mean 'to do history'. Although by no means unique, this is less than usual as, whilst 'both philosophy and literature . . . have engaged very seriously with the question of what is the nature of their own nature', historians have often been resistant to the very idea that this is a valid question. See Keith Jenkins, *Rethinking History* (Oxford: Routledge Classics, 2003), p. 2.

8 Here endnotes not only provide the traditional references, clarifications and acknowledgements of connected ideas and research, but also proffer further explanations, discussions and musings. This approach to annotation is self-consciously adopted not least because of the range of sources and fields of knowledge drawn upon within these pages; in

a multidisciplinary text, which potentially addresses readers from a variety of backgrounds, there is often a need for more by way of sign-posting and elucidation. Also, the use of notes to contain such references and clarifications (as well as the occasional aside) serves to 'unburden' the body of the text, hopefully allowing it to be relatively accessible. This is not, of course, to say that notes (including these) are ever entirely distinct from 'the body of the text'. Instead one might better ask 'Where does a text stop and a footnote begin? What is hors d'oeuvre?' (literally 'What is "outside the work"?'). Stephen A. Barney (ed.), *Annotation and Its Texts* (Oxford: Oxford University Press, 1991), p. vii.

Despite evidence that there has of late been something of a backlash against noting, with some concern that the annotation is an endangered species (see Chuck Zerby, *The Devil's Details: A History of Footnotes* (New York: Simon & Schuster, 2002), chap. 1, especially pp. 2–3), to some people, like Zerby, not only do notes allow the reader to trace the origins of an idea or locate a source, they can also sometimes be the most engaging and revealing parts of texts (unsurprisingly, I am firmly of this camp). Beyond this (and given the importance of stories in *Telling Tales*), '[they] can allow you to create a kind of secret second narrative, which is important if, say, you're writing a book about what a story is and whether stories are significant' – John Green, www.sparksflyup.com/2006/08/footnotes.php (accessed in November 2008).

9 Only a few comparator texts are mentioned in this section precisely because *Telling Tales* differs so greatly from those works on COs which precede it. For the moment writings specifically about Great War objectors (not least works by these men and their support-ers) include: Henry Wood Nevinson, 'The conscientious objector', *Atlantic Monthly* 103:695 (November 1916), 686–94; Albert Venn Dicey, 'The conscientious objector', *Nineteenth Century* 83: 492 (1918), 357–73; No-Conscription Fellowship, *The No-Conscription Fellowship: A Souvenir of its Work During the Years 1914–1919* (London: No-Conscription Fellowship, 1920); John W. Graham, *Conscription and Conscience: A History 1916–1919* (London: George Allen and Unwin, 1971 reprint – first published 1922); Julian H. Bell (ed.), *We Did Not Fight 1914–1918: Experiences of War Resisters* (London: Cobden Sanderson, 1935); Alistair R. Mack, 'Conscription and Conscientious Objection in Leeds and York During the First World War' (MPhil thesis, University of York – History Department, 1983).

Other works, including autobiographies, biographies, novels and a range of histories touch upon objectors during the Great War to a greater or lesser degree. For example, see: John Buchan, *Mr Standfast* (Ware: Wordsworth Classics, 1994 – first published London: Hodder

& Stoughton, 1919); Archibald Fenner Brockway, *Inside the Left: Thirty Years of Platform, Press, Prison and Parliament* (London: Allen and Unwin, 1942 – reissued with a new preface in 1947); Denis Hayes, *Conscription Conflict: The Conflict of Ideas in the Struggle For and Against Military Conscription Between 1901 and 1939* (London: Sheppard Press, 1949); Martin Gilbert, *Plough My Own Furrow: The Story of Lord Allen of Hurtwood as Told Through his Writings and Correspondence* (London: Longman, 1965); Arthur Marwick, *Clifford Allen: The Open Conspirator* (London: Oliver and Boyd, 1964); Constance Braithwaite, 'Legal problems of conscientious objection to various compulsions under British law' *Journal of the Friends Historic Society* 52:1 (1968) 3–18; Keith Robbins, *The Abolition of War: The 'Peace Movement' in Britain, 1914–1919* (Cardiff: University of Wales Press, 1976); Raymond Challinor, *John S. Clarke: Parliamentarian and Lion Tamer* (London: Pluto Press, 1977); Ralph James Q. Adams and Philip P. Poirier, *The Conscription Controversy in Great Britain, 1900–1918* (London: Macmillan, 1987).

10 David Boulton, *Objection Overruled* (London: MacGibbon and Kee, 1967), see pp. 11, 12.

11 John Rae, *Conscience and Politics: The British Government and the Conscientious Objector to Military Service 1916–1919* (London: Oxford University Press, 1970).

12 Thomas C. Kennedy, *The Hound of Conscience: A History of the No-Conscription Fellowship* (Fayetteville: University of Arkansas Press, 1981).

13 Cyril Pearce, *Comrades in Conscience: The Story of an English Community's Opposition to the Great War* (London: Francis Boutle, 2001).

14 James Scott Duckers, *Handed Over: The Prison Experiences of Mr. J. Scott Duckers, Solicitor of Chancery Lane, Under the Military Service Act, Written by himself. With Foreword by T. Edmund Harvey* (London: C.W. Daniel, 1917).

15 George Baker, *The Soul of a Skunk: The Autobiography of a Conscientious Objector* (London: Eric Partridge at the Scholartis Press, 1930).

16 Frank G. Jannaway, *Without the Camp: Being the Story of Why and How the Christadelphians were Exempted from Military Service* (London: F.G. Jannaway, 1917).

17 Friends Library, London, Picture Collection, 86/A 80.

18 As such, it can be positioned alongside other leftish histories of the period and, in particular, those which focus upon trade union war resistance – such as: Malcolm I. Thomis, 'The Labour Movement in Great Britain and Compulsory Military Service, 1914–1916' (MA

dissertation, University of London, 1959); Ken Weller, *'Don't be a Soldier!': The Radical Anti-War Movement in North London, 1914–1918* (London: Journeyman Press, 1985).

19 Stanley Bloomfield James, *The Men Who Dared: The Story of an Adventure* (London: C.W. Daniel, 1917).

20 Will Ellsworth-Jones, *We Will Not Fight: The Untold Story of World War One's Conscientious Objectors* (London: Aurum Press, 2008).

21 A.T. Fitzroy [Rose Allatini], *Despised and Rejected* (London: C.W. Daniel Ltd, 1918 – reproduced London: The Gay Men Press Publishers Ltd, 1988)

22 Felicity Goodall, *A Question of Conscience: Conscientious Objection in Two World Wars* (Stroud: Sutton Publishing Limited, 1997).

23 Goodall, Preface, *A Question of Conscience*.

24 Thomas C. Kennedy, 'Public opinion and the conscientious objector, 1915–1919', *The Journal of British Studies*, 12:2 (1973), 105–19.

25 In contrast, there has been a range of feminist work on women within the peace movements of the period such as Anne Wiltshire's *Most Dangerous Women: Feminist Peace Campaigners of the Great War* (London: Pandora, 1985). However, the gender of objectors has been studied in other periods – see Timothy Stewart-Winter, 'Not a Soldier, Not a Slacker: Conscientious Objectors and Male Citizenship in the United States during the Second World War', *Gender and History*, 19:3 (2007), 519–42. There is also Daniel Conway's work on sexuality and objection ('"Every Coward's Choice"? Political Objection to Military Service in Apartheid South Africa as Sexual Citizenship', *Citizenship Studies*, 8:1 (2004), 25–45) and there is scholarship on female conscientious objectors to assisting war: Rachel Waltner Goossen, *Women Against the Good War: Conscientious Objection and Gender on the American Home Front* (London: University of North Carolina Press, 1997); Hazel Nicholson, 'A disputed identity: women conscientious objectors in Second World War Britain', *Twentieth Century British History*, 18:4 (2007), 409–28. Beyond this, gender has been studied in relation to objection and the Vaccination Acts in Britain (Nadja Durbach, 'Class, gender, and the conscientious objector to vaccination, 1898–1907', *The Journal of British Studies*, 41:1 (2002), 58–83).

26 Notably see: David Newsome, *Godliness and Good Learning* (London: John Murray, 1961), p. 195; James Anthony Mangan, '"Muscular, Militaristic and Manly": the British middle-class hero as moral messenger', *International Journal of the History of Sport*, 13:1 (1996), 28–47, especially pp. 29–30.

27 For example, see Joanna Bourke's discussion in relation to the Boer War, *Dismembering the Male*, pp. 171–2.

28 On the notion of the soldier hero see further Dawson, *Soldier Heroes: British Adventure, Empire and the Imagining of Masculinities* (London: Routledge, 1994).

29 George Mosse, *Fallen Soldiers: Reshaping the Memory of the World Wars* (Oxford: Oxford University Press, 1990).

30 Ilana R. Bet-El, *Conscripts: Lost Legions of the Great War* (Stroud: Sutton: 1999); 'Men and soldiers: British conscripts, concepts of masculinity, and the Great War' in Billie Melman (ed.), *Borderlines: Genders and Identities in War and Peace 1870–1930* (London: Routledge, 1998).

31 David Morgan, *'It Will Make a Man of You': Notes on National Service, Masculinity and Autobiography*, Studies in Sexual Politics, No. 17 (Manchester: Manchester University, Department of Sociology, 1987).

32 David Morgan, 'Theatre of war: combat, the military and masculinities', in Harry Brod and Michael Kaufman (eds), *Theorising Masculinities* (Thousand Oaks, CA: Sage, 1994).

33 See also Higate, 'Peacekeepers, masculinities and sexual exploitation', *Men and Masculinities*, 10:1 (2007), 99–119.

34 Michael Paris, *Warrior Nation: Images of War in British Popular Culture, 1850–2000* (London: Reaction Books, 2000).

35 John Tosh, 'What should historians do with masculinity? Reflections on nineteenth-century Britain', *History Workshop Journal*, 38:1 (1994), 179–202.

36 *Ibid.*, 181–2.

37 Michael Roper and John Tosh, *Manful Assertions: Masculinities in Britain since 1800* (London: Routledge, 1991). In addition, there is Tosh's article collection, *Manliness and Masculinities in Nineteenth-Century Britain: Essays on Gender, Family and Empire* (Harlow: Pearson Educational, 2005).

38 It is perhaps useful to situate the present text within the genres of gender/sexualities scholarship which have most informed it. Key influences include: Richard Collier *Masculinity, Law and the Family* (London: Routledge, 1995) and *Masculinities, Crime and Criminology* (London: Sage, 1998); Judith Butler's work, in particular *Gender Trouble*; R.W. Connell's writings, in particular *Masculinities* (Cambridge: Polity, 2nd edn, 2005).

39 The autobiographical turn in feminist and gender studies is an influence here. See, for example: Tess Cosslett, Celia Lury and Penny Summerfield (eds), *Feminism and Autobiography: Texts, Theories, Methods* (London: Routledge, 2000); David Jackson, *Unmasking Masculinity: A Critical Autobiography (Critical Studies in Men and Masculinities 1)* (London: Unwin Hyam, 1990); Morgan, *'It Will Make a Man of You'*. In contrast, historian Alistair Thomson uses

autobiography in a different way to illustrate the theory he develops in *Anzac Memories: Living With the Legend* (Oxford: Oxford University Press, 1994).

This approach is also informed by the idea of changing voice as a method by which attention is drawn to the text as a human construction (that is as a metafictional device). On metafiction generally see, for example, Linda Hutcheon, *The Politics of Postmodernism* (London: Routledge, 1989), chaps 2, 3; Patricia Waugh, *Metafiction: The Theory and Practice of Self-Conscious Fiction* (London: Methuen, 1984).

Part II

Telling tales about objectors

Prologue: a conscientious tale – a brief linear history of conscientious objectors to military service 1914–1918

The text below offers what is to be the first of a number of tales about conscientious objectors (COs) included within these pages. This narrative provides a guide and reference point in a text which is primarily organised in terms of thematic conceptions of objector men. In order to serve this purpose, it is organised into a brief chronological and linear overview.

Voluntary recruitment

From the outbreak of war in August 1914 until early 1916 the sole method of recruitment in England was one of voluntarism, 'voluntaryism' or 'volunteerism' as it was variously called.[1] During this period the need for more men in the military was addressed by a series of official drives reinforced by the press, other cultural institutions and by individuals. These efforts sought to encourage and cajole men to do their duty and voluntarily join up. However, as the months passed there was a growing concern (encouraged by those who supported military conscription) as to whether enough men were coming forward. In the first instance this led to a census, the National Register of August 1915, to assess the total human resources.[2] The idea was to construct a register of all individuals (male and female) between the ages of fifteen and sixty-five who were not in the forces (with some exceptions).[3] In particular, the register aimed to discover the number of eligible men who remained in civilian life and could be spared from maintaining the war effort on the Home Front. The results, according to Lord Derby who oversaw it, showed

unacceptable numbers of civilian men of military age who had no
excuse for not joining up.[4] Unsurprisingly, the figures were exploited
and manipulated by those pressing for compulsion and, in particular,
the influential National Service League.[5] Following this and, in part,
as a result of attempts to placate both the pro-conscriptionists and
those who supported voluntarism, the government implemented a
new voluntary scheme under the supervision of Lord Derby.

The Derby Scheme was introduced in the autumn of 1915.[6] It
allowed men to 'attest' rather than to enlist. To attest meant merely
to profess a willingness to join up at some future date if required to
do so. The Scheme also carried the promise that married men would
only be called upon when all eligible single men had enlisted. When
attested men were called up they could apply for a postponement
via the Local Derby Tribunal and appeal to a Central Tribunal.[7]
Pressure for conscription from the National Service League continued, however, as did a public perception that not enough men
were coming forward and, as a consequence, the war was being
prolonged. Accordingly, some felt that dramatic action was needed
in order to change the course of the war.[8] Furthermore, there were
concerns about the need to manage manpower in order to ensure
the most efficient use of the male population. As a result of these
concerns and a coalition cabinet compromise, by late 1915 the decision to introduce conscription was made.

Conscription and the 'conscience clause'

The Military Service Act, 1916 imposed conscription within
Britain but not to Ireland. The legislation applied to single able-
bodied men between the ages of 18 and 41 along with childless
widowers.[9] Amongst other things, subsequent Military Service
Acts extended compulsion to married men and made other amendments and additions but the first Act remained the primary source
of law.[10] However, from the outset certain exceptions to and
exemptions from compulsion were recognised within the legislation.[11] Exemption was possible where it was in the national interest for the individual to be engaged in particular work, where
serious financial, business or domestic hardship would be caused
if a man were called up or where the man concerned was subject
to ill-health or infirmity.[12] Perhaps more remarkably, following
discussions and negotiations both within the coalition Cabinet and

Parliament, a very different ground of exemption was included in the legislation.

The 'conscience clause', as it continued to be called after the statute was passed, provided that those with a conscientious objection to military service could be granted various forms of exemption from conscription by (successfully) applying to a tribunal system.[13] Initially, there was some dispute as to which types of exemption were actually available to those successfully claiming objection. If the widest interpretation of the statute was taken such men could have been granted partial, conditional or absolute exemption from military service. The most limited form of exemption allowed for recognised objectors to be enlisted into the military but provided that they were only required to undertake non-combatant work in the Non-Combatant Corps (partial exemption). The Corps was created in March 1916[14] and objector members were required to perform a range of duties both at home and overseas. Tasks included stretcher-bearing, hospital portering and a range of manual jobs.[15] However, confusion as to the meaning of 'non-combatant' caused some difficulties with some men refusing to undertake certain tasks. For example, objectors were occasionally asked to handle munitions or other military supplies.[16] In addition, confusion resulted from the fact that unfit men were also placed within the Corps.[17]

Alternative service exempted men from the military on the condition that they undertake or continue to be employed in work that was deemed to be acceptable and of national importance (conditional exemption).[18] As it became clear that some guidance or oversight would be required in order to determine what constituted such tasks, the (Pelham) Committee on Work of National Importance was created to fulfil this role. It could make recommendations to tribunals and assist in a specific case if requested to do so by these bodies.[19] Absolute exemption completely absolved men from the terms of the legislation. However, some tribunals were reluctant to grant any exemption or more than partial exemption and a number disputed whether conditional exemption or absolute exemption was available in cases of conscience.[20]

The tribunals

Those men who were called up but wished to gain exemption on conscience (or other) grounds were required under the legislation to apply to their local (military service) tribunal to argue their claim. There was a right of appeal to the relevant regional appeal tribunal, which in turn had the power to grant a further appeal to the Central Tribunal. These bodies were created by the Act[21] and were overseen by the Local Government Board, which sent out circulars and letters including advice and guidance.[22] However, as local tribunals that dealt with military service had already been set up to adjudicate in applications for postponements of service under the Derby Scheme, the easiest way forward was to 'convert' these bodies into statutory tribunals that dealt with all applications for exemption from conscription in addition to their former work. This caused some confusion as to their role. Under Derby they were a part of the recruiting machine and were, therefore, directed that, given the large number of men in non-essential occupations, their duty was to 'assist the local Recruiting Authorities to secure these men for the Army'.[23] In contrast, under the 1916 Act they were cast as judicial bodies adjudicating claims for exemption from compulsion rather than solely being charged with recruiting work. Unsurprisingly, their conflicting duties caused some confusion. To make matters worse, the local tribunals included a mixed bag of worthies, those active in local politics, lawyers, labour representatives and magistrates who had varied views as to their roles. Despite recent evidence of such tribunals' lack of impartiality, competence and consistency in relation to their use in administrating the conscience provision in the Vaccination Act, 1898, a great deal of faith was placed in these bodies and their membership by the Local Government Board.[24] Given this, unsurprisingly their record of (in)justice was and has continued to be the subject of some debate.[25] The latter has perhaps also been encouraged by the destruction of the majority of tribunal records in 1921 when they were deemed not to be of 'sufficient public interest to justify preservation'.[26]

Although under the direction of the Local Government Board, the tribunals (and particularly the local tribunals) were often closely associated with the military, further confusing their role. The War Office paid their expenses and set up local Advisory Committees to scrutinise applications before tribunals heard the claim. These bodies then advised Military Representatives, who appeared before tribunals and presented the military case. Often the roles and interests of the military and the tribunals were confused, with, for example, tribunal members receiving and seeking to follow the Committee's advice and Military Representatives sitting with the tribunal and sometimes even retiring with them when they made their decision. The result of this and, amongst other things, members' sense of their patriotic duty and disagreement over the exemptions available, was a quality of justice that was often perceived to be highly variable. Consequently, particularly in the early days of conscription, it has been argued that many objectors went unrecognised or were granted a level of exemption that they were not prepared to accept.[27]

Some commentators have attempted to estimate the numbers of men who claimed conscience in front of a tribunal, with the largest figure topping 19,000 and the lowest not reaching 14,000.[28] However, not all objectors followed this route. Some men who called themselves COs failed or refused to appear before the tribunals and, consequently, found themselves subject to military service. Also, there were those who used different means to attempt to avoid compulsion (for example, they were performing or found work of national importance).

Any man whose claim was rejected outright remained subject to conscription, as did those men who refused to accept and comply with the tribunal decision or failed to apply for exemption. Some COs reported to the military but then announced their intention to refuse orders. Others failed to obey their call up papers and, if found, faced arrest, summary trial and a fine.[29] They would then be handed over to the military where some continued to refuse to be a soldier. Indeed, despite the fact that the tribunal system had failed to accord many of these men the legal status of 'conscientious objector', those who continued in their stance still tended to be referred to as objectors even by those who opposed them.

Objectors in the army

Once in the army, those men who refused to obey orders faced the harshness of army discipline, including a range of inventive techniques and punishments, court-martial, military detention and potentially execution if taken to the Front. Such men quickly became a nuisance and an embarrassment to the military authorities. However, no plans had been laid for objectors who, for whatever reason, found themselves in the military and persisted in their intransigence. In consequence, such men experienced repeated punishments, court-martials and terms of military detention because as conscripts they remained soldiers (unless they were adjudged unfit for service). It soon became clear that something needed to be done for these men, if only to relieve the military of their burden. A series of initiatives followed with the Government seeking to find new ways of dealing with the conscientious objector problem.

To further complicate matters both for the military and COs there was initially some confusion as to whether objectors in the army (whether classed as combatants or in the Non-Combatant Corps) were liable to face the death penalty should their disobedience warrant this penalty. A statutory safeguard had been inserted to prevent this possibility but its precise effect was unclear; the Army Council interpreted it to mean that only the first refusal to obey was exempted from the death penalty.[30] Reassurances were given in the House of Commons[31] but differences of opinion remained. A few COs in the army were taken to France in May and June of 1916 and, having refused to obey orders at the Front, were feared to be at risk of execution. As a consequence of anxieties about their fate, their supporters lobbied the Prime Minister and secured a clear direction to the military and statement in Parliament that executions were not to be carried out in the case of objectors without Cabinet approval.[32] In fact, no men who claimed to be COs from the outset and refused to comply with the military were executed in the First World War. However, groups of objectors taken to France were initially sentenced to death, although their sentences were immediately commuted.[33]

Transfer from military detention to civilian prisons

Subsequently, through a provision which came to be known as 'Army Order X' the Government allowed for those serving periods of military detention following court-martial to be transferred to civilian prisons.[34] However, once their sentences were completed these men were handed back to the military and, consequently, their continued disobedience could result in further court-martials and periods of incarceration. Thus, for example, Dennis Hayes estimates that 655 COs were court-martialled twice, 521 three times, 50 five times, and three six times.[35]

Once in prison objectors were subject to the harsh regime experienced by 'ordinary criminals'. This Third Division treatment meant that they had none of the privileges of other categories of prisoner serving terms of 'penal servitude' rather than 'hard labour'. Hard labour required a man to be kept in solitary for the first twenty-eight days, then he would be allowed to work alongside others (generally this amounted to sewing mailbags for between six to ten hours each day). If well behaved, two months into his sentence he could communicate with family and suitable friends and receive visitors. Also, the 'silence rule', which had by this time supposedly been replaced by a discretionary granting of permission to talk in some circumstances and for limited times, was still widely in evidence in relation to objectors.[36] Disobedience could result in solitary confinement for long periods and a punishment diet.[37] Moreover, as ordinary criminals objectors were initially denied the privileges which had eventually been granted to Suffragettes under Rule 243A.[38] This decision not to allow COs any concessions was a conscious one; conscience was not to be seen as allowing an easy way out of the military.[39] However, subsequently some dispensations were made for those who, because of their refusal to cooperate with the authorities, remained in prison long term (see below).

The Home Office Scheme and the Brace Committee

The repeated court-martial and imprisonment of COs failed completely to unburden the military and caused complaints about the treatment of objectors. Again the Government intervened by offering those objectors who had been court-martialled the chance to be 'reviewed' by the Central Tribunal. However, this did not constitute a reversal of earlier tribunal decisions. If a man agreed to be considered and was found to be 'genuine', he was to be offered the option of being transferred to section W of the Army Reserve. Should he accept this new status he would be released from prison and directed to work by the (Brace) Committee on Employment of Conscientious Objectors.[40] The Home Office Scheme, as it was known, initially placed objectors in work centres or camps around the country but subsequently moved to a policy of dispersal. The work and conditions on the Scheme were meant to be sufficiently difficult to discourage others from viewing a claim of conscience as a means to evade conscription. Some objectors did join the Scheme but a number rejected the offer or opted to return to prison once they found that the work they were doing aided the military or the war effort. Others were returned to gaol following their failure to cooperate with the authorities.[41] There they would serve out their sentences, be returned into military hands, disobey orders, face court-martial and then be returned to prison again.

Objectors in prison

Those who refused to co-operate with the authorities technically remained in the military for the duration of the war, serving repeated terms in prison as at the end of each sentence they would be released into military hands, court-martialled for further disobedience and returned to gaol. These included men who were militantly anti-authoritarian and those known as the absolutists, the 'extremists of peace', who rejected any form of alternative service but had different views in relation to cooperation with the authorities (official figures put the number in the latter category as 985).[42] Thus, some men tried to disrupt the authorities as much as possible, whilst others endeavoured to be obedient in so far as their consciences would allow.

In 1917 privileges under Rule 243A, which ameliorated the harshness of incarceration, were granted to COs who had spent a substantial period in prison and had behaved well.[43] A further concession allowed for the release of unfit COs in prison and their transfer to the Army Reserve.[44] Also, some men were released from prison under the Prisoners (Temporary Discharge for Ill-Health) Act, 1913 (the 'Cat & Mouse' provisions introduced to deal with Suffragettes). As in the case of those other (gender) dissidents, release sometimes followed hunger-strikes and force-feeding. However, force-feeding was halted in 1919 when increased protests from the objectors remaining in prison and demanding release brought a wave of hunger-strikes and an increased risk of deaths occurring.[45]

Release, discharge and disenfranchisement

Once the Armistice was signed in November 1918, recruiting under the Military Service Acts was suspended and the work of the tribunals ended. After the war objectors were gradually and often reluctantly discharged from the military, and released from prison, from the Home Office Scheme or from alternative work. Men undertaking work under the directions of the tribunals or the Pelham Committee were released from their duties by February 1919.[46] The Home

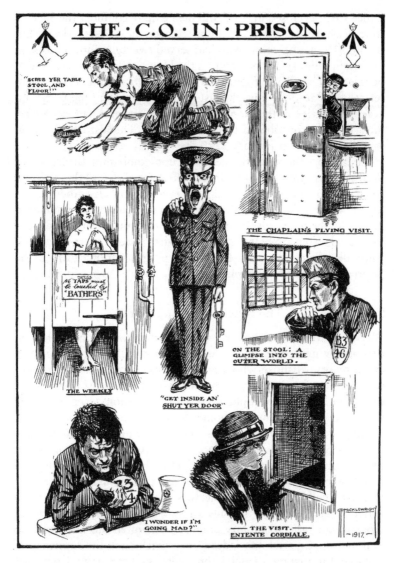

2 G.P. Micklewright, 'THE C.O. IN PRISON', 1917. Friends Library, London, Picture Collection, 86/AL 11.

Office Centres closed in April and men employed under the Scheme were discharged.[47] Objectors in prison were next. It was decided in April 1919 that objectors who had served twenty months in total in prison, in military custody and on the Home Office Scheme were to be released.[48] By early August all the men remaining in prison were released.[49] Paradoxically, the last to be set free were the COs who accepted service in the Non-Combatant Corps and had, therefore, most directly contributed to the war effort. The last of these men was demobilised in January 1920.[50]

Apart from the men who accepted non-combatant service, those in the army were dishonourably discharged from the military with the warning that, should they ever try to enlist, they would face court-martial. After the war objectors faced discrimination in employment because of their stance and those who had been exempted from military service or had been court-martialled were disenfranchised for five years under section 9(2) of the Representation of the People Act, 1918.

The conscientious objectors

Who then were the COs? As a starting point, technically only men of military age could fit the legal description. However, limiting the category to those who were recognised by, or even to those who appeared before, the tribunals would be unjustifiably limiting. John Rae, for example, prefers the definition accepted by the Government of the time, although he accepts that it is 'imperfect': for him, conscientious objectors were men who were granted some level of recognition of conscience in the tribunals or who, having not appeared before a tribunal or refused its decision, continued to refuse combatant service.[51] However, this leaves out a range of men who called themselves objectors. Those who were already on active service with the Friends Ambulance Unit or were abroad working for other voluntary organisations often did not return to appear before a tribunal; indeed, men working in the former were exempted following a special agreement with the Army Council.[52] As suggested above, some objectors undoubtedly evaded compulsion in other ways. For example, their work of national importance allowed them to gain exemption or they actively sought such employment before conscription was introduced. Some men applied for exemption on a number of different grounds including conscience simultaneously and may have been granted exemption on another basis, whilst others refused to go before a tribunal or attempted to avoid conscription by going on the run, going into hiding or leaving Britain.[53]

Also, objectors came from a range of social, economic and educational backgrounds and based their objection on varied grounds.[54] There were those whose objection was founded in socialism or the teachings of Tolstoy on non-violence and there were men who based their objection on anarchism or saw themselves as Bolsheviks. In contrast, for some their stance came from the tenets of their religion or their personal spiritual beliefs. These included Quakers, Christadelphians, Plymouth Brethren, Jehovah's Witnesses, Methodists, Anglicans and Catholics as well as a few men of the Jewish faith, some Spiritualists, at least one Buddhist and members of numerous small non-conformist groups. Other objectors founded their beliefs on a variety of moral, political or humanitarian grounds and, indeed, sometimes there was more than one basis for a man's objection and some men shifted the basis of their stance.

Thus, the ranks of COs included those who tried to bring about chaos or revolution, together with devoutly religious, law-abiding men, who practised passive resistance and strove not to be too troublesome for the authorities. For example, alongside COs who eschewed all violence there were men who would not hesitate to use it against those who challenged them. When one objector was waylaid by four or five 'roughs' at Wakefield he left them lying on the pavement; the man in question was an amateur boxer.[55] There were also those belonging to Christian sects whose behaviour could sometimes be bizarre and difficult to handle both from the perspective of the authorities and their fellow COs. Incidents at Princetown Prison on Dartmoor, which was 'deprisoned' (locks were removed from doors, for example) and transformed into a Home Office Centre, illustrate this point. During the war there were two outbreaks of 'mass hysteria' amongst some of the religious objectors. On these occasions the various factions of the Plymouth Brethren,[56] along with the Seventh Day Adventists,[57] the Sandamanians,[58] Muggletonians,[59] and the Swedenborgians[60] as well as adherents of the Anglo-Israelite movement[61] decided that Judgement Day was upon them and prepared accordingly. The whole Centre was affected as weeks of prayers and supplications ensued. When fire and brimstone failed to rain down and the last trumpet remained silent, the men returned to work.[62]

The nature of the objections and consequently what COs were prepared to do also varied greatly; some objected to state compulsion, some objected to war, some to this war, others objected to anything they felt amounted to killing by proxy, while a number refused to take part in any battle save the final conflict foretold in the Book of Revelation. As one CO, B.N. Langdon-Davies, explains:

> There were class-war men who had no objection to killing capitalists, but whose consciences baulked at fellow workers. There were this-war men, who had no objection to many wars that had or might occur, but who objected to this particular war for one reason or another. There were men who would do anything but actually kill with their own hands and there were men who tried to give up or avoid everything which directly or indirectly contributed to the financing or conduct of the war. One such . . . [man] went to prison for refusing to accept exactly the work he had for years been trying to get.[63]

Thus, the tasks that objectors were prepared to undertake in wartime also differed. For example, there were the absolutists in prison, numbering about 985 according to Rae,[64] who refused to be compelled, there were those who rejected alternative service but varied in the extent of their resistance beyond this, there were those who were happy to serve in the military so long as they were in the Non-Combatant Corps, men who went to the Front as part of the Friends Ambulance Unit but would have refused to undertake the same work in the Army Medical Corps and men who were happy to produce food. There were also the Christadelphians who were prepared even to manufacture munitions for the war as their objection related largely to being in the military and not to the war or alternative work.[65] As a consequence, following widespread non-recognition by the tribunals and negotiations with the authorities, special provision was made for men who were members of this denomination.[66] Moreover, objectors were not beyond changing their views, deciding for example that passive resistance was not sufficient, that the Home Office Scheme work which they were directed to did not accord with their objections or even that they would retract their claim and fight.

These vast differences between objectors meant that they were far harder to deal with than had been initially anticipated by the state. In particular, as the policy shifts and various concessions discussed above demonstrate, the differences between them made it impossible to deal with COs as a class of men. Moreover, the wide variety of objectors and objections also caused these men and their supporters to fall out amongst themselves. Indeed, a number of authors, notably Thomas C. Kennedy, depict the kind of splits that occurred as a consequence.[67] The satirical press also picked up on this. Thus, a *Punch* cartoon of early 1916 shows a passerby watching two men brawling. He suggests that they should be fighting in the war but a second observer responds with the words 'THEY WON'T GO, SIR. THEY'RE CONSCIENTIOUS OBJECTORS.'[68]

Beyond this, various authors have felt it necessary to attempt to calculate the overall number of objectors and those in different circumstances. For example, using his definition John Rae estimates that in total there were 16,500 COs of all kinds within the jurisdiction of the Military Service Acts, whilst Cyril Pearce, using a more liberal approach, has suggested that the figure may be 20,662 or 23,032.[69] However, my focus here is not upon numbers but rather upon multiple often overlapping and sometimes contradictory constructions of

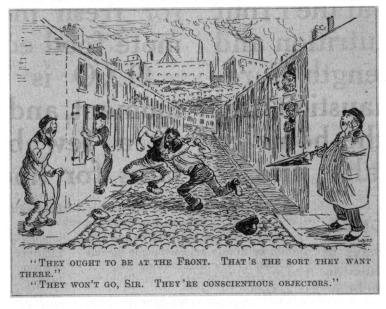

"THEY OUGHT TO BE AT THE FRONT. THAT'S THE SORT THEY WANT THERE."
"THEY WON'T GO, SIR. THEY'RE CONSCIENTIOUS OBJECTORS."

3 W. Bird, 'THEY OUGHT TO BE AT THE FRONT . . .' *Punch*
(2 February 1916), p. 81.

objectors, so no estimation of figures is offered in the text, although at points those proffered by others are referred to. Indeed, the fuzziness in terms of the definition of conscientious objection means that any estimation of numbers serves little purpose.

Organisations that supported and worked with objectors

Peace and anti-militarist groups existed before August 1914; however, with the declaration of war and moves towards conscription new organisations joined their ranks and many individuals with experience of peace campaigning joined and, in some cases, helped run the newer initiatives. A number of these pacifist, anti-war and anti-conscription groups along with democratic, political and religious organisations and elements of the trade union and labour movements supported objectors. People were often associated with more than one of these groups and, indeed, there was often support between different organisations. The most notable in terms of its focus upon resisting conscription and supporting objectors, its range of members, its national profile and potential influence was the No-Conscription Fellowship (N-CF or the Fellowship). Consequently, this text focuses upon this umbrella organisation.

The Fellowship was formed in November 1914 following the call by the editor of the Independent Labour Party's *Labour Leader*, Fenner Brockway, for men of enlistment age who opposed conscription to join the organisation.[70] Its aim was initially to prevent the introduction of conscription and, once the Military Service Act was passed, to bring about its repeal, although there were significant disagreements about a whole range of other related matters.[71] Brockway became its Secretary with Clifford Allen, another Independent Labour Party man, as Chairman and other prominent people amongst its supporters, although full membership was restricted to men of military age.[72] Prominent helpers included: philosopher and mathematician Bertrand Russell, who, in his early forties, was too old for conscription (Russell was acting Chairman for a time whilst Allen was in prison); penal reformer and Quaker Edward Grubb; and bacteriologist Dr Alfred Salter. Women, some of whom had been active in the fight for female suffrage, the women's movement and the various pre-war peace societies also came to play a prominent role in the organisation.[73] Thus, when most of the men were imprisoned Catherine Marshall, a prominent Suffragist,[74] took over running the organisation, Violet Tillard ran the Maintenance Organisation that helped support the relatives of objectors and was to become N-CF General Secretary in 1917 and Lydia Smith edited the organisation's journal, *The Tribunal*.[75]

N-CF members included men who based their objections on very different foundations and had various reasons for resisting compulsion. Indeed, not all shared the Fellowship's central aim of bringing down conscription. They included Independent Labour Party socialists and adherents of other less prominent leftwing organisations, trade unionists, Quakers, and members of other religious movements and churches. Most, however, were probably either Friends or members of the Independent Labour Party.[76]

Once the organisation was created, a National Committee was quickly established along with shadow officials (men not eligible for the military and women) who would take over the running of the organisation should its leadership be arrested for their activities or handed over to the military in the event of conscription. Based upon the models provided by the Suffragettes and Sinn Féin, the idea was to ensure the work could continue regardless of arrests, imprisonment, police surveillance and prosecution.[77] In addition, a network of local branches of the N-CF were established around the country.

Amongst other things, the organisation vigorously campaigned against conscription and strove to publicise the injustices and suffering that some COs experienced. The Fellowship also provided advice and support to COs and their families and kept meticulous records of their situation. It also produced the weekly *C.O.'s Hansard*, which collected relevant excerpts from debates in both Houses of Parliament, along with numerous pamphlets in order to inform its membership of developments.

There were other organisations that supported COs. For example, the Union of Democratic Control, founded in 1914, opposed conscription and anything it saw as 'Prussian' and anti-democratic. It worked closely with the N-CF and the Fellowship of Reconciliation.[78] The latter was a religious-based organisation which one 'sympathetic Quaker' describes as 'an organisation which works by prayer and the propagation of a right spirit, which eschews political action and is not in any immediate hurry to count up results'.[79] The organisation held religious meetings, led discussion circles, published pamphlets advocating the New Testament basis for pacifism and published a journal, the *Venturer*.[80] It co-operated with the N-CF and campaigned against and then supported resistance to the Military Service Act.

Another body, the National Council against Conscription was formed in London in the closing days of 1915 with the initial aim of preventing the introduction of compulsion, and local branches of the Council formed around the country. Once the Act passed the national body changed its name to the National Council for Civil Liberties and it, along with its local branches, worked against compulsion, amongst other things, producing pamphlets, campaigning and providing networks of support for COs and others who opposed the war. It included support from people with a range of political and religious beliefs, and also worked closely with the N-CF.[81]

Of the religious groups that supported objectors, the most notable was the Society of Friends. In May 1915 the Quaker's Yearly Meeting set up its own anti-conscription body, the Friends Service Committee. The Friends and the N-CF also worked together and in July 1915 a Joint Advisory Council was set up with representation from the N-CF, the Friends Service Committee and the Fellowship of Reconciliation so that organisation and information, along with efforts to support objectors, could be shared.[82]

In terms of leftwing organisations, the Independent Labour Party was the most prominent of those opposed to conscription, as its connection with the founding of the N-CF would suggest. Many members were active in the anti-war as well as the anti-conscription organisations and some were objectors. Despite some disagreement in the ranks, other leftwing groups, such as the British Socialist Party, also continued to fight against conscription.[83] In contrast, the trade union leadership were generally supportive of the war, but whilst they were initially opposed to conscription they were forced to accepted it once their major objection, industrial conscription, was ruled out.[84] However, at the grassroots level, around the country pockets of resistance to both the war and compulsion continued amongst the left including within unions.[85]

The trade union movement, labour and socialist organisations' objections to compulsion rested upon a number of linked concerns. There were the general objections to forcing men to fight fellow workers in an imperialist war and it was felt that conscription tended to make the working-class man suffer more than other classes both at the Front and at home. In the military it was assumed that he would be the first to the slaughter at the Front, whilst those men who remained would lose their hard-earned rights and that profiteering bosses would exploit their workers as well as the war. Also, as suggested above, there were concerns that industrial conscription would follow military conscription or that the former would be introduced by stealth should the tribunals be left free to specify that a worker conditionally exempted on grounds of national importance be required to labour for a particular employer.[86]

Notes

1 See War Office, *A Reprint of the Amendments Manual of Military Law* (London: War Office, 1914), Ch. IX. On volunteer forces before and during the war, see: M.H. Hale, *Volunteer Soldiers* (London: Kegan Paul and Co, 1900) – this was a new edition of *Amateur Soldiers* (London: Wyman and Sons, 1886); John Morton Osborne, 'Defining their own patriotism: British Volunteer Training Corps in the First World War', *Journal of Contemporary History*, 23:1 (1988), 59–75; John Morton Osborne, *The Voluntary Recruiting Movement in Britain, 1914–1916* (New York: Garland, 1982).

2 See further National Registration Act, 1915 and National Archives, London (hereafter NA), RG, which includes papers relating to the preparations for and the administration of the system of National Registration during the First World War (including records of several committees concerned with its operation) and to the tribunals set up under the Military Service Acts 1916–1918.

3 *Ibid.* s.12.

4 NA, CAB 37/139/26, Lord Derby 'Memorandum on recruiting', 13 December 1915.

5 On the work of the League see, for example, Denis Hayes, *Conscription Conflict: The Conflict of Ideas in the Struggle For and Against Military Conscription Between 1901 and 1939* (London: Sheppard Press, 1949), pp. 36–50; Ralph James Q. Adams and Philip P. Poirier, *The Conscription Controversy in Great Britain, 1900–1918* (London: Macmillan, 1987), pp. 10–48.

6 See Earl of Derby, KG, Director-General of Recruiting, *Report on Recruiting*, Cd. 8149, 1916. The Scheme was known by the name of the man who headed it, Lord Derby. Edward George Villiers Stanley, 17th Earl of Derby was to be Secretary of State for War 1916–18.

7 The tribunals were loosely overseen by the Local Government Board – for letters and circulars see NA, MH 10/79–84, 'Local Government

Board Circulars, 1914–1919'. The instruction to set up the local bodies is directed to Local Registration Authorities and dated 26 October 1915.

8 Alan John Percival Taylor describes the existence of this pressure for a major shift in policy – see *English History, 1914–1945* (Oxford: Clarendon, 1965), p. 53.

9 S.1(1)(a). It applied to those who were 18 (or subsequently reached the age of 18) and had not yet reached the age of 41.

10 The Military Service (No. 2) Act, 1916 extended conscription to married men and clarified the nature of the exemption available to objectors. The Military Service (Review of Exceptions) Act, 1917 dealt with exceptions to the operation of conscription. The Military Service Act, 1918 provided for the cancellation of certificates of exemption granted upon occupational grounds. Finally, the Military Service (No. 2) Act, 1918 allowed for the extension of the upper age limit to those who had not yet reached 51, and to those under 56 if necessary (s.1; s.1(1)(a)) and included other emergency powers (the extension of conscription to Ireland and the withdrawal of certificates of exemption unless these were granted on grounds of ill-health or conscientious objection).

11 S.1(1)(b) and sch. 1, para.2

12 Military Service Act, 1916, ss.2(1)(a), 2(1)(b), 2(1)(c).

13 *Ibid.*, s. 2(1)(d).

14 See NA, WO 293, 'Army Council Instruction No. 456', 4 March 1916 and 'Army Order 112', 10 March 1916. See also 'NON-COMBATANT CORPS: A NEW BRANCH OF THE ARMY', *The Times* (11 March 1916), p. 6.

15 On the work of the Corps see, for example: John Rae, *Conscience and Politics: The British Government and the Conscientious Objector to Military Service 1916–1919* (London: Oxford University Press, 1970), pp. 192–3; Peter Brock, 'Weaponless in the British Armed Forces: The Non-Combatant Corps in the First World War' in *Against the Draft: Essays on Conscientious Objection from the Radical Reformation to the Second World War* (Toronto: University of Toronto Press, 2006). John W. Graham estimates that there were about 3,300 objectors in the Corps: *Conscription and Conscience: A History 1916–1919* (London: George Allen and Unwin, 1971 reprint – first published 1922), p. 348.

16 See further Constance Braithwaite, *Conscientious Objection to Compulsions Under the Law* (York: William Sessions, 1995), p. 157. Unsurprisingly, the War Office view was that munitions handling was part of this form of military service. See Rae, *Conscience and Politics*, pp. 192–3.

17 The Government was keen to emphasise at the outset that this was not a penal unit created solely for COs. See, for example, 'THE NON-COMBATANT CORPS', *The Times* (14 March 1916), p. 7.

18 From Graham's estimates about 6,250 objectors were conditionally exempted and complied with their certificate (this figure includes a few hundred who were exempted by the Government rather than the tribunals because they were already serving in the Friend Ambulance Unit by early 1916). *Conscription and Conscience*, pp. 346–7.

19 See: NA, MH 10/79–84, 'R.70 Local Government Board Circular', 23 March 1916; Friends Library, London, Temp MSS 835/8/1, Pelham Committee Papers, 'Report of the Pelham Committee' (hereafter 'Report of the Pelham Committee'), 1919, 1 (in T. Edmund Harvey: Correspondence with COs from 1916–1920).

20 See Rae, *Conscience and Politics*, pp. 117–28.

21 Military Service Act, 1916, s.2(7) and sch. 2.

22 See NA, MH 10/79–84.

23 NA MH 10/79–84, Local Government Board to Local Registration Authorities, 26 October 1915.

24 For example, see John Burns, 4 HC 174, cols, 1275–84, 24 May 1907.

25 For example, see Cyril Pearce, *Comrades in Conscience: The Story of an English Community's Opposition to the Great War* (London: Francis Boutle, 2001), pp. 168–9 and Rae, *Conscience and Politics*, p. 131.

26 See NA MH 47/3.

27 For example, Graham takes the view that the Tribunals were generally unjust and unfair in their treatment of objectors. See *Conscription and Conscience*, ch. 3.

28 For example, see Pearce, *Comrades in Conscience*, p. 168.

29 See Military Service Act, 1916, s.1(2)(a) and War Office, 'Registration and Recruiting', August 1916, pp. 13–15.

30 See War Office, 'Registration and Recruiting', p. 14.

31 See David Lloyd George and Walter Long 5 HC 81, cols 308 and 327, 22 March 1916.

32 See H.J. Tennant, 5 HC 83, col. 492, 22 June 1916.

33 For example, Harry E. Stanton's account ('Will You March Too? 1916–1919', unpublished account of a CO's experiences (privately owned), volume 1, pp. 126–30).

34 Army Order 179, 25 May 1916, reproduced in *The Tribunal* – 'NEW ARMY COUNCIL ORDER' (1 June 1916), p. 4.

35 Hayes, *Conscription Conflict*, p. 8.

36 See Stephen Hobhouse, 'The Silence System in British Prisons', 52 (July 1918) *Friends Quarterly Examiner*, 249–63, p. 263; David Garland, *Punishment and Welfare: A History of Penal Strategies* (Aldershot: Gower House, 1985), pp. 23–4.

37 For descriptions of COs' prison experiences see, for example, Stephen Hobhouse, *An English Prison From Within* (London: Allen and Unwin,

1919). Garland's analysis of the developments relating to prisons during the late nineteenth and early twentieth centuries provides a useful context within which to consider the imprisoned objectors (see Garland, *Punishment and Welfare*, ch. 1). Two former objectors subsequently used their experiences in prison to work for prison reform. Stephen Hobhouse and Archibald Fenner Brockway (eds), *English Prisons To-Day: The Report of the Prison System Committee* (London: Longmans, 1922). Victor Bailey examines, amongst other things, these efforts and Garland's work in 'English prisons, penal culture, and the abatement of imprisonment, 1895–1922', *Journal of British Studies*, 36:3 (1997), 285–324.

38 See *Report of the Commissioners of Prisons and Directors of Convict Prisons*, Cd. 6406, 1912, p. 10; Sylvia Pankhurst, *The Suffragette Movement: An Intimate Account of Persons and Ideas* (London: Longmans, 1931), p. 376.

39 For example, see Home Office, 'The Home Office and Conscientious Objectors: A Report Prepared for the Committee of Imperial Defence 1919: Part II, Conscientious Objectors in Prison', p. 1 (subsequently 'Conscientious Objectors in Prison').

40 See Prime Minister Herbert Henry Asquith, 5 HC 83, cols 1014–15, 29 June 1916.

41 See, for example, Graham, *Conscription and Conscience*, pp. 350–1.

42 See Rae, *Conscription and Politics*, p. 167.

43 NA, CAB 23/4/257(3), Minute of War Cabinet meeting, 24 October 1917.

44 Lord Curzon, 5 HL 27, col. 53–6, 4 December 1917.

45 'Conscientious Objectors in Prison', p. 6.

46 See 'Report of the Pelham Committee'.

47 War Office, 'Statistics of the Military Effort of the British Empire in the Great War 1914–1920' (London: War Office, 1922), p. 673.

48 See NA, CAB 23/10/553(I), 3 April 1919.

49 See 'Conscientious Objectors in Prison', p. 6.

50 See further NA, WO 32/5490, 'Employment of Military Forces: Mobilisation and Demobilisation (Code 53(E)): Problems arising out of demobilisation of non-combatant corps', 1919–20.

51 Rae, *Conscience and Politics*, p. 70.

52 For the agreement see Friends Library, London, Temp MSS 977/1/2, Friends Ambulance Unit letter to members, 17 May 1916 (in Arnold Rowntree Papers). The work of the Unit in the First World War is described in Meaburn Tatham and James Edward Miles, *The Friends Ambulance Unit 1914–1919* (London: Swarthmore Press, 1920).

53 The state sought to locate, recruit and capture those men who sought to evade compulsion – whether they claimed to be doing so on conscience

or other grounds. See further NA, NATS 1/909 'Army Reservists normally resident in Great Britain who have proceeded to Ireland in order to evade military service', 1918 and NA, NATS 1/935 'Men of military age escaping to Ireland to evade call up', 1917–18.

54 Class is, thus, a significant factor in the analysis in this text.

55 James Primrose Malcolm Millar, 'A socialist in war time' in Julian H. Bell (ed.), *We Did Not Fight 1914–1918: Experiences of War Resisters* (London: Cobden Sanderson, 1935), p. 249.

56 On this group see, for example, William Blair Neatby, *A History of the Plymouth Brethren* (London: Hodder & Stoughton, 2nd edn, 1902, reprinted Stoke-on-Trent: Tentmaker Publications, 2001).

57 The organisation's objection was based upon their interpretation of the Old Testament commandments; see Francis McLellan Wilcox, *Seventh Day Adventists in Time of War* (Washington, DC: Review and Herald Pub. Association, 1936), p. 256. The latter was reprinted (Whitefish, MT: Kessinger Publishing, 2006). For information on this organisation see, for example, Mahlon Ellsworth Olsen, *A History of the Origin and Progress of Seventh-day Adventists* (Washington, DC: Review and Herald Publishing Association, 1932).

58 This group, also known as Glasites, based their objection upon their striving for separation from secular and political life. See James Hastings (ed.), *Encyclopaedia of Religion and Ethics*, volume 6 (Edinburgh: T. and T. Clark, 1913), p. 230.

59 Muggletonians tended to base their objection upon the expectation of the imminent arrival of the Son of God, although their literalist approach to biblical interpretation was also a factor. See James Hastings (ed.), *Encyclopaedia of Religion and Ethics*, volume 8 (Edinburgh: T. and T. Clark, 1915), p. 871.

60 The religious beliefs associated with adherents include a reinterpretation of biblical texts and a focus upon the second coming of the messiah via the writings of Emanuel Swedenborg. In the case of those men mentioned above, presumably their actions related to their readings of the Book of Revelation and the belief that Swedenborg had special knowledge of both the second coming and the Day of Judgement. On this organisation see, for example, Herbert Newell Morris, *The Creed of Swedenborgian* (London: New Church Press, 1932).

61 This movement is discussed in Chapter 2 below.

62 John Rodker, 'Twenty years after' in Bell (ed.), *We Did Not Fight*, p. 288.

63 B.N. Langdon-Davies, 'Alternative service' in Bell (ed.), *We Did Not Fight*, pp. 189–90.

64 Rae, *Conscience and Politics*, pp. 167, 201.

65 On this group see, for example: Andrew R. Wilson, *The History of*

the Christadelphians, 1864–1885: The Emergence of a Denomination (Australia Square, New South Wales: Shalom Publications, 1997); Harry Tennant, *The Christadelphians: What they Believe and Preach* (Birmingham: The Christadelphian, 1986). For a historical overview of the group's stance on military service see John Botten, *The Captive Conscience: An Historical Perspective of the Christadelphian Stand Against Military Service* (Birmingham: Christadelphian Military Service Committee, 2002).

66 They were granted special conditional exemption by the Army Council. See Frank G. Jannaway, *Without the Camp: Being the Story of Why and How the Christadelphians were Exempted from Military Service* (London: F.G. Jannaway, 1917) chs 30, 31; NA, MH 47/1, 'Minutes of the Central Tribunal', 4, 6 April 1916.

67 Thomas C. Kennedy, *The Hound of Conscience: A History of the No-Conscription Fellowship* (Fayetteville: University of Arkansas Press, 1981). See especially ch. 10.

68 W. Bird, 2 February 1916, p. 81.

69 See Rae, *Conscience and Politics*, pp. 70–1; Pearce, *Comrades in Conscience*, pp. 168–9.

70 Letter headed 'In Case of It', *Labour Leader*, 12 November 1914, p. 6. See further Archibald Fenner Brockway, *Inside the Left: Thirty Years of Platform, Press, Prison and Parliament* (London: Allen and Unwin, 1942 – reissued in 1947), p. 66.

71 By April 1916 the N-CF was claiming to have a membership of 15,000 (N-CF letter to Asquith, 15 April 1916, cited by Rae, *Conscience and Politics*, p. 11). A short account of the Fellowship's work is given by Brockway 'The Story of the NCF' in No-Conscription Fellowship, *The No-Conscription Fellowship: A Souvenir of its Work During the Years 1914–1919* (London: No-Conscription Fellowship, 1920), pp. 22–6. See further Kennedy, *The Hound of Conscience*.

72 See David Boulton, *Objection Overruled* (London: MacGibbon and Kee, 1967), pp. 100–9.

73 However, members of the female suffrage movement were by no means united in their stance towards the war. See further Anne Wiltshire, *Most Dangerous Women: Feminist Peace Campaigners of the Great War* (London: Pandora, 1985).

74 See further Jo Vellacott, *From Liberal to Labour with Women's Suffrage: The Story of Catherine Marshall* (London: McGill-Queen's University Press, 1993).

75 Wiltshire, *Most Dangerous Women*, pp. 144–5.

76 Boulton, *Objection Overruled*, p. 109.

77 *Ibid.*, p. 115.

78 See further: H. Hanak, 'The Union of Democratic Control during the

First World War', *Bulletin of the Institute of Historical Research*, 36 (November 1963), 94; Helena M. Swanwick, *Builders of Peace: Being Ten Years History of the Union of Democratic Control* (London: Swarthmore Press, 1924); Marvin Swartz *The Union of Democratic Control in British Politics during the First World War* (Oxford: Clarendon, 1971).

79 Quoted in Boulton, *Objection Overruled*, p. 52.
80 On the Fellowship, see: Jill Wallis, *Valiant for Peace: A History of the Fellowship of Reconciliation 1914–1989* (London: Fellowship of Reconciliation, 1991); Vera Brittain, *The Rebel Passion: A Short History of Some Pioneer Peace-makers* (London: Allen and Unwin, 1964).
81 See Boulton, *Objection Overruled*, pp. 119, 138, 217, 278; Pearce, *Comrades in Conscience*, pp. 152–4.
82 *Ibid.*, Boulton, pp. 112–13.
83 See Henry Pelling, *The British Communist Party: A Historical Profile* (London: Adam and Charles Black, 1958), p. 3.
84 G.D.H. Cole, *A History of the Labour Party from 1914* (London: Routledge, 1948), pp. 26–7.
85 For example, see Pearce's study of Huddersfield in *Comrades in Conscience*.
86 See, for example, Beatrice Webb's comments. Webb to Betty Balfour, 28 October 1915, Passfield Papers, II.4.g.f.45, quoted in Rae, *Conscience and Politics*, p. 10.

I

'Despised and rejected'[1]

This chapter looks at the construction of conscientious objectors (COs) as outsiders and outcasts, who were hated, ridiculed and viewed as mad. It sets their experiences within a conception of the war as an endeavour that was supported by the majority of the population.[2] In this context, the idea of conscientious objection was unfathomable. Thus, both attitudes towards COs and their treatment tended to reflect, at the very least, incomprehension or misunderstanding. What is more, objectors tended to be blamed for all manner of ills. Unsurprisingly, such attitudes, along with the unjust and harsh treatment they resulted in, were especially pronounced when the war was perceived to be going badly for the nation.

It is with a brief sketch of the idea of mass support for the war that this chapter begins. Then, building upon this scene setting, a range of contemporary notions, which fed and were consciously used in propaganda to bolster support for the conflict, are introduced. Finally, the CO is positioned within this milieu, as the text explores some of the ways in which he was despised and rejected.

Narratives of enthusiasm and support for the war

In the early days, weeks and months the Great War was a popular endeavour, with men, women, boys and girls all clamouring to join in. Enthusiasm was the order of the day and the vast majority of the population were swept away by it. Moreover – whilst the intensity of feeling may have waned as time passed, was sometimes replaced by weariness and occasionally resisted – for the most part the war was at least broadly supported if not always eagerly celebrated. This idea of widespread support for the fighting is, unsurprisingly, the picture portrayed in wartime jingoism and propaganda.

However, this is not a view limited to such texts. Indeed, a range of commentators (including objectors and their supporters), whether writing at the time or looking back upon the period, adopt a similar view of the nation's mood. In addition, this is how some historians, not least those writing about objectors, depict the social context.[3]

Turning first to the initial days of the war, various accounts of the sense of expectation in August 1914 as people waited to see what would happen and of the wild celebrations on the streets which followed the declaration of war convey a picture not only of widespread pro-war feeling, but also of an excitement that was contagious. Even in the days before war was declared some reports record a wave of 'mass hysteria'. Thus, one commentator notes that on 3 August 1914 in London '[a] vast procession jammed the road from side to side, everyone waving flags and singing patriotic songs . . . We were swept along . . . bitten by the same hysteria'.[4] Another version of the events at this time tells how on 4 August '[a]ll of London was awaiting Germany's reply to our Ultimatum, the excitement was intense, and it was plain that a large Majority were in favour of war'.[5]

According to this war narrative the early enthusiasm was demonstrated not only by crowds of people publicly celebrating in early August but also by the numbers of men who enlisted in the military. In the early weeks of the war accounts tell of the flood of volunteer soldiers and of recruiting offices inundated to such an extent that various buildings served as temporary facilities to process the men.[6] Thus, on the day that war was declared a 'seething mass' of men crowded round the Great Scotland Yard recruiting offices seeking to join up.[7] Indeed, official sources suggest not only an initial rush of men but also that large numbers continued to come forward throughout the period of volunteerism. Military statistics support this version of events, suggesting that around two and a half million men and boys enlisted in the first sixteen months of the war.[8] In addition, the introduction of the National Register, the Derby Scheme and ultimately conscription were, in part, said to be necessary precisely because of the vast numbers of men who had and continued to join up. Not only were the authorities finding it difficult to cope with so many raw recruits (they were at times unable to dress or equip them) but also many skilled workers had been lost as a result of the voluntary system, so some form of manpower management was deemed necessary.[9]

Thus, working-class men walked out of their jobs, often without informing their employer, leaving the latter in some difficulty because of the sudden and sometimes considerable depletion in their workforce.[10] The upper and middle classes came forward too. Writing in 1915, Edgar Wallace describes the great public schools as contributing 'almost to their last man to the call for officers'[11] and subsequently Reginald Pound estimates that nearly all the boys who left Winchester College between 1909 and the end of 1915 joined the military.[12]

Apparently the desire to be a soldier could be such that even men who were ineligible or unfit sought to be accepted. Wilfrid Wilson Gibson tried to enlist four times before he was accepted despite poor eyesight, although he served as a non-combatant in England.[13] The author of *Peter Pan*, J.M. Barrie, who had been recruited by the Propaganda Bureau at the start of the war[14] and, therefore, was charged with boosting support for the conflict, refers to this phenomenon in a short story. In 'The New Word', first published in 1918, a man past enlistment age describes his feeling towards another who dyed his hair in order to appear younger and be accepted by the military:

> [t]he thing that makes me wince most is that some of my contemporaries have managed to squeeze back: back into youth . . . though I guess they were a pretty tight fit at the turnstile.[15]

Moreover, the need to be part of the fight could apparently sometimes take a more desperate turn. According to Paul Fussell in *The Great War and Modern Memory*, on 9 August 1914 *The Times* included the following report:

> At an inquest on the body of Arthur Sydney Evelyn Annesley, aged 49, formerly a captain in the Rifle Brigade, who committed suicide by flinging himself under a heavy van at Pimlico, the Coroner stated that worry caused by the feeling that he was *not* going to be accepted for service led him to take his life. [emphasis added][16]

Whilst this has the ring of an apocryphal jingoistic tale, the story is, nevertheless, reflective of the dominant feeling in those early days both as it was frequently portrayed at the time and has often been depicted since.

Meanwhile, men who could not join the military sought to be part of the fight in some other way. Many satisfied their desire for the forces by setting up or joining self-generating paramilitary home defence units. Whilst these organisations pre-dated the war, from August 1914 new corps sprang up all over the country. Men joined out of patriotism and so that they might be in a kind of army, wear some sort of uniform and practise drilling as well as route-marching. These units continued to be popular throughout the war.[17]

Boys too desired to be soldiers. Particularly in the early months of the war, lads thronged the places where soldiers collected, enjoying 'the vicarious thrill of hanging about the troops'.[18] Indeed, some worried that if, as expected, the war had ended by Christmas, then they would 'miss out' on all the fun. A *Punch* cartoon in late 1914 both illustrated such anxieties and reinforced the sense that all the male population wanted to join up. A boy and his parents are pictured sitting at the breakfast table, the father dressed in uniform. The caption reads:

> Michael (gloomily). "MUMMY, I DO HOPE I SHAN'T DIE SOON."
> Mummy. "DARLING! SO DO I – BUT WHY?"
> Michael. "IT WOULD BE TOO AWFUL TO DIE A CIVILIAN."[19]

Some teenage boys who were below the age for enlistment tried to join up and in at least a few cases succeeded. For example, Victor Silvester (well-known later for his orchestra and television dancing club) recalls that he was fourteen and nine months when he played truant from school, told the recruiting sergeant he was eighteen and nine months and joined up.[20] Thus, for those nearer to manhood there was at least a chance of being accepted if they lied about their age. For younger boys a popular option was to join one of the militaristic boys' organisations, such as the Scouts or Boys' Brigade, where at least they could prepare themselves for soldiering.[21]

However, the urgent desire to be part of the war and, if possible, the military effort was not restricted to the male population. As Rose Macaulay's 1919 poem 'Many Sisters to Many Brothers' suggests, in this conception of the nation's response to the Great War women and girls often envied the men in khaki:

> Oh it's you that have the luck, out there in blood and muck:
> You were born beneath a kindly star;
> All we dreamt, I and you, you can really go and do,
> And I can't, the way things are.[22]

Some women did, of course, become a part of the war effort;
increasingly as the war progressed they worked in jobs left vacant
by men who had joined up or took over their work in order to
release them for the military. Others turned to nursing, joined the
pre-existing Voluntary Aid Detachments or laboured in the munitions and other essential industries. Indeed, as the conflict progressed women gained new opportunities to access the thrill offered
by being directly involved in the war effort; they laboured in paramilitary organisations (such as the Women's Army Auxiliary Corps,
Women's Royal Naval Service and Women's Royal Air Force), in
the Red Cross or Voluntary Aid Detachment, in factories, shops,
offices, on the land or on the buses.[23]

Those females who were not able to serve could at least express
their fervour for the war by encouraging their more fortunate men
folk. Thus, families and communities supported and were proud of
their men going off to fight. Mrs Beveridge, writing in *The Morning
Post* on 30 September 1914 celebrates '[t]hose gallant boys of
whom we, their mothers, and, I venture to think, the whole British
nation are justly proud'. She adds that she would 'not lift one finger'
to stop her own son from serving or 'take from him his grandest
privilege'.[24] For other younger women and girls the lure of the
uniformed man became an obsession and he became an object of
desire; if a girl could not be a soldier she could at least idolise them
and perhaps seek to acquire one.[25]

Another sign of this ostensible enthusiasm or backing for the war
was that during the conflict men, women and children seemed to
feel the need to wear a uniform or some visible signification of their
support for and involvement in the conflict even if they could only
approximate the look and had no claim to a direct military connection.[26] Most obviously, the various boys' organisations along with
the paramilitary home defence units to some degree allowed boys
and men to dress up as if they were soldiers – even if this was only by
wearing some small form of insignia.[27] Even the Women Patrols who
policed the female population had their own armbands to indicate
their role.[28] Similarly, for young men, armbands and badges demonstrating their status as wounded or engaged in essential war work
were also a symbol of their patriotism and involvement in the war.[29]

Beyond this, throughout the conflict men, women, boys and girls
engaged in a whole range of other activities in the name of patriotism and the war effort. They collected funds for war relief, in shops

and restaurants they refused to be served by foreigners and some, including the King, vowed to give up alcohol for the duration of the war.[30] Indeed, there are many stories of the (occasionally slightly bizarre) things that people apparently did in order to demonstrate their backing for the conflict, including the efforts of Miss G. Storey who set up a fund to provide soldiers at the Front with Bovril.[31] In addition, there were those women who took it upon themselves to try to recruit men for the military or at least berate those who looked both fit and young enough but wore no uniform.[32]

Thus, in these and other similar narratives about attitudes towards the First World War the vast majority of the population, it seemed, were not only in favour of the conflict but were also excited by it and keen to be a part of it; or, at the very least, they were supportive of it. This is shown even in some more measured responses to the war. For example, George S.C. Swinton in a letter published in the 5 August 1914 edition of The Times describes a very different, less hysterical but nevertheless committed mood:

> All over these islands to-day individuals of every class are saying to themselves, 'What can I do to help?'
> It is said quite quietly, with no panic, perhaps with no great enthusiasm, but with a real sense of responsibility.[33]

Significantly, as this and the next three chapters will illustrate, the construction of the war as a popular enterprise was a particularly common theme in accounts of the war by COs and those who backed them – whether these were set down during or after the conflict. For example, this chapter borrows its title from Rose Allatini's 1918 novel, which follows the lives of men who refused military service. Her characters speak about the ill-treatment and social ostracism they suffered as a consequence of following views which not only were often far from the apparent norm of war enthusiasm in society but also challenged it.[34] Likewise, in a wartime article Henry Wood Nevinson constructs his argument in support of COs upon the premise that there was a mass of popular opinion in favour of the war and that this resulted in their poor treatment.[35] In a similar vein, in 1917 Stanley Bloomfield James writes of the 'popular feeling' in favour of both the war and the military and the pressure this put COs under.[36] Moreover, from Bertrand Russell's anti-war and pro-objector perspective, 'most people were happier than in peace-time, because they enjoyed the excitement'.[37]

The foundations of enthusiasm and support for the war.

All this enthusiasm and backing for the conflict was unsurprising given contemporary ideas about the benefits of war, the holiness of fighting, the greatness of the nation, along with suspicions of German territorial intentions and hatred of Prussianism. Indeed, such ideas both produced and supported the popularity of the First World War. What is more, they were utilised by the state in order to sustain it. Thus, whilst these notions were fed to the populous through propaganda, they were already very much a part of the national psyche.[38]

For example, in some quarters in the early twentieth century war was felt to be a boon – offering the possibility of individual and national regeneration.[39] In '"The Blessings of War": The Depiction of Military Force in Edwardian Newspapers', Glenn R. Wilkinson examines this tendency.[40] He considers the imagery used to convey the 'idea of warfare' in the pre-1914 period, concluding that:

> The dominant perception of war was that it was not such a terrible event and that it would likely bring with it positive benefits to those engaged in it individually and as members of a nation.[41]

Also, an assumption of 'racial' and/or national superiority, promoted through various discourses, led many to believe that if war came 'we' would win; regardless of any racial connections between nations, 'we' were a breed apart. Here the greatness of England and the English 'race' (or Britain and the British) was often taken for granted; this was part of the nineteenth-century Anglo-Saxon myth. Indeed, Anglo-Saxonism 'attached a special merit to being English, to belonging to a people not just peculiar but privileged, blessed by its inheritance and its mission to the world'.[42] As one volunteer explains:

> We had been brought up to believe that Britain was the best country in the world and we wanted to defend her. The history taught us at school showed us that we were better than other people (didn't we always win the last war?) . . . and we wanted to show the Germans what we could do.[43]

Such beliefs could only reinforce the idea that war was to be welcomed. If the outcome was certain then the country could only benefit and men could be proud to fight for the greatest nation. The pride in England's imperial lands (which were sometimes taken to include Wales, Ireland and Scotland) also supported this confidence, which was in turn reinforced in school classrooms around the country where children studied the pink lands, owned by England, which dominated the globes and maps. Moreover, these acquisitions were secured through conflict: '[t]he British Empire is built up on good fighting by its army and its navy; the spirit of war is native to the British.'[44]

In addition, suspicion of and hatred for Germany and Prussianism had been encouraged prior to the war. This meant that for many this fight was an expected, a necessary and possibly a desired one. For example, fictional accounts and predictions of war with Germany or invasion and infiltration by the Kaiser's forces were widespread within the press, novels and pamphlets in the years before the war.[45] Thus, in early August 1914 Arthur Ponsonby MP talks of 'a deep animosity against Germany's ambition' which he said had been 'rankling all these years', linking this to the already present 'war fever'.[46] In addition, as another contemporary commentator notes, this 'anti-Germanism' was being encouraged by papers such as *The Times* and the *Daily Mail*.[47] Whether such texts caused or merely fed pre-existing anti-Prussianism, it seems that such feeling was not uncommon in the pre-war years and resulted in occasional attacks upon Germans.[48]

Religion also tended to support the conflict and feed the enthusiasm. Mainstream Christianity allied with patriotism had encouraged boys and men to see serving their country by joining up in a positive light as well as emphasising England's greatness. Establishment Anglican (pro-war) notions of Christianity also propounded the idea of fighting as a noble and necessary act as war was justified by the teachings of Christ.[49] Beyond this, as William Joseph Reader notes, '[i]f, as [some] claimed, war was part of God's plan for the ethical improvement of mankind . . . pacifism was a wrong-headed delusion and war service became legitimate'.[50]

It is, therefore, unsurprising that between 1914 and 1918 the Anglican Church and, to a large degree, other non-pacifist Christian denominations supported the conflict and clergy often used their position to call for active support of the national effort.[51] This pro-military stance led David Boulton to note subsequently that nine out of ten pulpits had turned into 'high pressure recruiting platforms'.[52] Indeed, on behalf of the government Lord Derby had called upon ministers of religion to use their influence to boost the number of men joining up[53] and clerics contributed to the recruiting efforts of the press. *The Times Recruiting Supplement*, 3 November 1915, included exhortations from the Archbishop of Canterbury, the Bishops of London and Birmingham, the Archbishop of Armagh, Cardinal Bourne, the Reverend F.B. Meyer (on behalf of the Free Churches), General Booth (of the Salvation Army) along with the Chief Rabbi and other prominent figures.

As this suggests, the Church of England was especially active in preaching a Christian patriotism that required that men did their duty for God, King and country and joined up. To take an extreme example of this tendency, Bishop Moule of Durham talked in 1915 of the 'holiness of patriotism' and, hence, encouraged people to support the war effort.[54] At the same time mainstream Anglican opinion, in particular, was almost unanimous in rejecting pacifism.[55]

In addition, in terms of the dominant interpretations of Christianity, the First World War was often portrayed as 'primarily a holy war' in which those who fought for Germany would be on the side of 'the devil and all his works'. In this context those fighting against the Hun would, of course, 'be fighting in the holy cause of humanity and the law of love.'[56] If this was true then, of course, victory was assured. Robert Bridges often expressed this view. For example, his poem 'Wake up England' is a religious call to arms:

> Thou careless, awake!
> Thou peace-maker, fight!
> Stand, England, for honour,
> And God guard the Right
>
> . . .
>
> Up, careless, awake!
> Ye peacemakers, Fight!
> ENGLAND STANDS FOR HONOUR.
> GOD DEFENDS THE RIGHT![57]

God then was on 'our' side and soldiers were often depicted as being rescued or tended to by celestial apparitions. The transformation of the short story 'The Bowman', by Arthur Machen, into the myth of the Angels of Mons and, thence, purportedly into a number of supposedly factual accounts, was an extreme but not unrepresentative example of this belief.[58] Similarly, other cultural forms reflected such ideas, portraying those opposing and victimised by Germany as God's people. Hence, Charles Ernest Butler's wartime painting 'Blood and Iron' shows Jesus tending dead, wounded and dying civilians whilst the Kaiser, along with the angel of death, look on.[59]

Thus, England or Britain was often portrayed as being on the side of right, fighting Germanic devilishness in a just war. Such binary depictions of 'our' side as good and the enemy as bad were common in various contexts and were exploited to legitimise the war and encourage a hatred which would instil, incite and maintain support for the war-effort. Further, propaganda and, in particular, atrocity propaganda was to feed upon and encourage this sense that Germans should be hated and feared as evil, satanic or, at least, un-Christian.[60] A number of papers carried such stories, including unsubstantiated reports of German soldiers cutting off Belgian children's hands.[61] Consequently, Henry Wickham Steed, foreign editor of *The Times*, describes how the enemy came to be portrayed and often viewed during the war: 'Germany had become virtually pagan, worshipping a deity more akin to Odin than to Christ.'[62]

Religious celebrations of English greatness, along with the belief that we could not lose as God was on 'our' side, were reinforced through the ideas promulgated by the Christian Anglo-Israelite or British Israelite movement (subsequently also known as the (Christian) Identity Movement). There were differing schools of thought, but the fundamental idea here was that England[63] was the geographical home of the true descendants of the ten lost tribes of Israel who, upon their escape from Assyrian captivity, travelled across Europe ending up in the British Isles. It followed that the Anglo-Saxon (and sometimes Celtic) 'race' were God's chosen people, England/Britain was the 'new Israel' and the monarch sat upon the throne of David.[64]

The movement was attractive because it allowed the English to believe that biblical prophecy was specifically directed at them and that, consequently, they were a chosen elite. As a result, their enemies were believed to be always at a disadvantage. Anglo-Israelism spread through different denominations[65] and acquired a degree of cultural currency within public debates and numerous publications advocated, refuted or developed the claims.[66] The ideas provided a justification for imperialism along with the proof, reassurance and security of knowing that England/Britain would always be great as God would see to the future. Thus, Edward Hine, one of the most prominent promoters of these teachings said: '[i]t is an utter impossibility for England ever to be defeated. And this is another result arising entirely from the fact of our being Israel.'[67] Similarly, Admiral John Arbuthnot Fisher, First Sea Lord for some of the First World War, recorded his belief in Briton's greatness in

The Times, 7 May 1919: 'Why we win, in spite of incredible blunders, is that we are the "lost" Ten Tribes of Israel'.[68]

The objector and the national mood

Amidst all this apparent excitement about and support for the conflict as well as the pro-war propaganda and recruitment drives that encouraged this conception of the enthusiastic and supportive national mood, there were, of course, various voices of dissent. However, merely expressing doubts about the war beyond the safety of like-minded circles could be expected to cause problems for the individual concerned, and declaring oneself to be a CO could lead to all sorts of difficulties even before conscription was introduced. Such men were at best greeted with puzzlement, incomprehension, suspicion or derision, at worst by hatred, ill-treatment and violence. Alongside this they were often viewed as outcasts, rejected by family, friends and mainstream society.

Incomprehension, along with a linked suspicion of objectors' motives, was a common response to these men and their ideas. Indeed, in a number of respects, given contemporary attitudes to war, the CO's stance in opposing the conflict, refusing to join up and resisting conscription was unfathomable. His lack of enthusiasm for the conflict was not only completely at odds with the apparently predominant air but also went against the idea that war was beneficial. From this standpoint, not supporting the war and failing to join up was considered to be at least nonsensical. A similar conclusion about COs was suggested by a general sense of confidence in the country's greatness and, as a consequence of this, a feeling that victory was assured in any conflict.

Indeed, given that war was portrayed as something the English or British had an inherent aptitude for, COs' thinking and actions seemed to be totally inexplicable. These men were rejecting not only war, which was held to be beneficial to the nation, but also fighting, which was both a key part of the national identity and the basis of the country's imperial greatness. Incomprehension of the CO in this and other regards was common. For example, one tribunal member could not fathom the man before him and asked a CO applicant in incredulity '[d]o you really mean to say you wouldn't kill anybody?' When the applicant agreed that this was the case the response was '[w]hat an awful state of mind to be in!'[69]

Moreover, if there was no doubt that the war would be won, then why should it be resisted? Consequently, objectors' various stances in opposition to these ideas about war and national superiority suggested, for example, that they were un-English or did not deserve to be English; patriotism demanded that they support the war, embrace their superiority and fight. Indeed, it was often assumed that conscience excluded patriotism, as the following passage from the pages of the *Daily Mail* demonstrates: '[i]n the schools where he [the CO] has been bred the word "patriotism" has been suppressed as something obscene. It is a word which may not be heard upon conscientious lips.'[70]

Following on from such sentiments one tribunal member declared that a man had no right to live in a country unless he was prepared to fight for it,[71] and at Tunbridge Wells Tribunal an objector was refused exemption 'because the chairman said he could not consider his conscience, but must subordinate it to the conscience of the country he lived in'.[72] Further, the fact that many objectors rejected the very idea of nationality as well as the importance of patriotism confounded those around them. At another tribunal in Huddersfield the Military Representative was astounded to hear the applicant, Arthur Gardiner, declare 'I have no country'. The former's response was to ask '[w]hat are you doing here, having no country? Why are you receiving all the benefits of a citizen when you have no country?'[73] This was a commonly held view, as the following passage taken from 'THE LETTERS OF AN ENGLISHMAN' column in the *Daily Mail* illustrates: 'If there be justice still left in this world, assuredly the Conscientious Objector shall never be allowed again to approach the polling-booth. How shall he be permitted to use the rights of citizenship who did not think that citizenship was worth fighting for?'[74]

Suspicion of and hatred for all things German not only reinforced support for the war but also made the objector's stance hard to grasp and meant that it could also be perceived to be unpatriotic or even pro-German. Thus, the CO sometimes came to be associated with the enemy in the popular imagination and was, consequently, often referred to as a traitor. For instance, the *Daily Express* described objectors as, amongst other things, 'agents of the enemy',[75] and Harry E. Stanton records COs in prison being seen as traitors who had been 'convicted of espionage'.[76] Similarly, there were apparently those who suspected that the No-Conscription Fellowship (hereafter N-CF or the Fellowship) was financed by Germans.[77]

What then of the objector in the context of religious views on war and soldiering in the opening decades of the twentieth century? Given that, in the establishment version of Christianity, war was justified because 'our' side was in the right and a duty to God was intimately connected with loyalty to king and country – and to be English/British was to be Christian and to accept the dominant interpretation of the scriptures – the CO's position was a difficult one. Indeed, it is arguable that Christianity, fighting, patriotism and English/Britishness had become so intertwined and firmly entrenched in many people's minds that to suggest their separation or to propose a differing version of the Faith was not only deeply offensive, it was quite simply wrong. Indeed, it challenged the very basis of their belief in God, their country and the war.

In the light of this, it is unsurprising that in terms of mainstream Christian thinking during the war, the objector was conceived of in a negative light or as incomprehensible; he was selfishly saving his own soul, misinterpreting the Bible, blaspheming, adopting heretical beliefs or supporting the devilish enemy. Moreover, the idea that 'we' were on the side of right also reinforced the sense that the CO should be castigated for his refusal to fight against evil (which was often identified with Prussianism) and the devil (who was frequently equated with the Kaiser), as reports show that some tribunal members were keen to point out.[78] Even if a more lenient view was taken, given the widely circulating atrocity stories, his refusal to support the war was incomprehensible to many, and Christian objectors were accused of using religion to conceal their less honourable motives. CO William Campbell records that it had been hinted to him that he was 'trying to hide cowardice behind . . . Christianity'.[79]

Accounts from tribunal hearings also demonstrate that members' and military representatives' knowledge of the scriptures was often severely tested in exchanges with such men, again highlighting the lack of understanding of objectors' beliefs. A tribunal member at Worcester felt that one applicant was a heretic who failed to see or wilfully ignored the true teachings of the Bible. His refusal to fight was to 'turn Christianity upside down' as 'the very essence of Christianity is to fight'.[80] At a Lancashire tribunal one member told an applicant that his claim was 'nothing but deliberate and rank blasphemy'.[81] Shoreditch Local Tribunal allowed Stephen Hobhouse to make a statement as to his beliefs but interrupted him whenever his views on Christianity and Socialism became too much to bear. Thus, he was able to assert that 'Germans, like Englishmen, have the spirit of God in them' but was stopped when he suggested that the British Empire had been built up by an 'aggressive war' and when he later tried to quote the Bible one of the tribunal members interjected, 'this is blasphemy'. The Military Representative then proceeded to maintain that 'an eye for an eye, and a tooth for a tooth' was one of Jesus's fundamental teachings.[82]

Sometimes the pronouncements from the tribunals on biblical matters took a more bizarre turn. For example, the Chairman of 'a tribunal near London', who had perhaps half-heard something of Anglo-Israelism, took the link between Christianity and the national identity to extreme lengths. When a CO applicant began to explain the meaning of a New Testament passage in the Greek the Chairman indignantly exclaimed 'Greek, you don't mean to tell me that Jesus Christ spoke Greek. He was British to the backbone'.[83]

In this context, non-religious objectors were even further beyond the pale than Christian men who adopted a very different creed from that espoused by the mainstream but were at least associated with it. Such men, by failing to embrace the nations' faith were even more un-English and incomprehensible. In one instance, a member of Burnley Local Tribunal informed an applicant that '[a] socialist cannot have a conscience'. The applicant was also told that 'HE CANNOT CLAIM TO BE A SOCIALIST AND A CONSCIENTIOUS OBJECTOR'.[84] Moreover, when an applicant informed a tribunal that he was an atheist, the tribunal Chairman, Major of Huddersfield, asked '[h]ave atheists consciences do you think?'[85] Further, non-religious political objectors were sometimes viewed as holding 'foreign' and, therefore, distasteful views[86] and were often rejected out of hand.[87]

Beyond such incomprehension of COs and their stance and partly as a result of this response to them, objectors were sometimes treated with derision as crackpots or madmen. This tendency to belittle objectors through ridicule and to view them as cranks or lunatics was a continuance of the pre-war view of peace campaigners, as James Primrose Malcolm Millar explains:

> During peace time . . . a man who declares himself an anti militarist may simply be laughed at, but during a war which the vast bulk of his fellows believe to be necessary, he ceases to be an object for amusement, ridicule or toleration, and becomes an object of bitter and unreasoned hatred.[88]

However, as he suggests, during the war ridicule was far less likely to be used in relation to such men.[89]

Nevertheless, some of the newspaper cartoons of the time seek to poke fun at the objector, although often the comedy has a malicious edge.[90] Perhaps the best example of light-hearted ridicule is a series of stories in the *Daily Sketch*. The paper followed the progress of

4 'CONSCIENTIOUS "PERCY'S" PROGRESS. – chapter III', *Daily Sketch* (17 April 1916), p. 1.

'Percy' the CO in the military, portraying him as a nonsensical figure, grinning maniacally and wrapped in an army blanket.[91] Such ridicule mirrored, to some extent, the way in which Germans were often portrayed.[92] In both contexts the idea was, of course, to express derision and dislike as well as to undermine, sideline and belittle.

Instances of madness being associated with the CO are, however, more common. Indeed, insanity was often used as a term of abuse. Thus, the Chairman of Aldershot Tribunal informed an applicant that he was 'qualifying for the lunatic asylum'.[93] At Gower Tribunal in Wales the Military Representative asked if the man before him had ever been detained in such a place.[94] The press also often branded objectors as mad. For example, the *Daily Express* argued that if they were not enemy agents then they must be 'crazy', describing them as 'neurotic curiosities'[95] and on 30 November 1915 the front cover of the *Daily Sketch* carried the banner line 'THE PLACE FOR THE PEACE CRANKS – THE LUNATIC ASYLUM'.

The absolutists, the 'extremists of peace', who persistently refused to co-operate in any way with the war and, consequently, remained in prison between their court-martials, were perhaps most frequently described as cranks or mad men. Their decisions to exist beyond the normal parameters of humanity meant that many questioned their sanity. For example, Herbert Fisher MP, President of the Board of Education, in discussing what to do with the men in prison felt that '[t]hese men are *ex hypothesi* cranks. They are morbid, obstinately tenacious of opinion, intractable, in many cases vain to the verge of lunacy . . .'[96] Indeed, N-CF Chairman Clifford Allen, himself an absolutist, recognised that most people felt that such men had 'a mania for being in prison'.[97]

The dissonance of the CO's ideas in terms of contemporary thought, the resultant incomprehension of his stance along with the tendency to deride or dismiss him as a crank, meant that the objector became an Ishmaelitish figure. Indeed, he was often rejected by society and, consequently, came to represent an outcast identity. Thus, in a 1916 editorial in *The Times* the paper denounces objectors who refused even non-combatant work and argues that any such man 'deserves to be treated as a pariah'.[98] Caroline Playne highlights this social ostracism:

> In general society you could scarcely mention their existence, much less claim acquaintance with individual COs, so great was the

disgust and abhorrence called forth . . . Some families expelled the
Conscientious Objector members from their midst, so keenly did they
feel the disgrace of the connection.[99]

Similarly, Allen recalled that '[o]ur utter isolation in the nation
was a very real thing'.[100] A man who was offered conditional
exemption and accepted alternative work, B.N. Langdon-Davies,
also wrote of the problems of being against war during the conflict. He describes several really serious effects including 'the clean
sweep of all one's friends except the very few who were more or
less of the same views' and 'the association almost exclusively with
people who were in deadly earnest, angry and plunged in gloom'.[101]
Indeed, for some objectors their circles decreased considerably and
could be limited to those in the same situation whether they were in
prison, at a Home Office Centre or in the community. Millar recalls
working on a market garden as a CO on the Home Office Scheme.
He was the only objector there and describes his isolation: 'I . . .
had all the loneliness of a pariah.' Soon the other employees let it be
known that unless he was sent away they would go on strike, so the
job lasted only a week. Indeed, he felt that his decision to be a CO
turned him into 'an Ishmael'.[102]

Objectors quickly became aware that people in their circle might
react unfavourably to their stance and may even eject them from
their midst. For example, 22-year-old William Campbell's letter
to his parents in November 1915 illustrates such concerns. The
document explores his thinking about enlisting, war and soldiering.
Willie (as he signs himself and was always known) was anxious
about the reactions of his friends, family and, in particular, his
parents to his views. He describes how recent hints to his aunts
(with whom he was staying) that 'England could not be all in the
right & Germany all in the wrong' came as a 'thunder-clap' to them
as they had no idea of his view before this and refers to their reaction as 'a regular tornado & all sorts of things were said against
me which I know were not meant'.[103] Willie attempted to explain
his views to one of the women but 'saw that she could not see my
position at all & could not sympathise in the slightest with me'.
Consequently, he came to the conclusion that 'my presence in the
home is intolerable'.[104] He also records that his aunts had written
to his cousin, Boyd, about his views and that the latter had already
sent him two letters urging him 'to have nothing to do with passiv-

ist [*sic*] views, but to be a man & . . . enlist'.[105] In the light of these reactions, Willie expresses concern about his parents' response to his opinions on war and soldiering, not least as he reveals that he is aware that one of his aunts has written to them and has undoubtedly mentioned recent events.[106]

The disagreement with his aunts and cousin took place even before the advent of conscription and at that time it appeared that a family split was a not unlikely result of his stance. Indeed, the rift between Willie and his cousin Boyd, with whom he had been brought up in Ireland, was to be particularly severe. The two men had been very close but, following Willie's decision to be an objector, according to his family they never spoke again.[107] In this instance the ill-effects of pacifism were permanent.

Dorothy Bing, whose brother Harold was a CO, describes a similar split. Her mother's sisters wrote saying they would not be speaking to the CO branch of the family. As Dorothy explained:

> You see, if you met somebody and said: "my brother is a conscientious objector", they looked aghast. It was the last thing anybody did in respectable society. You just didn't go to prison.

Indeed, so strong was their feeling and refusal to be associated with an objector that her maternal aunts continued to act as if their sister's family no longer existed after the war. In addition, her immediate family were asked to leave the Unitarian Church that they had long attended and Dorothy was told to stop teaching in the Sunday School.[108]

Where families and friends did not ostracise their objector relatives but rejected their views, they often felt humiliated and disgraced by the connection. Thus, having an objector and what is more, in the case of those who went to prison, a convict in the family could, as Dorothy Bing suggests, be difficult for respectable relatives to deal with. George Baker, in his autobiography *The Soul of a Skunk: The Autobiography of a Conscientious Objector*, recalls his delay in telling his parents about his failure to gain recognition at the tribunals, his decision to go to prison and their reaction once he revealed all:

> I knew that they would be beyond measure distressed at the idea, though I did not guess that they would be overwhelmingly ashamed as well as distressed. I argued that it was both cruel and useless to bring this distress upon them, until it could no longer be avoided.[109]

Indeed, his sense of desperation at the effect of his stance upon his family was such that while he was awaiting arrest he decided to end his own life rather than inform them. On 24 April 1916 he wrote letters to his family and a close friend, put his affairs in order, left home and hid in a narrow hollow, waiting for death from exposure, starvation or dehydration. His attempt was unsuccessful as three days later he was found and brought home.[110]

Some families sought to hide the fact that they had an objector in their midst as if this were a guilty secret. When Baker was released from prison and discharged from the military at the end of the war he returned home to find that '[o]utside my [immediate] family, no relative or family friend knew of my imprisonment: the shame of it had been kept a secret.' His father, brother and sister had evaded answering questions about him. His mother had been forced to lie 'to hide my shame' and, after his return, she worried that others seeing him walk 'would guess in what place I had got into the habit of shuffling'.[111] The family's sense of shame lasted throughout the war and continued beyond it. Moreover, whilst Baker was away in the military and in gaol, his father, knowing that the family disgrace would at some point be revealed, had decided to try to mitigate it in some way. Despite his poor health and age (his son describes him as being 'over fifty'), he had joined his local home defence unit, and Baker notes that the drilling, route-marching and burden of rifle and kit had taken their toll.[112]

Thus, it was not only COs who were affected by such attitudes. Those who supported them along with their families often also experienced hardship. Fenner Brockway, N-CF Secretary, describes the experience of the women left behind by their men and those women and men who continued the work of the N-CF whilst key members were in prison: '[t]hey had to live in the middle of a war-mad world and to undergo the contumely which opposition to the war and relationship to an imprisoned "conchy" involved'.[113]

Another consequence of objectors' ostracism was that in civilian life they often lost their jobs, as employers, fellow workers, customers or their community forced them to leave. The N-CF found that many men were reporting 'loss of employment, loss of positions, closing of prospect [sic]'.[114] Similarly, sometimes the Pelham Committee on Work of National Importance encountered a resistance to taking on objectors or a desire that any COs that were taken on would be kept separate from other employees.[115] As a result, John

Rodker recalls that prison at least 'solved the problem of getting employment at a time when no civilian jobs were open to us'.[116]

Those who were incarcerated but were subsequently released by the Central Tribunal to labour under the Home Office Scheme were also unpopular workers. When private firms were initially approached to employ objectors on the Scheme they refused 'either because of their prejudice against them or because of the risk of trouble with *ordinary* workmen' (emphasis added).[117] In addition, when the War Agricultural Committee was offered the services of these men it preferred to use German soldiers as:

> . . . while prisoners of war rapidly established themselves in favour, it was impossible to make much use of conscientious objectors; the feeling against them in county districts was strong and efforts to place them on farms met with little success.[118]

This sense of rejection continued for a while after the war both in the sphere of work and beyond, with some employers shunning former objectors. State and private employment practices reflected this hostility towards and rejection of COs. For example, the civil service had imposed restrictions upon the promotion and employment of objectors during the war, freezing the wages of those who were allowed to remain in their jobs of national importance, and continued with various types of discrimination until 1929, although these were gradually relaxed. The Ministry of Defence, however, maintained a complete ban on objectors.[119] Consequently, COs sometimes struggled to re-establish themselves after the conflict. Fred Tait, who was held in Leicester Prison until he accepted release on health grounds and joined the Friends Ambulance Unit, found it difficult to find a job after the war and ended up taking a number of 'trivial jobs', although previously he had been a teacher.[120]

Along with and linked to incomprehension and derision, hatred and violence were also common responses to COs. Moreover, people saw it as their patriotic duty and part of their war effort to challenge or insult any able-bodied young man who was not wearing a uniform and seek to persuade, embarrass or humiliate him into enlisting. A known objector was an obvious target for their attentions. The handing out of white feathers (to symbolise cowardice) was just one relatively mild example of the form that such an approach might take.[121] Another more extreme illustration of this type of behaviour was reported to have taken place in Bath following a CO's tribunal hearing. According to one report, local residents 'paraded last night with an effigy, which was burned in front of his house amid loud groans for the objector and cheers for the Army and Navy'.[122] Thus, in this view of their wartime experiences objectors were widely despised and often suffered harsh treatment, from harassment and injustice to abuse and attack. Consequently, they were by no means totally ignored by pro-war elements in society; indeed, for some mere ostracism might have been easier to bear.

Unsurprisingly, it was the political objectors and, in particular, the militants who tended to be the most despised of all COs, being castigated and variously described in colourful terms as 'lawless', 'subhuman' and 'unmanly'.[123] However, most if not all objectors experienced some degree of loathing and ill-treatment. Millar, reflecting on his experiences as a CO, remembers that:

> C.O.s got very few kind words during the war years . . . How one longed for friendly company – in place of the hatred and contempt that the ordinary citizen showered on us.[124]

Similarly, Rodker recalls how COs awaiting their call-up papers spent an unpleasant time 'in which we went about, shipwrecked as it were, on sufferance, all men our enemies'.[125]

Propaganda and the pro-war press encouraged hatred of as well as verbal and physical assaults upon COs. For example, at various points during the war there were inflammatory stories in the local and national press about the Princetown Home Office Camp and the objectors who had been placed there, as well as pictures of their antics.[126] Indeed, the press and the pro-war establishment seemed to delight in reporting examples of objectors' misdeeds, as such stories not only made good headlines but also reaffirmed anti-CO feeling.[127] More generally, the jingoistic press reinforced a patriotic fervour which tended to promote a violent hatred of all those who thought differently about the war. As Harold D. Lasswell notes, '[t]here must be no ambiguity about whom the public is to hate' if the abhorrence of the people is to be mobilised.[128] Thus, jingoism, which (as J.A. Hobson comments) in its most extreme form acts as '[a] coarse patriotism fed by the wildest rumours and the most violent appeals to hate and the animal lust of blood',[129] played a role here. During the First World War this bloodlust was directed primarily towards the 'Hun' but, to a lesser extent, it also targeted the anti-war movement and, more specifically, the objector. Hence, CO Langdon-Davies recalls the problems of being against war during the conflict as including 'the general difficulties, intellectual, moral and physical, of the propaganda'.[130]

In this context, it is unsurprising that the N-CF was particularly unpopular. Indeed, because of the amount of ill-feeling and hatred, those attending meetings were advised not to draw too much attention to their presence and to avoid enflaming passers-by and opponents. For example, men at the second N-CF National Convention in April 1916 were asked to refrain from clapping lest it announced their presence – instead handkerchiefs were to be waved.[131] Similarly, Millar describes the advice given on the printed notice for the event. Those looking for the venue were warned that '[o]nly policemen should be asked for directions to find the hall' so as to avoid notifying others as to the location.[132] Despite such caution a hostile crowd gathered outside.[133] In this instance the crowd had been encouraged by the pro-war press to disrupt the meeting and to give the COs a suitable reception.[134]

Not infrequently this hatred of COs spilled over into violence as vigilantes sought out objectors as well as others suspected of being, in particular, pro-German. Indeed, there were reports of objectors being attacked around the country. In May 1918 local youths assaulted COs at Knutsford Home Office Camp[135] and on Dartmoor parties of objectors from the Princetown Camp were attacked in the village, leading them to be confined to the prison grounds.[136] Thus, as Bertrand Russell observes, whilst the patriots feared the Germans, the pacifists feared the patriots – 'I can remember sitting in a bus and thinking: "These people would tear me to pieces if they knew what I think about the war"'.[137] As was suggested above, such violence was also often encouraged by the press. When some of the objectors at Knutsford were moved to Wakefield Camp there was further violence, in part incited by the local press, which expressed strong views concerning the arrival of the 'white-feathered crew'.[138]

It was not only in general society but also in their dealings with the state and its institutions that COs experienced hatred. Expressions of loathing and instances of ill-treatment were experienced by COs in the military, in prison and on the Home Office Scheme. For example, in the military in the most extreme incidents objectors were subjected to physical abuse including kickings and beatings along with a variety of more inventive tortures.[139] Appearing before a tribunal, which was supposedly charged with judiciously interpreting and applying the Military Service Acts, was also no guarantee that an objector would be fairly treated. These bodies often expressed their prejudice against and hatred of objectors openly. In a hearing at Hammersmith the Chairman angrily stated that he had 'had enough of these conscientious objectors', adding '[s]erve them all alike'.[140] The N-CF organ, *The Tribunal*, often conveys an extremely negative picture of these bodies, arguing that '[they] seem to take the view that a conscientious objector, whatever his statement of belief, is a person to be rebutted, bullied and condemned'.[141] Similarly, Philip Snowden MP, a supporter of COs, notes that 'a great many of the Tribunals seem to take delight in heaping scorn and insults upon the applicants who appear before them for exemption on this ground [conscientious objection]'.[142] Consequently, some examples of tribunal practice would suggest that hearings (where there was a hearing) often operated as a denunciatory rather than an investigatory process.

Indeed, hatred interlinked with bigotry and jingoism inhabited some of the hearings, arguably influencing their treatment of objectors not just through expressions of hatred and denunciations but also in the form of various kinds of unfairness including refusals to hear applications on conscience grounds, the unjustified rejection of genuine claims or the refusal to grant adequate levels of exemption or any exemption. Thus, tribunal members sometimes objected to or refused to accept the 'conscience clause' and, therefore, failed to apply it. The Chairman of Wirral Local Tribunal announced:

> I wish the Government had not put this clause about conscientious objectors in the Act at all. I do not agree with it myself.[143]

A member of Hudderfield Tribunal was opposed to the idea of exemption from military service and he, along with a like-minded colleague, was vocal in criticising CO applications and, when recognition was granted, threatened to challenge the decision on appeal.[144] Some tribunals sought various means to prevent men from appealing. Thus, a number of appeal tribunals refused to grant leave to appeal to the Central Tribunal. At Manchester all certificates of exemption were directed to be marked '[l]eave to appeal refused', and in Liverpool a man who lodged an appeal was told by the Tribunal's clerk that his application would be acknowledged but 'no leave to appeal was being granted'.[145] Tribunals also sought to prevent appeals by not sending out papers until the deadline had passed.[146]

Sometimes, as a consequence of hatred, CO's hearings could be extremely brief. This was reflected in the rejection of objectors out of hand or with the slightest excuse as well as in instances of abuse. For instance, Stanton records that his appearance on 8 March 1916 at Luton Local Tribunal lasted less than three minutes,[147] and at another tribunal the Chairman rushed a CO's hearing saying 'we are not paid for this sort of work'.[148] Indeed, these bodies seemed to seize the slightest justification for refusing a claim. Harold Frederick Bing's application was dismissed within moments once the Tribunal realised that he was only 18 years old and, they concluded, was too young to possess a conscience.[149]

There was even some state recognition of the prejudice against and harsh treatment of objectors within tribunals as a 1916 circular from Walter Long, President of the Local Government Board which was responsible for the constitution and procedure of the tribunals, demonstrates. Directed at the local tribunals, who were most often perceived as being the worst culprits, the document noted that '[s]ome tribunals are alleged to have subjected applicants to somewhat harsh cross examination with respect to the grounds of their objection' and called for an end to such practices.[150] The circular was not binding upon the tribunals, and complaints continued. Thus, even when directed to behave fairly some tribunals continued to treat objectors in accordance with their prejudices against them rather than in accordance with the law. The result was often a gap between the statutory rhetoric of recognition and the realities of tribunal practice, which made the 'conscience clause' take on the appearance of a symbolic rather than a genuine provision.[151]

So in this conception of the popularity of the war and the unpopularity of the CO, hatred and prejudice was common within the tribunals as well as in society, and the majority of commentators on the treatment of objectors during the war seem to support this view. For example, writing in 2001, Cyril Pearce estimates that there was a refusal to grant any form of exemption to applicants on conscience grounds in around 40 per cent of tribunal cases and suggests that his figures are by no means inconsistent with the view that 'the majority of tribunals allowed prejudice or intolerance to dictate their decisions'.[152] Writing during the war Beatrice Webb describes their work as 'a scandalous example of lay prejudice'.[153] James expresses a similar view, comparing some of the tribunals' unjudicial and illogical pronouncements to quotations from *Alice in Wonderland*.[154] Moreover, this conception of the tribunals lived on and was to become so notorious amongst politicians that when the Military Training Bill was debated in 1939, members recalled the First World War experience.[155] Indeed, their unfairness was also fictionalised in J.A. Cronin's 1935 novel *The Stars Look Down*.[156] Consequently, in 1970 even John Rae, despite his attempts to 'rescue the reputation of the Tribunals from the criticisms of Boulton, Moorehead, Graham and others',[157] recognises the ill repute in which these bodies were held, concluding that 'not since Lord Jeffrey's Bloody Assize have judicial bodies left to posterity a reputation so closely identified with injustice and bias'.[158]

Conclusion

Amidst the narratives of enthusiasm and support for the war, the objector was sometimes conceived of as a perplexing eccentric and was sometimes cast as the fool or charged with lunacy. He also tended to be spurned by family and friends and treated as an outcast by society. However, COs were not entirely rejected but were often subjected to special attention including deliberate injustice, verbal abuse and violence attacks. Wartime fiction reflects this picture of the ostracism, hatred and ridicule of objectors. For example, as mentioned above, *Despised and Rejected*, written by Rose Allatini under the pseudonym A.T. Fitzroy, was published in May 1918.[159] The text's two main characters, a gay CO and a lesbian, become part of a pacifist subculture revolving around a London café. The work provides a powerful account of objectors' early wartime experiences, with characters dissecting the stance of the CO and objectors describing their self-exposure to 'ridicule and vilification'.[160]

Indeed, to some extent, the objector was also seen as a scapegoat for contemporary concerns about, amongst other things, the conflict and the plight of men at the Front; he was a suitable target for patriotic citizens to blame.[161] The CO, for example, could be held responsible for the prolonging of the war (if all eligible men fought then surely it would end in a swift victory) or even for causing the conflict. Thus, a Military Representative at Huddersfield Tribunal, when faced with the father of two socialist CO applicants, felt that '[i]t's people like him who got us into the war'.[162] A member of Tipton Tribunal in Staffordshire told an applicant:

It is such people as you who are the cause of all wars. If I had my way I should try to abolish you Christadelphians . . .[163]

Similarly, T. Anderson felt that COs had caused the war and bemoaned the 'pacifist cranks and international faddists' with their 'peace at any price prattle'.[164] This scapegoating of objectors provided a further justification for their ill-treatment; if they were multiply culpable then they deserved to suffer.

Moreover, as suggested above, the negative effects of COs' stance did not end with the armistice. Thus, Baker recalls how he became

> . . . a pacifist, a Skunk, an Ishmael (except that his hand was not against all men's), who before prison, wore the white feather; in prison, the broad arrow, and after prison (according to some) the badge of matricide, the mark of Cain.[165]

Indeed, as *The Times* notes in 1917, having placed themselves 'permanently outside the community', COs were often considered to have 'no title either to its protection or to the enjoyment of civil rights'.[166]

Intertwined with these negative conceptions of objectors there were other notions associated with these men. There was, for example, an underlying sense of the unmanliness of COs. Thus, their refusal to adhere to contemporary ideas about war, fighting, Christianity and patriotism meant that their masculinity was called into question. The next chapter picks up this theme, focusing upon the idea of objectors as 'unmen'.

Notes

1 This is the title of Rose Allatini's novel, published under the pseudonym A.T. Fitzroy in 1918 by C.W. Daniel Ltd. It was reissued in 1988 – The Gay Men Press Publishers Ltd: London.

2 Thus, here notions of the war as a positive endeavour are deployed as a construct or device to assist in constructing and forming a background to the argument. Indeed, these broad notions form a backdrop not only to this chapter but also (to varying degrees) the next three. They are also a presence in Chapters 5 and 6, when the concepts associated with this way of seeing the war as well as COs are reconsidered and disrupted. Indeed, Chapters 5 and 6 will show that the use of this narrative about the war is by no means the only lens through which the war and COs can be conceptualised.

3 A range of histories take this perspective on initial attitudes and/
or long term support. See, in particular: Henry Stuart Hughes,
Consciousness and Society (New York: Knopf, 1958), pp. 336–91;
John Terraine, *Impacts of War, 1914 and 1918* (London: Hutchinson,
1970), p. 47; Keith Robbins, *The First World War* (Oxford: Oxford
University Press, 1984), p. 17; Brock Millman, *Managing Domestic
Dissent in First World War Britain* (London: Frank Cass, 2000), p.
7 (who writes that 'such few voices as were raised in dissent were
overwhelmed by a chorus supportive of the decision to resort to
arms'). See also William Joseph Reader, *'At Duty's Call': A Study
in Obsolete Patriotism* (Manchester: Manchester University Press,
1988). Beyond this, as Cyril Peace notes, influential cultural histories
have also accepted the enthusiasm thesis (*Comrades in Conscience:
The Story of an English Community's Opposition to the Great
War* (London: Francis Boutle, 2001), p. 25). See, for instance: Jay
Winter, *Sites of Memory, Sites of Mourning* (Cambridge: Cambridge
University Press, 1995); Paul Fussell, *The Great War and Modern
Memory* (Oxford: Oxford University Press, 25th anniversary edn,
2000 – first published 1975).
  A number of authors who have written about objection have also
tended, more or less explicitly, to take a similar line. For example,
John W. Graham's account dwells at length upon expressions of
hatred and instances of cruelty in the context of mass patriotic
support for the war (*Conscription and Conscience: A History 1916–
1919* (London: George Allen and Unwin, 1922, reprinted 1971)).
Similarly, David Boulton's 1967 *Objection Overruled* casts socialist
COs as loathed by general society because they rejected mainstream
conceptions of the war (London: MacGibbon and Kee, 1967). Also
in John Rae's more state-centred approach, published in 1970, there
is a strong sense of objectors having a difficult time during the war
because of negative societal attitudes towards them (*Conscience and
Politics: The British Government and the Conscientious Objector
to Military Service 1916–1919* (London: Oxford University Press,
1970)). Thus, behind all these narratives lies an assumption that
the majority went along with the propaganda and was supportive
of, if not entirely enthralled by, the idea of an all-encompassing war
fever.
  In addition, some writers on COs specifically describe an initial
excitement for war (for example, see Will Ellsworth-Jones's *We Will
Not Fight: The Untold Story of World War One's Conscientious
Objectors* (London: Aurum Press, 2008), p. 16). Thomas C. Kennedy,
in *The Hound of Conscience: A History of the No-Conscription
Fellowship*, notes '[t]he overwhelming popular support for the war

in August 1914' – seeing this as a 'terrible and inexplicable blow' to pacifists and anti-militarists, and he talks of '[t]he jubilant exhilaration that prevailed among the English bank-holiday crowds awaiting the news that their country had gone to war' (Fayetteville: University of Arkansas Press, 1981), pp. 22, 28.

On this tendency to depict or presume enthusiasm and support in the context of the study of COs, see further Cyril Pearce, who considers a number of the texts mentioned above (*Comrades in Conscience*), pp. 23–25, 69–75. Pearce sees Trevor Wilson's *The Myriad Faces of War: Britain and the Great War 1914–1918* (Cambridge: Polity, 1985) as being the 'high water mark' of this so called 'old consensus' scholarship on the war and, in particular, war enthusiasm (p. 24). Indeed, the 'war enthusiasm' thesis is now the subject of some controversy as a number of histories have sought to debunk, qualify or explore the conception of the war as a popular endeavour (along, in some cases, with other 'myths' about the war). For discussions and critiques of this enthusiasm thesis see, in particular: Niall Ferguson, *The Pity of War* (London: Allen Lane, 1998), ch. 7; Hew Strachan, *The First World War, Volume I: To Arms* (Oxford: Oxford University Press, 2001), pp. 103–4; David Silbey, *The British Working Class and Enthusiasm for War* (London: Frank Cass, 2005), chs 4–7; David Stevenson, *1914–1918: The History of the First World War* (London: Penguin, 2005), pp. 38–40. In rebutting the old consensus view Ferguson, for example, refers to the idea of war enthusiasm as 'an axiom of historiography' (p. 174) – as Grant Mansfield explains, this entails 'a belief so strong that it has almost entered historical folklore; a simple yet self-evident truth' ('"Unbounded enthusiasm"': Australian historians and the outbreak of the Great War', *Australian Journal of Politics and History*, 53:3 (2007), 360–74, 361). See further Chapter 5 below.

4 Imperial War Museum, London (hereafter IWM), Document Collection, PP/MCR/37, Microfilm copy of First World War memoir of E.C. Powell, pp. 2–3.

5 Basil Williams, *Raising and Training the New Armies* (London: Constable, 1918), p. 6. Other similar accounts of the crowds of early August 1914 are, for example, provided by Ferguson, *The Pity of War*, p. 176. On 5 August 1914 the press also included accounts of the crowds and their excitement. For one of the more measured contemporary versions of this story see 'AWAITING THE DECLARATION. THE SCENE AT THE FOREIGN OFFICE. PATRIOTIC DEMONSTRATIONS', *The Times*, p. 6. Papers such as the *Daily Sketch* and *Daily Mail*, which were, amongst other things, much more populist in their tone and approach, tended to be far less

restrained in both describing and encouraging the sense of excitement (see especially the 3, 4, 5 August 1914 issues).

6 For example, see Williams, *Raising and Training the New Armies*, p. 8.

7 *Ibid.*, p. 6. Other accounts of large numbers of men at recruiting offices in the early days are, for example, to be found in the press. Thus, *The Times* carried regular articles reporting this. See, for example: '"BOOM" IN RECRUITING' (5 August 1914), p. 3; 'GROWTH OF THE ARMY' (13 August 1914), p. 4.

8 *General Annual Reports of the British Army for the period from 1 October 1913 to 30 September 1919*, Cmd 1193, p. 9. See further Silbey, *The British Working Class*, p. 27.

9 See, for example: David Lloyd George, *War Memoirs of David Lloyd George*, vol. I (London: Odhams, 1938, first issued 1933), p. 427; Clement Kinloch-Cooke, 'National service: the National Register and after', *The Nineteenth Century*, 78:464 (1915), 792–807. Kennedy also discusses these problems, citing further sources (*The Hound of Conscience*, pp. 30–1).

10 James Maxton describes a trend that was visible around the country. In August 1914 he was visiting a fruit farm in Perthshire in order to support striking workers. However, he found that many of the men (who were from the slums of Dundee, Edinburgh and Glasgow) abruptly ended the action once war was declared: 'the male portion of our army of strikers vanished in twenty-four hours to line up at the recruiting offices to fight for the country which was giving them the meanest level of existence'. 'War resistance by working class struggle', in Julian H. Bell (ed.), *We Did Not Fight 1914–1918: Experiences of War Resisters* (London: Cobden Sanderson, 1935), p. 214. On working-class volunteering see further Silbey, *The British Working Class*.

11 Edgar Wallace, *Kitchener's Army and the Territorial Forces: The Full Story of a Great Achievement (In the King's Army)* (London: George Newnes, 1915), p. 186.

12 Reginald Pound, *The Lost Generation* (London: Constable, 1964), p. 151. Other sources estimate that large numbers of young men from Cambridge and Oxford served, although volunteers and conscripts are not distinguished. See: G.V. Carey (ed.), *War List of the University of Cambridge 1914–1918* (Cambridge: Cambridge University Press, 1921); Edwin Stewart Craig and W.M. Gibson, *Oxford University Roll of Service* (Oxford: Clarendon Press, 1920). On the conception of the rush of men from different classes, see further, Reader's argument and sources in '*At Duty's Call*'.

13 David Roberts, *Minds at War: The Poetry and Experience of the First World War* (Burgess Hill: Saxon, 1996), p. 207. Gibson's eventual

acceptance despite his unfitness was probably the result of the pressure to take as many men as possible, which was especially acute during perceived crises in the war and panics about the numbers in the military. For further examples of such efforts see Joanna Bourke, *Dismembering the Male: Men's Bodies, Britain and the Great War* (London: Reaktion, 1996), p. 81, fnt.2.

14 *Ibid.*, p. 54.

15 Reprinted in Trudi Tate, *Women, Men and the Great War: An Anthology of Stories* (Manchester: Manchester University Press, 1995), p. 236.

16 Fussell, *The Great War and Modern Memory*, p. 19.

17 The volunteer units that existed prior to 1914, known as the Volunteers and subsequently the Territorial Force, were mobilised in August 1914. The terms of their enlistment stipulated home defence but as events developed they were asked and, indeed, pressurised to volunteer for overseas service as at this time there was felt to be little need for home defence. This left a gap on the Home Front, which enthusiastic men sought to fill. See: M.H. Hale, *Volunteer Soldiers* (London: Kegan Paul and Co, 1900), which was a new edition of *Amateur Soldiers* (London: Wyman & Sons, 1886); John Morton Osborne, 'Defining their own patriotism: British Volunteer Training Corps in the First World War', *Journal of Contemporary History*, 23:1 (1988), 59–75, 60.

18 Angela Woollacott, '"Khaki Fever" and its control: gender, class, age and sexual morality on the British Homefront in the First World War', *Journal of Contemporary History*, 29:2 (1994), 325–47, 328.

19 (9 December 1914), reproduced in Roberts, *Minds at War*, p. 78.

20 Reconstructing the story years later, he records that he told his parents but they did not prevent him going. When his regiment found out his age they did not send him home but delayed drafting him to France. He describes both his sense of frustration because of this and the way he got round this barrier to his service abroad; he applied for a transfer to a different regiment where his youth was not known and was sent to France. Victor Silvester, *Dancing is my Life* (London: Heinemann, 1958), pp. 16, 19.

21 On such movements see further: John Springhall, 'Baden-Powell and the Scout movement before 1920: citizen training or soldiers of the future?' *The English Historical Review*, 102:405 (1987), 934–42; Springhall, *Sure and Stedfast: A History of the Boys' Brigade, 1883–1983* (London: Collins, 1983); Springhall, *Youth, Empire and Society: British Youth Movements 1883–1940* (London: Croom Helm, 1977); Paul Wilkinson, 'English youth movements, 1908–30', *Journal of*

Contemporary History, 4:2 (1969), 3–23; Richard A. Voeltz, '"...A good Jew and a good Englishman": the Jewish Lads' Brigade, 1894–1922', *Journal of Contemporary History*, 23:1 (1988), 119–27. In particular, Allen Warren posits the militaristic nature of the Scouts – see 'Sir Robert Baden-Powell, the Scout movement and citizen training in Great Britain, 1900–1920', *English Historical Review*, 101:399 (1986), 376–98. See further Chapter 2 below.

22 Reproduced in Roberts, *Minds at War*, p. 88.

23 On women's war work see, for example: Jenny Gould, 'Women's military services in First World War Britain', in Margaret Randolf Higonnet *et al.* (eds), *Behind the Lines: Gender and the Two World Wars* (New Haven, CT: Yale University Press, 1987); Angela Woollacott, *On Her Their Lives Depend: Munition Workers in the Great War* (Berkeley: University of California Press, 1994); David John Mitchell, *Women on the Warpath: The Story of the Women of the First World War* (London: Jonathan Cape, 1966); Susan R. Grayzel, '"The outward and visible sign of her patriotism": women, uniforms and national service during the First World War', *Twentieth Century British History*, 8 (1997), 145–64; Krisztina Robert, 'Gender, class and patriotism: women's paramilitary units in First World War Britain', *International History Review*, 19 (1997), 52–65; Doron Lamm, 'Emily goes to war: explaining the recruitment to the Women's Army Auxiliary Corps in World War I', in Billie Melman (ed.), *Borderlines: Genders and Identities in War and Peace 1870–1930* (London: Routledge, 1998). In addition, many women recorded their own accounts of their war work (although not all are equally enthusiastic about their experiences and/or the conflict). Not least of these are those within the IWM. For example, see Document Collection: 153 89/20/1 and 1A (Miss W. Adair-Roberts, private papers); 2364 86/20/1 (Mrs M. Harrold, private papers); 1899 92/49/1 (Mrs E. Wilby, private papers).

24 *The Morning Post*, 30 September 1914, p. 9.

25 See further, Woollacott, '"Khaki Fever"'.

26 See J.R. Raynes, *The Pageant of England, 1900–1920: A Journalist's Log of Twenty Remarkable Years* (London: Swarthmore Press, 1920), p. 169.

27 For example, Baden-Powell proposed elements of a uniform when formulating the idea of a boys' organisation. See Michael Rosenthal, 'Knights and retainers: the earliest version of Baden-Powell's Boy Scout scheme', *Journal of Contemporary History*, 15:4 (1980), 603–17, 606. Amongst other things, Osborne discusses defence units wearing of uniforms and the controversy that this caused, see 'Defining their own patriotism'.

28 Woollacott, '"Khaki Fever"', 335.

29 Badging, run by the Ministry of Munitions (under s.8(1) Munitions of War Act, 1915) was not wholeheartedly supported by the War Office – see Humbert Wolfe, *Labour Supply and Regulation* (Oxford: Clarendon Press, 1923), p. 37. However, such signs of men's involvement in the war effort were sometimes missed or failed to be understood. See further, Nicoletta F. Gullace, 'White feathers and wounded men: female patriotism and the memory of the Great War', *Journal of British Studies*, 36:2 (1997), 178–206, 199–200.

30 See Osborne, 'Defining their own patriotism', 59–60; Lloyd George, *War Memoirs* (1938), p. 196.

31 IWM, Document Collection, 2741 86/36/1 (private papers).

32 See further below.

33 George S.C. Swinton, 'PUBLIC SERVICE', *The Times*, p. 9.

34 Fitzroy [Allatini], *Despised and Rejected*.

35 Henry Wood Nevinson, 'The conscientious objector', *Atlantic Monthly*, 103:695 (November 1916), 686–94.

36 Stanley Bloomfield James, *The Men Who Dared: The Story of an Adventure* (London: C.W. Daniel, 1917), p. 13.

37 Bertrand Russell, 'Some psychological difficulties of pacifism' in Bell (ed.), *We Did Not Fight*, p. 331.

38 Some of the scholarship which depicts the pro-war national mood has also sought to trace the ways in which this supposed enthusiasm and support were founded upon such pre-existing ideas. For example, William Joseph Reader focuses upon the rush of men to volunteer for the military at the outset of the war, explaining this apparent phenomenon in terms of contemporary ideas about such things as nationality, soldiering, war and manliness (*'At Duty's Call'*) – he tends, however, to concentrate more upon middle- and upper-class than working-class men. See further Chapter 2 below.

39 For example, one medic argued in 1899 that drilling, in particular, could transform men's bodies. See Bourke, *Dismembering the Male*, p. 174.

40 Glenn R. Wilkinson, '"The Blessings of War": The Depiction of Military Force in Edwardian Newspapers', *Journal of Contemporary History*, 33:1 (1998), 97–115.

41 *Ibid.*, 115.

42 See, for example, Krishan Kumar, *The Making of English National Identity* (Cambridge: Cambridge University Press, 2003), p. 207.

43 Private George Morgan, 16th Battalion, Yorkshire Regiment, quoted in Malcolm Brown, *Tommy Goes to War* (London: Dent, 1978), p. 21.

44 Leading article, *Morning News* (20 October 1914), p. 1, quoted and critiqued by Bertrand Russell, 'The War and Non-Resistance: A Rejoinder to Professor Perry', *International Journal of Ethics*, 26:1

(October, 1915), 23–30, 26 (text available at http://fair-use.org/international-journal-of-ethics/1915/10/the-war-and-non-resistance#n1) (accessed November 2008).

45 For example, see further Ignatius Frederick Clarke, 'Forecasts of warfare in fiction 1803–1914', *Comparative Studies in Society and History*, 10:1 (1967), 1–25. The author explores this genre further (and within a wider historical and geographical frame) in *Voices Prophesying War: Future Wars, 1763–3749* (Oxford: Oxford University Press, 2nd edn, 1992).

46 See 'IMPERIAL PARLIAMENT', *Morning Post* (4 August 1914), p. 4.

47 A.G.G., 'WHY WE MUST NOT FIGHT' 'ENGLAND AND THE CRISIS', *Daily News* (1 August 1914), p. 6.

48 For example, see Eberhard Demm, 'Propaganda and caricature in the First World War', *Journal of Contemporary History*, 28:1 (1993), 163–92, 184.

49 Article XXVII, *Church of England Articles of Faith*.

50 Reader, *'At Duty's Call'*, p. 23.

51 See, for example, Alan Wilkinson, *The Church of England and the First World War* (London: Society for Promoting Christian Knowledge, 1978), pp. 32–7.

52 Boulton, *Objection Overruled*, p. 96.

53 See Wilkinson, *The Church of England*, p. 32. The Archbishop of Canterbury, however, refused to appeal for recruits from the pulpit (see Wilkinson, ch. 2). Also, the official Church of England Prayers for wartime were more restrained and did not claim that God was on our side. This resulted in some criticism – see, for example, Artifex, 'The Church's Opportunity', *Manchester Guardian* (20 August 1914), p. 10.

54 Wilkinson, *The Church of England*, p. 33 and see ch. 2 on the Church's role in the war effort.

55 *Ibid.*, pp. 54–5.

56 Robert Bridges, 'A HOLY WAR' (letter to the editor dated 1 September) *The Times* (2 September 1914), p. 9.

57 Robert Bridges, 'Wake Up England!', *The Times* (8 August 1914), p. 7.

58 The story was first published in the *Evening News* (29 September 1914) – see Fussell, *The Great War and Modern Memory*, pp. 115–16. The original version describes the bowmen of Agincourt coming to the aid of English soldiers, but people came to view these shining shapes as angels. On war myths see further: Arthur Machen, *The Angel of Mons: the Bowmen and Other Legends of the War* (London: Simpkin, Marshall and Co., 1915); David Clarke, *The Angel of Mons: Phantom Soldiers and Ghostly Guardians* (Chichester: Wiley, 2004). The Mons myth is described by Tate, *Women, Men and the Great War*, pp. 2–3 and her collection also includes a version of the Machen story (pp. 252–4).

59 IWM, Art Collection, 6492. The picture was exhibited at the Royal Academy in 1917.

60 Depictions of the Kaiser as Satan or a devil were not uncommon. For example, see IWM, Art Collection: 'Let Me Congratulate Your Majesty!' PST 13536; 'A Good Month's Business' PST 13537.

61 For example, see 'BELGIANS' ADDRESS TO THE KING: GRATITUDE TO ENGLAND: HIS MAJESTY AND GERMAN BRUTALITY', *The Times* (2 September 1914), p. 10. The stories of the Belgian atrocities were investigated. See Trevor Wilson, 'Lord Bryce's investigation into alleged German atrocities in Belgium, 1914–15', *Journal of Contemporary History*, 14:3 (1979), 369–83.

62 Henry Wickham Steed, *Through Thirty Years, 1892–1922: A Personal Narrative* (London: Heinemann, 1924), p. 37.

63 Sometimes Great Britain and occasionally Ireland were also referred to in this context – although England alone was spoken of often.

64 See further, John Wilson, *Lectures on Ancient Israel, and the Israelitish Origin of the Modern Nations of Europe* (Cheltenham (privately published), printed in Liverpool, 1840).

65 The beliefs of those within the movement varied considerably. For example, as mentioned in the Prologue, some Anglo-Israelites were conscientious objectors and others supported the war.

66 See, for example: Charles Dent Bell, *Anglo-Israelism true, not false. Being an answer to . . . Canon C. D. Bell. By Philo-Israel* (London: R. Banks, 1882); Bourchier Wrey Savile, *Anglo-Israelism and the Great Pyramid: an examination of the alleged claims of H.M. Queen Victoria to the throne of David; and of the reasons for fixing the end of the age in 1882* (London: Longmans and Co, 1880); Robert Roberts, *Anglo-Israelism refuted. A lecture . . . in reply to a lecture . . . by Mr. Edward Hine, . . .* (London: F. Pxitman, 1879; Birmingham: R. Roberts, 1884); H.J.D., *Anglo-Israelism. The English People Gentiles* (Durham: printed at the *Durham Advertiser* Office, 1878); Anon. ('By a Watcher'), *Christ in Joseph. A reply to "Anglo-Israelism" in the Church Quarterly Review of July, 1880* (London: Rivington, 1880); David Baron, *The History of The Ten "Lost" Tribes: Anglo-Israelism Examined* (London: Morgan and Scott, 1915).

67 Edward Hine, *The British Nation Identified with Lost Israel* (London: Robert Banks and Son, 1910), p. 73.

68 John Arbuthnot Fisher, '"A FINE OLD HEN THAT HATCHED THE AMERICAN EAGLE"', *The Times* (7 May 1919), p. 13. The British-Israel World Federation still exists. See www.britishisrael. co.uk (accessed July 2008).

69 Quoted in Graham, *Conscription and Conscience*, p. 89.

70 'THE LETTERS OF AN ENGLISHMAN' column, '"CONSCIENTIOUS" SHIRKERS' (28 April 1917), p. 2.

71 Philip Snowden, *British Prussianism: The Scandal of the Tribunals* (Manchester: National Labour Press, 1916), p. 11. The local tribunal in this example was in Aberavon, Wales.

72 Snowden, *British Prussianism*, p. 12.

73 Quoted in Pearce, *Comrades in Conscience*, p. 253.

74 '"CONSCIENTIOUS" SHIRKERS' (28 April 1917), p. 2.

75 'CONSCIENCE HUMBUG' (10 April 1916), p. 4. See further Chapter 3 below.

76 Harry E. Stanton, 'Will You March Too? 1916–1919', unpublished account of a CO's experiences, 2 volumes (privately owned). vol. 2, p. 183. In some instance objectors were also conceived of as being worse than the Germans. For example, see 'THE CASE AGAINST THE APPEAL TRIBUNALS: An Exhibition of Tolerance', *The Tribunal* (Thursday, 6 April 1916), p. 2.

77 For example, see: 'SOME CASES OF "FAIR DEALING"', *The Tribunal* (15 March 1916), p. 2; 'CONSCIENCE HUMBUG', *Daily Express* (10 April 1916), p. 4.

78 For example, see: 'WHAT THE TRIBUNALS ARE DOING: Impartial Consideration!', *The Tribunal* (8 March 1916), p. 2; 'SOME CASES OF "FAIR DEALING"', *The Tribunal* (15 March 1916), p. 2.

79 Letter from William Campbell to his parents, dated November 1915, p. 7, privately owned.

80 Quoted by Graham, *Conscription and Conscience*, p. 89.

81 Quoted by Graham, *Conscription and Conscience*, p. 71 and referred to in 'SOME CASES OF "FAIR DEALING"', *The Tribunal* (15 March 1916), p. 2.

82 Stephen Hobhouse, 'Fourteen months service with the colours', in Bell (ed.), *We Did Not Fight*, p. 166.

83 Quoted in Graham, *Conscription and Conscience*, p. 71; R.L. Outhwaite, 5 HC 80, cols 2435–37, 16 March 1916.

84 'A Socialist Cannot Have a Conscience', *The Tribunal* (6 April 1916), p. 3.

85 Quoted in Pearce, *Comrades in Conscience*, p. 256.

86 For example, see the Military Representative's comment quoted in *ibid.*, p. 256.

87 For example, see: *The Tribunal* (8 March 1916), p. 2; Snowden, *British Prussianism*, p. 12.

88 James Primrose Malcolm Millar, 'A socialist in war time' in Bell (ed.), *We Did Not Fight*, p. 226.

89 *Ibid.*

90 See, for example, the cover illustration to *Telling Tales* – 'Taking

Cover', signed F.H. – 'AFTER Lawson Wood', *John Bull* (5 February 1916), p. 17.

91 See, 'A CONSCIENTIOUS OBJECTOR'S FIRST DAY IN THE ARMY' (14 April 1916), p. 1; '"PERCY'S" PROGRESS IN THE ARMY' (15 April 1916), p. 12; 'CONSCIENTIOUS "PERCY'S" PROGRESS. – chapter III' (17 April 1916), p. 1. 'Percy' was a real objector named Eric B. Chappelow; see Kennedy, *The Hound of Conscience*, p. ii. The choice of nickname may have been significant given its resonance with the Victorian 'cult of chivalry' explored in Chapter 3 below. Although there are different versions of the tale, in Arthurian myth Percival became one of the King's knights but is sometimes initially portrayed as an innocent who was raised in ignorance of the ways of men. After meeting some knights, he decides he wants to be one, proves himself an excellent warrior and is invited to join the Knights of the Round Table. Chappelow acquired some notoriety and was referred to in *The Times* as the 'RECRUIT IN A BLANKET' (21 April 1916), p. 2.

92 See, for example, Cate Haste, *Keep The Home Fires Burning: Propaganda in the First World War* (London: Allen Lane, 1977), pp. 103–5

93 Quoted in James, *The Men Who Dared*, p. 15.

94 *Ibid.*

95 *Daily Express* (10 April 1916), pp. 4, 1.

96 Fisher in a letter to Curzon, 15 November 1917, Curzon Papers 72, cited in Rae, *Conscience and Politics*, p. 220. Here Fisher was actually arguing for their release from prison.

97 Allen in a letter from Maidstone Prison to Catherine Marshall, 21 April 1917, quoted in Martin Gilbert, *Plough My Own Furrow: The Story of Lord Allen of Hurtwood as Told through his Writings and Correspondence* (London: Longman, 1965), p. 71.

98 'Conscience and Conduct' (editorial/leader), *The Times* (8 April 1916), p. 9.

99 Caroline Playne, *Britain Holds On, 1917–1918* (London: George Allen & Unwin, 1933), p. 303.

100 Clifford Allen, 'Pacifism: then and now' in Bell (ed.), *We Did Not Fight*, p. 26.

101 B.N. Langdon-Davies, 'Alternative service', in Bell (ed.), *We Did Not Fight*, p. 185.

102 Millar, 'A socialist in war time', pp. 264–5.

103 Campbell letter, pp. 5–6.

104 *Ibid.*, p. 6.

105 *Ibid.*, p. 8.

106 *Ibid.*, p. 7.

107 Interview with one of Willie's sons, Professor Alastair V. Campbell,

12 April 2005. Campbell is Director of the Centre for Biomedical Ethics, National University of Singapore.

108 Caroline Moorehead, *Troublesome People, Enemies of War: 1916–1986* (London: Hamish Hamilton, 1987), pp. 30–1. Bing also talks about the ostracism of COs' families and her own experiences in IWM, Sound Collection, 555/9, Reel 1, Dorothy Bing ('British civilian pacifist in Croydon and London, GB, 1914–1945').

109 George Baker, *The Soul of a Skunk: The Autobiography of a Conscientious Objector* (London: Eric Partridge at the Scholartis Press, 1930), p. 119.

110 *Ibid.*, pp. 120–7.

111 *Ibid.*, pp. 263–4.

112 *Ibid.*, p. 264.

113 Cited in Sheila Rowbotham, *Friends of Alice Wheeldon* (London: Pluto, 1986), p. 36.

114 Cited in James, *The Men Who Dared*, p. 92.

115 See, for example, Friends Library, London, Temp MSS 835/8/1, Pelham Committee Papers, Home Grown Timber Committee, 'Employment of conscientious objectors in forestry operations' (in T. Edmund Harvey: correspondence with COs from 1916–1920).

116 John Rodker, 'Twenty years after', in Bell (ed.), *We Did Not Fight*, p. 288.

117 Home Office, 'The Home Office and Conscientious Objectors: A Report Prepared for the Committee of Imperial Defence 1919: Part I, The Brace Committee', p. 6 (subsequently 'Brace Committee').

118 Thomas Hudson Middleton, *Food Production in the War* (Oxford: Clarendon Press, 1923), p. 222.

119 See: National Archives, London (hereafter NA), CAB 23/4/298(18), Minute of War Cabinet meeting, 14 December 1917; Report of Select Committee on the Civil Service, 'Employment of Objectors' (London: HMSO, 1922); NA, Civil Service Commission: Files Series II CSC 5/85/, Treasury Circular E.1206/4, 'Civil Service and Conscientious Objectors', 10 September 1929.

120 Friends Library, London, Temp MSS 907, Nancy Martin, Epilogue, in Fred Tait 'Diary of a Conscientious Objector' (unpublished, 1992), p. 68.

121 See further, Gullace, 'White feathers and wounded men' and Chapter 2 below.

122 'Objector Burned in Effigy', *Evening Standard and St James Gazette* (1 March 1916), p 8.

123 See further Chapters 3, 4 and 5 below.

124 Millar, 'A socialist in war time', pp. 259–60.

125 Rodker, 'Twenty years after', p. 291.

126 By way of illustration see *Daily Mail*: '"HA HA! YOU CAN'T CATCH US!" SAY THE DARTMOOR DO-NOTHINGS' (23 April 1917), p. 8; 'PRISONERS ABROAD AND "OBJECTORS" AT HOME – OFFICIAL AND EXCLUSIVE PICTURES' (24 April 1916), p. 8; 'OUR DESTROYER HEROES IN HOSPITAL' AND 'THE "CONSCIENCE" SCANDAL' (27 April 1916), p. 8; 'OUR WONDERFUL WOUNDED – DARTMOOR'S ARTFUL DODGERS' (30 April 1916), p. 8.

127 The *Daily Express* was at the forefront of the production of such copy (but was by no means alone) – for instance, see: (7 April 1916), p. 5; (10 April 1916), p. 1; (8 April 1916), p. 5.

128 Harold D. Lasswell, *Propaganda Technique in World War I* (Cambridge: Massachusetts Institute of Technology, 1971), p. 47. This was initially published as *Propaganda Technique in the World War* (London: Kegan Paul and Co., 1927).

129 J.A. Hobson, *The Psychology of Jingoism* (London: Grant Richards, 1901), pp. 8–9.

130 Langdon-Davies, 'Alternative service', p. 185.

131 Allen, 'Pacifism: then and now', p. 27.

132 Millar, 'A socialist in war time', p. 225.

133 See for example Allen, 'Pacifism: then and now' pp. 26–7.

134 For example, Mr Cossip in 'Echos of the Town', 'No-Conscriptionists At Work', *Daily Sketch* (27 March 1916), p. 5 reported whispers of a planned meeting somewhere in London early the next month and referred with approval to 'efforts which are being secretly made to arrange for "hospitality" in London for these delegates'. See also 'SECRET MEETING OF PEACE CRANKS', *Daily Express* (7 April 1916), p. 5. The *Daily Sketch* was also active in encouraging its readers to act against any anti-war activities in London – see Mr Cossip, 'Echoes of the Town' (7 April 1916), p. 5.

135 'Brace Committee', p. 7.

136 *Ibid.*, p. 6.

137 Russell, 'Some psychological difficulties of pacifism', p. 330.

138 *Wakefield Express*, 18 May 1918, cited in Rae, *Conscience and Politics*, p. 189.

139 See further Chapters 3 and 4 in this volume.

140 See Snowden, *British Prussianism*, p. 18.

141 Clifford Allen, 'Our Point of View' (8 March 1916), p. 1.

142 Snowden, *British Prussianism*, p. 8.

143 Quoted in *ibid.*, p. 11.

144 See Pearce, *Comrades in Conscience*, pp. 162–3.

145 Snowden, *British Prussianism*, p. 19.

146 *Ibid.*, p. 5.

147 Stanton, 'Will You March Too? 1916–1919', volume 1, p. 8.

148 Snowden, *British Prussianism*, p. 13.

149 IWM, Sound Collection, 358/11, Reel 2 (transcript, p. 7), Harold Frederick Bing ('British civilian absolutist conscientious objector imprisoned in Kingston Barracks, Wormwood Scrubs and Winchester Prisons, GB, 1916–1919').

150 NA, MH 47/142, R.70, 23 March 1916.

151 On the idea of a gap between legislative rhetoric and practice see, for example, Doreen McBarnet, *Conviction: Law, the State and the Construction of Justice* (London: Macmillan, 2nd edn, 1983), pp. 159–63. On the concept of 'symbolic legislation' see Vilhelm Aubert, 'Some social functions of legislation', *Acta Sociologica*, 10:1–2 (1966), 98–120.

152 Pearce, *Comrades in Conscience*, pp. 168–9. This challenges John Rae's earlier view that, despite obvious instances of unfairness, ill-treatment and non-recognition, the tribunals were not as unjust and prejudiced when it came to COs as most had previously claimed (*Conscience and Politics*, p. 131).

153 British Library of Political and Economic Science, Passfield Papers, Beatrice Webb Diaries, 9 March 1916.

154 James, *The Men Who Dared*, p. 12.

155 For example, see T.E. Harvey 5 HC 346, col. 2182, 4 March 1939.

156 Archibald Joseph Cronin, *The Stars Look Down* (London: Gollancz, 1935), p. 357.

157 Pearce, *Comrades in Conscience*, p. 169. The text refers to: Boulton, *Objection Overruled*; Moorehead, *Troublesome People*; Graham, *Conscription and Conscience*. All of these authors criticise the tribunal record of unfairness, prejudice and bigotry in relation to objectors.

158 Rae, *Conscience and Politics*, p. 60.

159 Fitzroy [Allatini], *Despised and Rejected*.

160 *Ibid.* (1988), p. 342.

161 On the notion of the scapegoat see, in particular: René Girard, *The Scapegoat*, trans. Yvonne Freccero (London: Athlone, 1986); Michiel Heyns, *Expulsion and the Nineteenth-Century Novel: The Scapegoat in English Realist Fiction* (Oxford: Clarendon Press, 1994).

162 Quoted in Pearce, *Comrades in Conscience*, p. 162.

163 Reported in *The Tribunal* – 'WHAT THE TRIBUNALS ARE DOING: Impartial Consideration!' (8 March 1916), p. 2.

164 Letter to the *Nelson Leader* (3 December 1915) quoted in Thomas C. Kennedy, 'Public opinion and the conscientious objector, 1915–1919', *The Journal of British Studies*, 12:2 (1973), 105–19, 107.

165 Baker, *The Soul of a Skunk*, p. ix.

166 'Conscience Recalcitrant', *The Times* (25 October 1917), p. 7.

2

Of cowards, shirkers and 'unmen'

Set against the backdrop of the overarching support for the war
sketched in the previous chapter, the focus here is upon the idea
of the conscientious objector (CO) as being in various respects
unmanly. The text does this by constructing a dichotomy which
juxtaposes the objector with the soldier. In doing so the narrative
argues that during the First World War one cluster of masculinities
swiftly dominated notions of English or British manhood. Here the
image of the soldier-male was the brightest star in this particular
masculinist firmament. This representation of the exemplary and
aspirational military man to some degree drew upon pre-existing
understandings but was also encouraged and supplemented by
propaganda and the pro-war press. Thus, a range of ideas about
what it was to be a man were drawn upon and manipulated in order
to assist in a redefinition of manhood 'in terms of soldiering' and
this was the case for all classes of men.[1] As a result, the military man
came to be a much celebrated and desired identity.[2]

Unsurprisingly, in this context the CO fared extremely poorly.
By rejecting the military, even when compelled by legislation to
be a part of it, he seemed to represent the antithesis of the soldier.
Consequently, at best he was assumed to be selfish as opposed to
self-sacrificing and a coward rather than a hero. Indeed, he came
to be seen to embody a whole range of unmanly qualities and was
frequently cast as shirking, lazy, spineless, un-Christian, unpatriotic
and un-English/British. Moreover, sometimes he was perceived of
as womanly and sexually undesirable to women or was suspected
of sexual inversion.

The chapter begins by examining positive constructions of the
soldier. Utilising these dominant ideas about manliness, the text
then moves on to consider the CO. It explores the various ways in

which he was felt to be lacking in comparison to the masculine ideal embodied by the military man.

Manliness and the soldier

Both before and during the war the soldier was constructed as exemplary and aspirational in a range of cultural forms, and the characteristics which he was supposed to embody were celebrated. In addition, exposure to militaristic ideas or paramilitary training in a variety of environments meant that many young men had both been prepared for the possibility that they might be needed as soldiers and taught not only to revere the military man but also to embrace the notions of patriotism, duty and responsibility which he was meant to represent. Thus, his manliness was an idea rooted in contemporary discourses and experiences.

Many texts elevated the triumphant soldier to the pinnacle of aspirational manliness in their patriotism and dangerous adventures. They used a language of utopian heroism which created a tantalising and longed for warrior manliness and by the late nineteenth century they took place outside the (feminine) domestic sphere: such tales were about men, male camaraderie and intra-masculine rivalry.[3] In particular, boys' adventure stories focused upon links between manliness as a virtue and fighting, glamorising the adventure, heroism and honour to be gained from military service and promoting a sense of duty and patriotism.[4] Thus, G.A. Henty's stories are depicted in the following terms:

> [t]hey are essentially manly and he used to say that he wanted his boys to be bold, straightforward and ready to play a young man's part . . . He had a horror of a lad who displayed any weak emotion and shrank from shedding blood, or winced at any encounter.[5]

Boys' magazines also utilised a discourse about manliness which had militaristic and patriotic associations.[6] In similar terms, a range of publications for men as well as boys told exotic tales of far-off lands and celebrated the exploits of intrepid military adventurers. Here fictional representations were supplemented by popular 'true' narratives about real imperial heroes, such as the inexpensive 1885 pamphlet *Lives and Adventures of Great Soldiers in the British Army*,[7] which reprinted press stories. Such accounts formed part of the myth of Empire, they were 'the story England told itself as it went to sleep at night'[8] and they celebrated not only the greatness of the nation but also the individual achievements of the warrior.

These ideas about military manliness were evoked, tapped into and supplemented by propaganda literatures during the war. Thus, the First World War was often described in recruitment materials as providing the opportunity to experience life as a storybook hero, or to become like the real-life imperial conquerors such as Kitchener, the hero of Sudan and Secretary of State for War.[9] At the same time, posters, leaflets and cartoons promised honours, quests and dare-devil exploits, warned that if men were slow to join in, they might miss this wonderful opportunity or depicted the envy of those not eligible for the military by reason of age or gender.[10]

In addition, both pre-1914 tales of adventure (whether fictional or 'true') drew upon a range of specific ideas about heroism.[11] One frequent influence was the Victorian revival of the Arthurian tradition and its gentlemanly and, therefore, largely class-specific, Christian 'cult of chivalry'.[12] This explored the Arthurian romance 'tradition' and celebrated the figure of the knight with his code of honour requiring him to protect women and children against often magical foes.[13] In this context, both fictional and more factual accounts of imperial military exploits were portrayed as patriotic knightly quests.[14] Moreover, '[b]y stressing the essentially chivalric nature of such "military virtues" as discipline, dedication and self-sacrifice it was possible . . . to interpret colonial skirmishes as Christian Crusades'[15] and the Empire as 'a place where adventures took place, and men became heroes'.[16] Here then soldiers were portrayed as knights in shining armour.

This cult was most accessible and, indeed, fashionable to the middle or upper classes, as the focus upon the knight meant that this was a vision of a particular sort of man; a gentlemanly male, of the middle or upper classes who was potentially officer material and who embraced truthfulness, courage, honour and obligation, viewing any violation of such qualities as 'unsporting' and 'bad form'.[17] However, the chivalric themes were echoed in more widely available forms. Consequently, men or boys of lower classes could enjoy such chivalrous motifs in the more accessible form of press reports, celebrations of colonial military achievements or in adventure stories as well as in the Scouts. For example, *Chums*, a boys' magazine along the lines of *The Boy's own Paper*, was aimed at a lower-middle- and upper-working-class readership and includes adventure stories which focus upon the 'good works' and 'unselfish sacrifice' expected of the lower orders.[18]

The chivalric romance tradition, thus, involved a reverence for a certain kind of mythic or legendary soldierly manhood, and in the 1914–18 conflict this construction of the military man was to continue. Thus, Paul Fussell describes the romanticised language used to talk about the war and the soldier as echoing such sources. Here 'high diction' and the language of knightly honour transformed the mundane and the gruesome into a euphemistic romance lexicon. Here a horse became a 'steed' or 'charger'; the enemy was 'the foe'; danger was 'peril'; to conquer was 'to vanquish'; to die was to 'perish'; and the blood of young men was, in the words of Rupert Brooke, 'the red / Sweet wine of youth'.[19] Indeed, such language had begun being used to glorify the soldier and militarism even before the war. For example, Baden-Powell, founder of the Scouts, saw Scouting as embodying a form of chivalrous manliness which offered suitable roles to all classes of boys:

> The knights of old were the patrol leaders of the nation, and the men-at-arms were the Scouts . . . the knight would daily ride about looking for a chance of doing a good turn to any needing help, especially a woman or a child . . . in distress.[20]

During the war this style of expression came to be used, as Fussell suggests, more frequently and often with a greater and more direct sense of purpose. Thus, Christabel Pankhurst encouraged men to enlist in the following terms:

> I want men to go to battle like the knight of old who knelt upon the altar and vowed that he would keep his sword stainless and with absolute honour to his nation.[21]

Mainstream conceptions of Christianity also often portrayed the soldier, along with fighting and the war, in idealised chivalric terms. Prior to and during the Great War the soldier was a shining Christian knight or 'a type of crucified Christ' sacrificing himself for the greater good, and the fallen achieved martyrdom through their actions.[22] Moreover, writers often extolled the godliness of the military man[23] and establishment Christianity's support for conflict in general and the First World War in particular. In addition, such texts stressed the spiritual benefits of soldiering. Reflecting this tendency, Robert Bridges's poem 'Wake up England', published in *The*

Times on 8 August 1914, draws upon notions of Christian sacrifice and the promise of glory, purging of sins and resurrection for those who fight:

> Much suffering shall cleanse thee:
> But thou through the flood
> Shalt win to Salvation,
> To Beauty through blood.[24]

Thus, it was argued that joining up would bring not only heroic glory but also divine deliverance.

What is more, various discourses about war and the national identity tended not only to posit the military man as an idealised figure but also to suggest that soldiering, along with fighting, came naturally to the English or British man. This in turn implied that men would naturally come forward through a sense of patriotism, duty and a willingness to serve. For instance, those who supported the 'English tradition' of voluntary military recruitment assumed that the nation's men, in contrast to the Prussian, required no measure of legislative compulsion as innately conscientious Englishmen would do their duty.[25] In addition, as the previous chapter suggested, advocates of war as regenerative for the nation also saw soldiering as beneficial for the individual man and viewed war as a project of remasculinisation.[26] Here then the soldier was romanticised, depicted as an innate masculine identity and portrayed as a way of instilling manliness into men.

Such reverence for and celebrations of the soldier had also been inculcated in a variety of settings including within many public schools,[27] in state elementary schools,[28] in boys' organisations[29] and in the home defence forces,[30] as well as on the sports field.[31] In these contexts boys and men were often encouraged to see themselves as potential soldiers and to enjoy the association. For example, as the possibilities for earning a living or establishing a career in the military had expanded with the growth of the Empire, public schools and universities set up Cadet Corps, Rifle Corps and Officer Training Corps.[32] By 1914 many middle- and upper-class young men had passed through this system of training and had been instilled from a young age with a sense of gentlemanly discipline, patriotism and duty and a reverence for the soldier who embodied these qualities.[33] Stephen Hobhouse, who was to become a well-known CO, had experienced this at Eton. He was 'persistent and patriotic', joining the 'bug-shooters' in the years before the Boer War, before membership became popular. He rose in the ranks in a uniform purchased from an old boy who, he was proud to read, subsequently died heroically in South Africa. At Oxford, 'the flame of patriotism, encouraged as it was by parents and teachers', led him to continue in his military training by joining the University Cyclist Corps. Subsequently his views changed but he could still recall the intensity of these early influences years later.[34]

Also, in government-funded schools drilling was a requirement, in part, because of fears about the perceived threat posed by Prussian militarism and male degeneration.[35] Here too boys had tended to be taught skills and ideas in a manner which prioritised the manliness of the soldier. Similarly, various organisations encouraged boys both to aspire to the image of the soldier and to see themselves in militaristic terms. Notably in the Scouts, founded by Robert Baden-Powell in 1907, the ethos, aims and activities meant that boys began to see soldiers in idealised terms and to view themselves as some sort of warriors.[36] In addition, within the various home defence units men were taught and, indeed, sought the glory of an association with the military man.[37]

On the sports fields, too, boys and men of all classes were encouraged to see the connection between games and war as well as to celebrate and aspire to the sportsmanship of the soldier. In the public schools there was a sense that boys had been trained to wait on the sidelines in readiness to 'play the game' of war. Thus, Colin Veitch argues that sport sought to prepare boys 'for the moral and military battles [they] might have to face in the wider world'.[38] In similar vein, in 1906 Dr J.E.C. Welldon, Bishop of Calcutta, former headmaster at both Dulwich College and Harrow School, explained both the importance of games and the link between the English sportsman and the soldier, stating that, as a result of his experience on the playing field, when an 'English gentleman . . . is put down in the face of duty . . . he will know what to do, and he will do it'.[39] Moreover, the image of the war as an international contest was popular.[40] As a result, amongst former public school boys this link between the battlefield and sports field as well as the soldier hero and the sporting hero was often made before 1914.[41] Indeed, such ideas were also encouraged within the working classes, particularly through the medium of football.[42]

Thus, in a range of spheres the manliness of the soldier was being portrayed and promoted even before the war, and once the conflict began these were a resource for propaganda to draw upon and exploit. For example, recruiting efforts, patriotic literature and the jingoistic press drew upon the connection between sport and soldiering to encourage such men to come forward and 'play the game', echoing Henry Newbolt's refrain in each verse of 'Vitai Lampada' ('The Torch of Life').[43] Moreover, writing in 1916 one commentator argues that '[m]en still regard battles as magnified football scrums: war is still for many men a glorified sport'.[44]

More specifically, however, it was the volunteer soldier who was at the apex of this hierarchical lexicon of manliness. In willingly coming forward he, in particular, was constructed as self-sacrificing, courageous and patriotic. Thus, whilst any man who wore a uniform, however it was acquired, could lay claim to this image of exemplary manliness, it was the conscientious volunteer soldier who was portrayed, implicitly or explicitly, as the ideal during the war.

In addition, as Ilana R. Bet-El maintains, there was during the war (and has continued to be) a 'rigid correlation between patriotism and voluntarism that excluded the conscripts from the prevailing imagery of both masculinity and soldiering . . . and also redefined the soldier . . . as a volunteer.' Consequently, the dominant construction of manliness revolved around the idea that 'a real man = a patriot = a volunteer = a soldier.'[45] In Bet-El's work this formation is depicted as seemingly colonising the way in which soldiering during the war was (and has since been) depicted; indeed, this image of the volunteer rushing to enlist was a dominant motif within the previous chapter. More specifically, this tendency for all soldiers who fought in the Great War to be seen and portrayed as volunteers[46] meant that notions of English manliness were confirmed and men's sacrifice was portrayed as one that was patriotic, heroic and, most significantly, freely made. Hence, despite the fact that some of his number were forced to serve, the sparkling image of the soldier remained untarnished.

Objector unmanliness

Both in the context of the narratives of enthusiasm and support for the war explored in the last chapter and the constructions of the idealised manliness of the soldier considered above, all men who were not in the military were, to varying degrees, excluded from exemplary notions of maleness. Thus, as Trudi Tate argues, in these renderings of the war story all 'civilian men found themselves in an odd negated space in relation to masculinity'.[47] However, the CO was a particularly marginalised figure in this portrait of unmanliness as he became the antithesis of the iconic figure of the soldier during the war. Indeed, at a time when war and soldiering were seen as offering the potential for adventure, competition, sport and heroism as well as being a natural choice for boys and men, the notion that some men would reject the military called their maleness into question. In addition, to do so at a time of national need was hard to fathom and, at the very least, was often taken to be a sign that the objector was less than a man. Moreover, he was not merely failing to come forward but was even refusing to be compelled to serve. Thus, some of the notions of the objector as variously despised and rejected explored in the previous chapter feed into the idea of him as lacking in terms of his gender.

Conceptions of the objector as unmanly abound and he was often juxtaposed with the soldier. Indeed, the CO's stance was commonly interpreted as evidence of unmanliness and of qualities which were diametrically opposed to those associated with the military man. Thus, characteristics such as cowardice, shirking and laziness tended to be used in connection with the objector. For example, writing in 1916 Henry Wood Nevinson argues that objectors tended to be refused recognition in the tribunals and harshly treated by the state in its different guises precisely because they were assumed to embody these unmanly traits and were seeking to disguise this 'under the cloak of conscience'.[48] Moreover, COs also sometimes came to be seen not just as unmasculine but also as womanly.

Unsurprisingly perhaps the most common portrayal of objectors' unmanliness was as cowardly rather than heroic and keen for adventures. Clifford Allen, Chairman of the No-Conscription Fellowship (N-CF) recognised this, stating that in the opinion of most people '[w]e are considered cowards'.[49] As a result, objectors' accounts of their wartime experiences record numerous stories about being denounced or castigated in these terms. Indeed, such conceptions of COs came from a variety of quarters. For example, the pro-war press frequently used this notion and arguably encouraged this view of objectors. Thus in March 1916 the *Evening Standard and St James Gazette* referred to the N-CF's 'hordes of cowards',[50] in April the *Daily Sketch* railed against COs as 'a feeble folk',[51] in May the paper published pictures of leading figures of the organisation under the headline 'THE FELLOWSHIP OF FAINT-HEARTS'[52] and in April 1917 the *Daily Mail* reported a protestor's view that most of the men at Princetown Home Office Camp were 'frauds, the crawling worms who stole the cloak of conscience to cover cowardice . . .'.[53] A slightly more sophisticated take on this construction of objectors

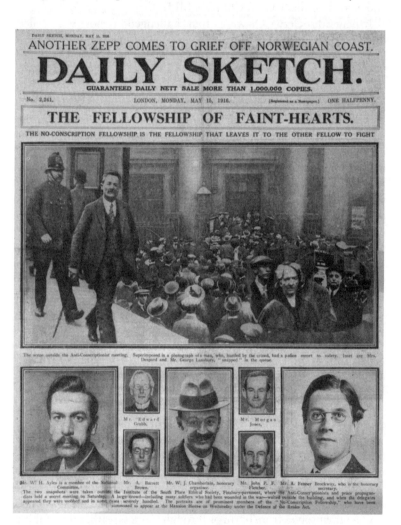

5 'THE FELLOWSHIP OF FAINT-HEARTS',
Daily Sketch (15 May 1916), p. 1.

was demonstrated in a cartoon entitled 'Taking Cover' published in *John Bull* and reproduced as the cover to the present text. A CO is pictured in civvies at a military camp. He cowers behind a soldier, hiding beneath the man's overcoat, whilst an officer, bearing more than a passing resemblance to Kitchener, walks by carrying a sword and a copy of the 'COMPULSION BILL'.[54]

In general society COs were often challenged by those who called them cowards for their stance. However, it was not only those who knew a man to be an objector who took this approach. Often the lack of a uniform would be taken to signify the linked ideas of conscientiousness, cowardice and unmanliness, leading patriotic strangers to approach young men in civvies in order to berate them or seek an explanation for their mode of dress. More specifically, the handing out of white feathers to COs or suspected COs as symbols of spinelessness became common. This activity was encouraged by the Organisation of the White Feather, which was created by Admiral Charles Fitzgerald in the opening month of the war and would often take place in public, but the objects were sometimes delivered in letters. This practice was so widespread that the feathers came to be closely associated with objectors. Consequently, they were often referred to as the 'white-feathered crew'.[55]

Friends and relatives also interpreted objectors' views as gutlessness. For example, Willie Campbell writes that one of his aunts, upon learning of his pacifist views, said that 'it was all very well for me to stand there talking but had not Tom died for me: had I not the courage to go and fight, too – I saw she felt that I was a coward'.[56] Once in the hands of the authorities, objectors experienced similar perceptions. Thus, a member of Oldham Tribunal accused an objector of possessing 'cowardice and insolence'[57] and Harry E. Stanton records instances where a prison chaplain along with warders accused COs incarcerated in civilian jails of being spineless for their refusal to fight.[58] Moreover, the idea of cowardice was reflected in the fact that the Non-Combatant Corps, in which partially exempted objectors were known to serve, came to be popularly referred to as the 'No-Courage Corps'.[59]

Alongside such perceptions, the idea of COs as men who were shirking or evading their duty in order to secure an easy life, to protect themselves from harm or through laziness, rather than taking the manly military route, continued to be fundamental to many people's thinking during the war. Freeloading on the sacrifices of

6 'THE WHITE FEATHER' issue, *The Union Jack* (26 December 1914), p. 1 (illustration by W. Taylor).

others, he was looking out for himself, and objection was really self-interest masquerading as conscience. Thus, as a 1916 letter to *The Times* argues, objectors were 'taking advantage of the self-sacrifice and patriotism of worthier men'.[60] Consequently, one objector felt that '[t]o the ordinary man or woman the Conscientious Objector . . . appeared to choose a very easy path'.[61] Indeed, such sentiments were frequently expressed. For example, the Chairman of Market Bosworth Tribunal, when faced with a CO, felt that '[t]his man put his own skin first', adding that the applicant was the first of the breed he had met and he hoped that this man would be the last.[62] Similarly, at a Lancashire tribunal one member told an applicant that 'I think you are exploiting God to save your own skin'.[63]

Moreover, as the latter comment suggests, in the case of Christian objectors their selfishness was often as seen as an offence against God, and it was commonly said that by refusing to kill they were looking after their own consciences but benefiting from others who were prepared to sully their own souls. In this vein the CO and former 'persistent and patriotic' 'bug-shooter', Stephen Hobhouse recalls that:

> It was often objected at the time that the religious or moral objector, however genuine, was out for a more or less selfish individualism, for the saving of his own soul, for the keeping of his own hands clean at the expense of the nation to which he owed so much.[64]

Indeed, the notion that the objector was really out to save his own skin by choosing an easier and safer course than that of the soldier was frequently expressed even before conscription was introduced. Thus, discussions about the possible inclusion of a 'conscience clause' within the future Military Service Act and the possible contents of any such provision revolved around concerns that the measure would be a 'shirkers' charter'.[65] Opponents of the clause, such as Captain Craig, MP for South Antrim, therefore, took the view that having any provision for conscience not only went counter to the very idea of compulsion but also risked undermining the policy.[66] Moreover, in the pro-conscription press compulsion was, unsurprisingly, portrayed as a means to compel unmanly shirkers 'skrimshanking' (sic) at home to do their duty.[67] Alternatively, those who accepted the need for some provision for a few genuine objectors feared that an Act with too many loopholes would prove to be 'a rotten mutilated piece of legislation'.[68]

Consequently, for some objectors were by definition shirkers, whilst others feared that some at least were feigning conscience in order to evade the military.

When constructed as selfish, shirking or cowards, objectors were often portrayed as representing a parasitic unmanliness, shirking responsibility and living off the efforts of others. In this vein a letter writer to *The Times* in 1916 complains that the objector who refused non-combatant as well as combatant service was 'a parasite'.[69] The idea of the parasite had had some cultural currency at the *fin de siècle*, and such descriptions of COs tapped into linked fears of loss of control, atavistic degeneration and the figure of the vampire – all of which suggested that objectors were less than men.[70] Thus, whilst the soldier was portrayed in terms of his Arthurian chivalry, COs were conceived of as preferring 'dirt, discomfort, and survival' to the 'gallant fight and death'.[71] For example, a wartime cartoon published in *John Bull* in May 1918 and reproduced here (page 102) epitomises this construction of the objector. Here he is pictured slouching lazily in an armchair, hands in pockets, smoking and sporting a self-satisfied grin. In the background 'Happy Families' playing cards show his father, brother and uncle in the army, a cousin in the navy, his mother as a nurse and a sister in uniform. The caption reads 'This little pig stayed at home'. All the other members of his family, even the women, are doing their bit, while he lounges smugly, presumably protected by the 'shirkers charter', and suffers no discomfort from the war – in fact, he is portrayed as being very comfortable with his lot.[72] Here the 'pig' benefits from the patriotic labours of others, including women. As a consequence, he is failing as a man by his refusal to chivalrously protect his womenfolk (who are instead effectively protecting him) and is, thus, portrayed as less than a man. He may also be seen as being feminised by his continued existence within the domestic sphere on the Home Front, and he is belittled and emasculated by the use of a caption taken from a children's rhyme. Rather than craving masculine adventure as a soldier out in the world, welcoming the opportunity to take 'flight from domesticity', he remains at home.[73]

Beyond this, COs were often portrayed as being feminised or unmanned by their situation. Their lives were to a large extent out of their own hands as, whether in the military, in prison, undertaking non-combatant duties or doing work of national importance, they were forced into some degree of passivity rather than adopting

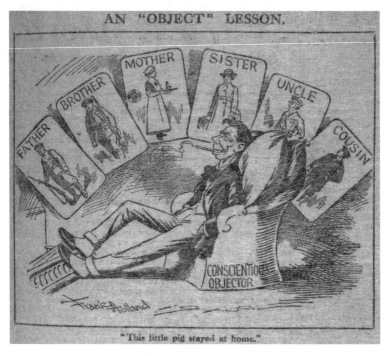

7 Frank Holland, 'AN "OBJECT" LESSON',
John Bull (4 May 1918), p. 5.

the active masculine role epitomised by the image of the heroic military man. Objectors themselves sometimes saw themselves in this way. Thus, CO George Baker recalls the boredom and the dehumanising effects of his situation: '[i]n prison, life is life suspended' and 'my manhood degraded into namelessness and numberdom'.[74]

In other instances too the unmanliness of the CO was emphasised by his display of supposedly feminine traits or his association with femininity. Thus, one tribunal member was astounded and horrified to hear a CO assert that he would not kill, seeing this as 'an awful state of mind [for a man] to be in'.[75] Similarly, a letter to *The Times* in 1916 expresses distaste that men could display such weak emotion as to refuse to kill and bemoans the 'faint and feeble souls' possessed by objectors.[76] Here then the reactions resonate with all that Henty's adventure tales stood against.

The popular pro-war press were particularly keen to portray objectors as unmanly. For example, one of the newspaper photographs of Percy, the reluctant (CO) conscript described and pictured in the last chapter (pp. 64–5), depicts him as lacking masculine attributes, in effect feminising him. This is the representation of a man emasculated by his undignified position and lack of control of his situation. He has been forced/persuaded into army boots but is draped in a blanket rather than proudly sporting a uniform and appears feminised by his seeming obsession with clothing and footwear rather than with the real business of war. Moreover, the ridicule to which he is subjected in this story also seems to unman him; he is not worthy of the serious and reverential consideration warranted by the soldier.[77]

COs were also unmanned by the sometimes explicit contrast presented by the romanticised image of the desirable and manfully sexual soldier and the shirker. This argument is made by Nicoletta F. Gullace, who observes that:

> [h]ighlighting the distinction between the sexually attractive recruit and the contemptible slacker, female music hall stars such as Vesta Tilly and Clara Butt became famous for their sexualized recruiting songs and their erotic impact on enlistment.[78]

Moreover, as the next chapter will suggest, the objector's heterosexuality was sometimes called into question, as there was a tendency to associate his perceived lack of masculinity with decadence. Here then the suggestion of sexual inversion was occasionally made.

Conclusion

This narrative begins to suggest that during the First World War the CO was cast in juxtaposition to dominant ideas about men. Indeed, he rejected popular notions of aspirational manliness by refusing to become a soldier even under legal compulsion. As a result, he was excluded from the image of patriotic masculine perfection epitomised by the conscientious (volunteer) soldier. Here the unconscientious conscientious objector came to represent not only an unpopular identity but also an extremely unmanly one. As a consequence, COs were conceived of as 'unmen'[79] in that they were emasculated by their stance. Thus, in terms of wartime ideas about the male, objectors had 'become not just No Men, nobodies, but *not* men'[80] and constructions of the CO often formed a stark contrast with that of the soldier and his association with adventure, heroism, duty and chivalry. In addition, the image of the objector fell far short of even those men, women, girls and boys who were, as the last chapter argued, apparently keen to support and aid the war in whatever way they were able. Thus, whilst the soldier was chased by girls, sought out and envied by boys and valorised by popular opinion, the objector was often spurned and attacked. But, as the next two chapters demonstrate, there were also darker conceptions of the CO which influenced his treatment and here too ideas about manliness played a role.

Notes

1 Trudi Tate, *Women, Men and the Great War: An Anthology of Stories* (Manchester: Manchester University Press, 1995), p. 5. See also John Tosh who argues that Victorian versions of manliness were not merely elite forms but filtered through to the working classes. 'What should historians do with manliness? Reflections on nineteenth-century Britain', *History Workshop Journal*, 38:1 (1994), 179–202, 181–2.

2 Images of an aspirational, yet apparently easily attainable, English manhood (all a man had to do was to wear a uniform) were also fortified by the assumption that, given this would be a speedily and victoriously concluded war, the sacrifice of service, if it were considered to be a sacrifice, would only be brief (enlisting did not mean choosing a career in the military) and the rewards great.

3 See Graham Dawson, *Soldier Heroes: British Adventure, Empire and the Imagining of Masculinities* (London: Routledge, 1994), pp. 62–6, 74–6.

4 As did many populist works of both fiction and non-fiction. William Joseph Reader, *'At Duty's Call': A Study in Obsolete Patriotism* (Manchester: Manchester University Press, 1988), p. 20.

5 George Manville Fenn, *George Alfred Henty: The Story of an Active Life* (London: Blackie, 1907), pp. 333–4. See also Reader, who discusses other authors, boys' magazines and annuals, along with collections of non-fiction, which all stress the themes of manliness and fighting (*'At Duty's Call'*, pp. 27–30).

6 See Robert H. MacDonald, 'Reproducing the middle-class boy: from purity to patriotism in the boys' magazines, 1892–1914', *Journal of Contemporary History*, 24:3 (1989), 519–39.

7 *Lives and Adventures of Great Soldiers in the British Army*, (London: General Publishing Company, 1885).

8 Martin Green, *Dreams of Adventure, Deeds of Empire* (London: Routledge, 1980), p. 3.

9 A series of posters featured Alfred Leete's image of Kitchener. For example, see Imperial War Museum, London (hereafter IWM), Department of Art (poster collection), PST 2734, 'Britons – Join Your Country's Army!'.

10 Notable posters include the following captions: 'Women of Britain Say "Go!"; 'Daddy What did YOU do in the Great War?'; 'Are YOU in this?'; 'COME ALONG BOYS AND JOIN THE ARMY ! (OUR CHEERY LADS NEED YOUR HELP)'; 'COME ALONG, BOYS! ENLIST TO-DAY. The moment the order came to go forward, there were smiling faces everywhere.'; 'He did his Duty – Will YOU do YOURS?' (under an image of the recently deceased military hero, Lord Roberts of Kandahar); 'The Veteran's Farewell' (which depicts an elderly military man congratulating a soldier with the words 'Good Bye my lad, I only wish I were young enough to go with you.'); 'WHO'S ABSENT? Is it you?' See IWM PST 2763, 0311, 2712, 12096, 5023, 11424, 0410, 0314.

11 As Dawson maintains in his text on imaginings of the soldier hero, the hero takes a 'plurality of forms', which vary from text to text and change with the contemporary cultural, social and political landscape. *Soldier Heroes*, p. 57.

12 See, for example, Mark Girouard, *The Return to Camelot: Chivalry and the English Gentleman* (New Haven, CT: Yale University Press, 1981), pp. 219–30.

13 See: Joan Winifred Martin Hichberger, *Images of the Army: The Military in British Art, 1815–1914* (Manchester: Manchester University Press, 1988), pp. 5–6; Girouard, *The Return to Camelot*, pp. 219–30.

14 Dawson, *Soldier Heroes*, pp. 108–9.

15 Hichberger, *Images of the Army*, p. 39.

16 Green, *Dreams of Adventure*, p. 37.

17 Reader, '*At Duty's Call*', p. 99.

18 See MacDonald, 'Reproducing the middle-class boy', 523–4.

19 Paul Fussell, *The Great War and Modern Memory* (Oxford: Oxford University Press, 25th anniversary edn, 2000 – first published 1975), pp. 21–3.

20 Robert Stephenson Smyth Baden-Powell, *Scouting for Boys: A Handbook for Instruction in Good Citizenship* (London: C. Arthur Pearson, complete edition, revised and illustrated, 1908 – reissued as a centenary print London: Scout Association, 2007), p. 211, see also p. 214.

21 Quoted in Andio Linklater, *An Unhusbanded Life: Charlotte Despard, Suffragette, Socialist and Sinn Féiner* (London: Hutchinson 1980), p. 177.

22 Fussell, *The Great War*, pp. 119, 117–20.

23 See Tate, *Women, Men and the Great War*, p. 1.

24 Robert Bridges, 'Wake Up England!', *The Times* (8 August 1914), p. 7. The quotation comes from the seventh, penultimate stanza.

25 Indeed, at the time of its introduction Prime Minister Herbert Henry Asquith depicted conscription as nothing more than a restating of the duty which (apparently) every English man knew that he had and which he would respond to voluntarily; in this view the Military Service Act, 1916 was supposedly an unnecessary formality. 5 HC 77, cols 949–62, 5 January 1916. See also the argument derived from J.S. Mill in 'Conscience and Conduct' (editorial/leader), *The Times* (8 April 1916), p. 9.

26 See for example, William Greenslade, *Degeneracy, Culture and the Novel 1880–1940* (Cambridge: Cambridge University Press, 1994), p. 213.

27 For example, see Geoffrey Best, 'Militarism and the Victorian public school', in Brian Simon and Ian Bradley (eds), *The Victorian Public School: Studies in the Development of an Institution: A Symposium* (London: Gill and Macmillan, 1975).

28 See further James Anthony Mangan, 'Military drill – rather more than "brief and basic" – English elementary schools and English militarism', in Mangan (ed.), *Militarism, Sport, Europe: War Without Weapons* (London: Routledge, 2003).

29 On such organisations and their militaristic tendencies see, for example: John Springhall, *Youth, Empire and Society: British Youth Movements 1883–1940* (London: Croom Helm, 1977), p. 58; Paul Wilkinson, 'English Youth Movements, 1908–30', *Journal of Contemporary History*, 4:2 (1969), 3–23, pp. 5, 8, 11, 14–15, 23; Richard A. Voeltz, '". . .A good Jew and a good Englishman": the Jewish Lads' Brigade, 1894–1922', *Journal of Contemporary History*, 23:1 (1988), 119–27.

30 On these forces before and during the war see: M.H. Hale, *Volunteer Soldiers* (London: Kegan Paul and Co, 1900), which was a new edition of *Amateur Soldiers* (London: Wyman & Sons, 1886); John Morton Osborne, 'Defining their own patriotism: British Volunteer Training Corps in the First World War', *Journal of Contemporary History*, 23:1 (1988), 59–75, 60.

31 On sport's role in public schools and links with militarism see James Antony Mangan, '"Muscular, militaristic and manly": the British middle-class hero as moral messenger', *International Journal of the History of Sport*, 13:1 (1996), 28–47, 33, 37–45. On sport in public schools more generally see Mangan, *Athleticism in the Victorian and Edwardian Public School* (Cambridge: Cambridge University Press, 1981).

32 This tended to be the case in the newer public schools that served parents who increasingly expected their sons to earn their living in the army. See Reader, *'At Duty's Call'*, pp. 88–9.

33 On militarism and private education see Best, 'Militarism and the Victorian public school'.

34 Stephen Hobhouse, 'Fourteen months service with the colours', in Julian H. Bell (ed.), *We Did Not Fight 1914–1918: Experiences of War Resisters* (London: Cobden Sanderson, 1935), p. 157.

35 See Mangan, 'Military drill'.

36 Baden-Powell always maintained that Scouting had no hidden military agenda, stating for example that: '. . . a Scout is not only a friend to the people round him, but "a friend to all the world". Friends don't fight each other' (Baden-Powell, *Scouting for Boys*, p. 264). Others dispute this. For example, Michael Rosenthal argues that Baden-Powell had militaristic aims from the outset ('Knights and retainers: the earliest version of Baden-Powell's boy Scout scheme', *Journal of Contemporary History*, 15:4. (1980), 603–17, 607–9). Certainly some of the imagery he used to describe the movement had military connotations. On Baden-Powell, Scouting and militarism see further: Rosenthal, *The Character Factory: Baden-Powell and the Origins of the Boy Scout Movement* (London: Collins, 1986), for example, pp. 226–7; John Springhall 'The Boy Scouts, class, and militarism in relation to British youth movements, 1908–1930', *International Review of Social History*, 16:1 (1971), 125–58; John Springhall, 'Baden-Powell and the Scout movement before 1920: Citizen Training or Soldiers of the Future?', *English Historical Review*, 102:405 (1987), 934–42; Allen Warren, 'Sir Robert Baden-Powell, the Scout movement and citizen training in Great Britain, 1900–1920', *English Historical Review* 101:399 (1986), 376–98.

37 See, in particular, Osborne, 'Defining their own patriotism'.

38 Colin Veitch, '"Play up! Play up! And Win the War!" Football, the nation and the First World War 1914–15', *Journal of Contemporary History*, 20:3 (1985), 363–78, 365.

39 Quoted by Reader, *'At Duty's Call'*, p. 133. See also p. 97.

40 See, for example, Fussell, *The Great War*, pp. 25–8; Eric J. Leed, *No Man's Land: Combat and Identity in World War I* (Cambridge: Cambridge University Press, 1979), pp. 40–2; David Roberts, *Minds at War: The Poetry and Experience of the First World War* (Burgess Hill: Saxon Books, 1996), pp. 162–6.

41 See, for example, Veitch, '"Play up! Play up! And Win the War!"', 365–6. Most notable in terms of scholarship on the history of sport is James Antony Mangan, some of whom's work is referenced in this volume.

42 Football, in particular, spread from the middle and upper classes to working-class boys and men, initially with the help of clergymen anxious to draw men away from the evils of drink and dancing and, thereby, guide them to salvation. Many of these men of the cloth had, of course, been taught the benefits of games and its links with war by

their experience in the public schools and, in seeking to use sport's 'civilising' influences to tame working men, also passed these associations on. Soon sports teams were set up without the oversight of religion at pubs and workplaces. Indeed, the enthusiasm spread quickly so that, although churches only began to organise teams in the latter half of the nineteenth century, by 1883 working-class teams dominated the Football Association Cup Final, which had originally been a contest for old public schoolboys (see Robert F. Wheeler, 'Organised sport and organised labour: the workers sports movement', *Journal of Contemporary History*, 13:2 (1978), 191–210, 192). By 1914 playing amateur and professional football as well as spectating was hugely popular (see Veitch, '"Play up! Play up! And Win the War!"', 367–9).

43 For example, 'BY OUR SPECIAL CORRESPONDENT', 'THE SCENE IN THE COMMONS: WHY WE MUST ACT', *Morning Post* (4 August 1914), p. 7, uses the phrase 'play the game' in the context of a report and comment on proceedings in Parliament the previous day regarding the ultimatum to Gemany from the Foreign Secretary, Sir Edward Grey. The poem, dated 1892, is reproduced in Roberts, *Minds at War*, pp. 20–1.

44 Mabel Annie Saint Clair Stobart, *The Flaming Sword in Serbia and Elsewhere* (London: Hodder & Stoughton, 1916), p. 315.

45 Ilana R. Bet-El, 'Men and soldiers: British conscripts, concepts of masculinity, and the Great War', in Billie Melman (ed.), *Borderlines: Genders and Identities in War and Peace 1870–1930* (London: Routledge, 1998), p. 74.

46 See further Chapter 5 below, where Bet-El's work is considered again.

47 Tate, *Women, Men and the Great War*, p. 5.

48 Henry Wood Nevinson, 'The conscientious objector', *Atlantic Monthly* 103:695 (November 1916), 686–94, 690.

49 Allen in letter from Maidstone Prison to Catherine Marshall, 21 April 1917, quoted in Martin Gilbert, *Plough My Own Furrow: The Story of Lord Allen of Hurtwood as Told through his Writings and Correspondence* (London: Longman, 1965), p. 70, see further pp. 70–3.

50 *Evening Standard*, (23 March 1916), quoted by Thomas C. Kennedy, 'Public opinion and the conscientious objector, 1915–1919', *The Journal of British Studies*, 12:2 (1973), 105–19, 112.

51 'The Man in the Street', *Daily Sketch* (10 April 1916), p. 5.

52 'THE FELLOWSHIP OF FAINT-HEARTS', *Daily Sketch* (15 May 1916), p. 1.

53 'CONSCIENTIOUS SHIRKERS', *Daily Mail* (26 April 1917), p. 3. The comment is attributed to Mr Shirley Benn. See also 'THE LETTERS OF AN ENGLISHMAN' column, headed '"CONSCIENTIOUS" SHIRKERS', *Daily Mail* (28 April 1917), p. 2: '[f]or it is cowardice, and cowardice alone, which holds back the "objector" from the duty

imposed upon all decent men. . . . He is afraid of discomfort, he is afraid of risk, he is afraid of death.' Indeed, the writer feels that '"conscience" . . . is "but a word that cowards use."'

54 Signed F.H. – 'AFTER Lawson Wood', *John Bull* (5 February 1916), p. 17.

55 See Nicoletta F. Gullace, 'White feathers and wounded men: female patriotism and the memory of the Great War', *Journal of British Studies*, 36:2 (1997), 178–206. There are numerous reports both of the challenging of men not wearing a uniform and the use of white feathers. See, for example, IWM, Sound Collection: 39/7, Reel 1, Recollections of Walter Glenn Ostler; 95/3, Reel 3, Recollections of William George Benham.

56 Letter from William Campbell to his parents, dated November 1915, privately owned, p. 6. Tom, the writer's brother, had enlisted.

57 Philip Snowden, *British Prussianism: The Scandal of the Tribunals* (Manchester: National Labour Press, 1916), p. 8; Stanley Bloomfield James, *The Men Who Dared: The Story of an Adventure* (London: C.W. Daniel, 1917), p. 15

58 'Will You March Too? 1916–1919', unpublished account of a CO's experiences (privately owned), 2 volumes, see, in particular, pp. 173, 183, 222.

59 For example, see Snowden, *British Prussianism*, p. 9.

60 Howard Spensley, 'PATRIOTISM IN SCHOOLS' (letter to editor), *The Times* (28 March 1916), p. 9.

61 James Primrose Malcolm Millar, 'A socialist in war time', in Bell (ed.), *We Did Not Fight*, p. 225.

62 Quoted in Snowden, *British Prussianism*, p. 9.

63 Quoted in John W. Graham, *Conscription and Conscience: A History 1916–1919* (London: George Allen and Unwin, 1971, first published 1922), p. 71. See also 'SOME CASES OF "FAIR DEALING"', *The Tribunal* (15 March 1916), p. 2.

64 Hobhouse, 'Fourteen months service with the colours' p. 167.

65 See for example, Conservative backbencher W. Joynson-Hicks, who voiced this view on behalf of his party during the committee stage of the first Military Service Act. He advocated limiting recognition to Quakers and members of similar religious organisations whose tenets included an objection to all war. 5 HC 78, col. 422–7, 19 January 1916.

66 5 HC 78, col. 460, 19 January 1916.

67 See for example, David Lloyd George, *War Memoirs of David Lloyd George*, vol. I (London: Odhams, 1938, first published in 1933), pp. 427–8.

68 Captain Craig, 5 HC 78, col. 460, 19 January 1916.

69 'Conscience and Conduct' (editorial/leader), *The Times* (8 April 1916), p. 9.

70 On the parasite, the vampire and degeneration see, for example, Greenslade, *Degeneracy*, pp. 18–19.

71 Herbert George Wells, 'Zoological retrogression', *Gentleman's Magazine*, 271 (September 1891), 246–53, 252.

72 The illustration is headed 'AN "OBJECT" LESSON', Frank Holland, *John Bull* (4 May 1918), p. 5.

73 See Dawson, *Soldier Heroes*, p. 63.

74 George Baker, *The Soul of a Skunk: The Autobiography of a Conscientious Objector* (London: Eric Partridge at the Scholartis Press, 1930), p. 165.

75 Quoted in Graham, *Conscription and Conscience*, p. 89.

76 R. Maguire and E.M. Lloyd, 'CONSCIENTIOUS OBJECTORS' (letter to the editor), *The Times* (5 April 1916), p. 9.

77 For example, see '"PERCY'S" PROGRESS IN THE ARMY', *Daily Sketch* (15 April 1916), p. 12.

78 Gullace, 'White feathers and wounded men', 193.

79 The term is taken from Sandra M. Gilbert, 'Soldier's heart: literary men, literary women, and the Great War', 8:3 (1983) *Signs*: 422–50 (see especially 423), and Gilbert and Susan Gubar, *No Man's Land: The Place of the Woman Writer in the Twentieth Century, Volume 2, Sexchanges* (New Haven, CT: Yale University Press, 1989), ch 7, see especially pp. 259–60. However, in these texts the term was being used in relation to the soldier – see further Chapter 6 below.

80 Gilbert, 'Soldier's heart', 423.

3

Deviance: degeneracy, decadence and criminality

The picture of the conscientious objector (CO) emerging so far within this volume posits him as a despised, rejected and emasculated figure. Other depictions of the objector, however, focused upon more specific conceptions of him. Building upon what has gone before, this chapter explores the ways in which the CO was seen as being multiply deviant. Here the analysis centres upon the degeneracy, decadence and criminality that was sometimes associated with him. These three overlapping notions of the CO all reinforced the sense that such men should be hated and contributed to, justified and were played out in the treatment which they experienced. For example, abusive or violent behaviour towards COs could be seen as attempts to punish them for, deter them from or cure them of their stance in a manner analogous to the penalties imposed upon criminals. Again the notion of mass support for the war is an underlying current here.

Degeneracy and decadence

The idea of degeneration,[1] along with linked premillennialist anxieties about decadence, sexual inversion, the female of the species and manhood being in crisis, were topics of frequent debate in the late nineteenth century and the early twentieth century. These narratives varied in terms of whether they saw the origins of these concerns as lying within the realm of the inherent or the acquired and, consequently, the solutions proffered also differed. However, whatever view was taken, the perceived problem remained: the English (or sometimes British) race and, in particular, English manhood were in moral and/or physical decline. For example, there were concerns about the sickliness, cleanliness and morality of the working classes[2] and anxieties about the effects of decadence upon the bodies and characters of upper-class men.[3] There were worries about a 'crisis of whiteness',[4] and various schools of eugenic thinking[5] argued that the English male, along with the nation's imperial might, was either failing or in peril.[6] Thus, alongside discourses which identified the inferior other in the 'savage races'[7] and 'our dusky cousins',[8] there were those who used similar language and ideas to talk about the degenerates 'near at home'.[9]

In the words of William Greenslade, 'degeneration was an important resource of myth for the post-Darwinian world'. In *Degeneracy, Culture and the Novel 1880–1940* he describes these ways of thinking as a 'loose assemblage of beliefs' or, more specifically, 'anxieties' concerning 'poverty and crime, about public health and imperial fitness, about decadent artists, "new women" and homosexuals'.[10] Moreover, in these contexts there were worries about human reversion, devolution and atavism. Such ideas were oft expressed. Thus, in 1880 Edwin Ray Lankester published *Degeneration: A Chapter in Darwinism*. As a zoologist, the author took a scientific approach and was concerned that natural selection would by no means guarantee that the human race would progress rather than regress.[11] In a more melancholic vein Max Nordau's classic text *Degeneration* (1892), first published in English in 1895, describes the age as being one of white western decline 'in which all suns and all stars are gradually waning, and mankind with all its institutions and creations is persisting in a dying world'.[12]

In the 1890s, in particular, such concerns were common currency.[13] However, their influence continued into the twentieth century with anxieties about male degeneration, particularly in the poorer sections of society.[14] These reached a peak during the Boer War when many recruits failed their medical examinations, and unease about physical fitness led to the setting-up of an Inter-Departmental Committee on Physical Deterioration in 1904 and calls for urgent action as the future of the Empire and the country were in doubt.[15] Thus, by 1914 ideas about decline were familiar to many and were, unsurprisingly, a more pressing issue once war was declared, when large numbers of healthy men were again needed for the military. Moreover, here again the soldier was conceptualised as an idealised figure; in this regard his iconic status arose from his image as a fit and active man – characteristics that were implicit in his depiction within the last chapter.

Decadence has been described as a mutation of degeneration theory[16] and, when used as a term of reproach, was often blamed upon foreign and, in particular, German influence.[17] Holbrook Jackson links these two concepts, describing decadence as 'degeneration arising . . . out of surfeit, out of the ease with which life was maintained and the desires satisfied', adding that '[t]o kill a desire . . . by satisfying it, is to create a new desire' for 'new experiences'.[18] A central issue was that sections of the upper classes were ruining themselves through the excessive indulgence in bodily pleasures and a focus upon beauty for beauty's sake rather than morality. Such worries about this form of decline had been intensified by the 'naughty nineties', with its notion of the 'New Hedonism'. Moreover, fears about the relatively newly categorised male sexual invert, who was beginning to be associated with the effeminacy and aestheticism of the dandy, which Oscar Wilde had in turn come to epitomise,[19] were linked to disquiet about degeneration and decadence.[20] Alongside such concerns about the male, the New Woman[21] with her greater independence was supposedly also posing a threat to the male, as were the female Suffragists and their militant Suffragette sisters.[22] In this latter regard, women it seemed were getting stronger whilst some men were in various respects weakening and were possibly even becoming more womanly.

Furthermore, debates about degeneracy and decadence stressed the benefits of healthy activity and warned of the dangers of 'morbid' introspection and 'habitual' self-absorption.[23] In the closing years of the nineteenth century such fears had heightened, particularly in writings about psychiatry. One contemporary sufferer cautioned as to the effects of these twin afflictions. Henry Maudsley writes of the '*morbid egoism*' they would foster, adding that such 'a tender conscience of that kind, overating its own importance, may easily pass into insanity, unless counterbalanced by the sobering influence of active outdoor preoccupations and interests'.[24]

As a consequence of such notions, sectors of the race and, in particular, the male population were often described as being under threat or in crisis. Indeed, such ideas were influential and several strands of contemporary thought embraced these notions of decline. Darwinian and eugenic as well as militaristic, philanthropic, medical, criminological and Christian thinking all engaged with debates about whether there was a deterioration and, if so, how best to rectify the situation. In particular, the Muscular Christianity

Movement[25] along with the National Service League[26] expressed such anxieties. The former called for sport and physical education by way of a solution, whilst the latter campaigned for the introduction of compulsory military training. Thus, George Richard Francis Shee advocated military conscription as a solution to the decline of the national male physique and encouraged worries about the effects of this upon the nation in order to further the case for compulsion.[27]

Other schools of thought developed these ideas. Some criminologists identified a degenerate criminal type whose savage, atavistic or subhuman characteristics were identified and studied,[28] and eugenic thinking focused upon the idea of racial imperfections, the throwback and male deterioration, suggesting, amongst other things, the need to limit reproduction amongst the poor and questioning the wisdom of welfare provision.[29] By the beginning of the twentieth century, the press was widely reporting such ideas about racial decline and positing different strategies aimed at averting the crisis. For example, *Lloyd's Weekly Newspaper* argued that the Boer War with its evidence of male unfitness was demonstrating that the 'great heart' of the Empire was suffering from 'fatty degeneration' and called for urgent action.[30]

Many of the conceptions of the CO considered in the previous two chapters resonate with the idea of the objector as degenerate and/or decadent. Thus, an applicant's presumed moral degeneracy and cowardice or laziness was often linked by tribunals. Laziness, in particular, was used by the press as an often implicit indication of degeneracy. When the *Daily Mail* published photographs of the men at Princetown, Home Office Camp describing them as the 'DARTMOOR DO-NOTHINGS' who enjoyed a 'slack life', this carried with it just such a suggestion.[31] Likewise, the Brace Committee's feeling that there was evidence of 'concerted idleness' amongst COs working on the Home Office Scheme would have suggested possible degeneracy and decadence.[32] Moreover, the construction of objectors as parasites or as vampiric, noted in the last chapter, connected with notions of degeneracy.[33] In this context, a danger was often conceived of as emanating from the outsider, the foreign other or from the female of the species.[34] Thus, conceptions of the objector as outcast, German or feminine resonate with these ideas.

Portrayals of COs as pathetic physical and/or moral specimens also echoed ideas about degeneration.[35] Thus, one CO was described at his tribunal hearing as 'a shivering mass of unwholesome fat',[36] echoing the prognosis in *Lloyd's Weekly Newspaper* mentioned above. In similar vein, an applicant at Holborn Tribunal seemed to have been refused exemption because of his failure to take healthy exercise and his supposedly unwashed appearance.[37] Another tribunal member told an objector that '[y]ours is a case of an unhealthy mind in an unwholesome body'.[38] Taking a more direct approach 'THE LETTERS OF AN ENGLISHMAN' column in the *Daily Mail* described the CO in the following terms: '[h]e bears upon him all the marks of the degenerate. He has an ill-balanced head and no chin.'[39]

Objectors were frequently perceived to be pathetic physical specimens who seemed to choose (unhealthy) thought over the action involved in becoming a soldier and sometimes they were depicted as madmen. Indeed, as was argued in Chapter 1, lunacy was sometimes associated with these men. Thus, in a letter to *The Times* A.W. Gough describes objectors as 'egotistical decadents', 'crank[s]' and 'neurotic curiosities'.[40] Meanwhile, the Chairman of Surrey Appeal Tribunal, Lewis T Dibdin, depicts 'sincere' absolutists in prison as being 'mentally abnormal', adding that they should be treated in a similar manner to people 'who suffer from other forms of mental perversity' and 'kept in confinement for the protection of society'.[41]

This tendency to hold a low opinion of objector's physical and mental health is frequently evidenced in official documents. In 1919 the Brace Committee, which organised work for men on the Home Office Scheme, felt that many of the men they dealt with were 'feeble in physique, weak of will or unstable of character . . . incapable of sustained collective effort, and cohering only to air their grievances or to promote queer and unusual ends'.[42] The Home Office also had concerns about COs' fitness and sent a memorandum to all local prisons directing them to consider the health of the men when imposing repeated dietary and other punishments, stressing that most objectors were poor specimens:

> It has been found that though here and there a man of good physique is to be seen amongst Conscientious Objectors yet the majority are below the average, and an appreciable amount of mental defect has also been observed.[43]

In addition, objectors' representation as being less than human resonated with theories of degeneration. In this conception of the CO they were seen as being of inferior stock or a breed apart.[44] Thus, CO George Baker describes the attitude of prison wardens in Wormwood Scrubs upon first encountering pacifist prisoners. Most, he writes, were ex-army Non-Commissioned Officers and their knowledge of objectors came from the press and the pulpit. As a result, they expected such men to embody 'the kind of obscene and crawling life to be found under a large stone, when it is lifted from the spot where it has lain for a long time'.[45] In the tribunals too such sentiments were expressed. Depicted as scavenging at the margins of society, objectors were described in the words of one tribunal member as 'the most awful pack that ever walked the earth'.[46]

Representations of the CO also utilised more specific concerns about decadence, effeminacy and sexual inversion. He was often described as a snivelling, pathetic, morally bankrupt inadequate, sometimes with the subtle suggestion of sexual inversion. In one telling cartoon from *John Bull* reproduced in these pages (p. 102) the 'pig' objector is depicted as a floppy haired, dandified figure, lazing whilst others around him laboured for the war.[47] Here he bears more than a passing resemblance to Wilde and to L. Raven-Hill's 1890s sketch 'A Voluptuary', which portrays a man living 'a life of pleasure'. Indeed, both the latter and the CO in *John Bull* seem to be striking the same pose, slouching back nonchalantly in a chair, smoking.[48] Indeed, cartoons often suggested that such men were womanly, as A.E.'s depiction of a CO and a German pictured on page 117 illustrates. Thus, there was sometimes a tendency to degenerate and demasculinise the CO in terms of his presumed unmanliness and supposedly questionable sexuality.

In like tones one worker in Princetown Home Office Camp reported missing the 'good old convicts', as objectors were a very different breed: 'long-haired, idle young men wandering about a respectable village with their arms around each other's necks. It makes me sick to look at them'.[49] Further, those attending a socialist meeting in Huddersfield, which aimed to secure more recruits for the anti-war movement, were referred to as 'skunks, scoundrels, cowards, pacifists, neuters, neither men or women'.[50] Or, as one journalist subsequently opined, they had 'something repellent and almost inhuman about them'.[51] Consequently, in this view the CO was cast as an unnatural man, a pointless man, an aberration who was not only unmanly and possibly an invert, but was also less than a woman; a subhuman breed.

More generally, the image of the objector as in various respects unmanly could be taken to suggest that he was an instance of a

8 A.E., 'THE CONSCIENTIOUS OBJECTOR AT THE FRONT!', 1916.

weakness in the race. Indeed, his failure to join in with the enthusiasm for the war when it seemed that everyone else shared in the excitement marked him out as different if not in some way suspect or lacking. Moreover, in refusing the solutions to degeneracy and decadence suggested by those advocating (re)masculinisation through some form of compulsory military service or training, the CO was actually providing support for his construction as in some way lacking as a man. Indeed, his rejection of the 'cure' to this apparent inadequacy suggested that he might be beyond redemption or alternatively this was taken as an indication that he required more drastic intervention in order to correct the deficiency in his manhood. Thus, the idea of harsh treatment and the use of force to ensure compliance was a common theme in COs' treatment – not least when associated with the idea of objectors as criminals.

Criminality and conscience

Another pervasive and linked thread in constructions of and attitudes towards the objector saw his deviance as a form of criminality. Technically, of course, conscientious objection was not in itself an offence. Rather, during the period of conscription it was, for the first time in the context of military service, a legal category.[52] Thus, far from being defined as a dissident identity, in terms of the statutory rhetoric a man was free to claim conscience without suffering as a consequence and genuine objectors could legitimately gain recognition. However, there were a number of offences which some objectors and their supporters fell foul of. Most obviously, failing to report to the military once called up was in itself a minor infraction[53] which some, but by no means all, COs committed. In addition, those who helped objectors could be liable for aiding and abetting the evasion of military service.[54] Some of these men and their supporters perpetrated other offences. Most notably convictions occurred under the Defence of the Realm legislation for producing or distributing anti-conscription materials.[55] More specifically, for those who found themselves in the military, refusing to obey orders meant that they were subject to a different species of law and, thus, could be found guilty of military offences. However, none of these crimes amounted to an offence of conscientious objection.

Nevertheless, whilst objection was not a crime in terms of the letter of the law, COs were often portrayed as criminal and in this sense their criminality was *cultural* and *ideological* rather than legal; conscientious objection, which parliament had not formally designated as criminal, nevertheless was most often assumed to be.[56] Indeed, COs' portrayal and treatment in society, in the tribunals, in the military, in prisons and on the Home Office Scheme frequently reflected this. As a result, objectors would seem to have been, for practical if not formal purposes, criminals.[57] For example, in April 1917 the *Daily Mail* referred to the men at Princetown as 'DARTMOOR'S ARTFUL DODGERS', drawing upon Dickensian imagery of thievery. Reproduced under this headline is a photograph of a CO in labouring clothes with hands in pockets, looking relaxed and fairly contented (see page 120 below).[58]

Sometimes the idea of objector criminality was linked to some of the notions of the CO already considered. For example, their perceived perversion of establishment Christianity appeared to be heretical or blasphemous and their association with sexual inversion seemed to suggest that some might have been guilty of sexual offences. Also, their failures in terms of manliness and Englishness were sometimes taken to mean that they were committing crimes against their gender and their country. Indeed, within the (supposed) climate of jingoistic fervour and enthusiasm for the war, their stand seemed to some to be taken to constitute 'an unpatriotic offence', as commentator Henry Wood Nevinson notes in 1916.[59] As a consequence of such views in April 1916, under the headline 'Take him to the Tower!', *John Bull* demanded No-Conscription Fellowship (N-CF or the Fellowship) founder and Secretary Fenner Brockway's arrest and execution.[60] More specifically, their perceived lack of support for the war made them traitors because they were assumed to be pro-German, Prussian spies or Bolshevik agitators. Thus, the *Globe* saw the Fellowship as an 'essentially treasonable' organisation[61] and the press along with *The Tribunal* frequently reported the castigation of 'treacherous' objectors in the tribunals.[62]

Further, in the context of public suspicions that objectors were pro-German, such men were sometimes seen as the enemy within.[63] The presence of such fears drew upon the pre-war stories of spies living or holidaying in the country and planning an invasion which formed a part of the 'forecasts of war' genre.[64] These tales were often written in such a way as to suggest that they might not have been entirely fictional, and they featured in novels, pamphlets and the press. For example, the powerful newspaper owner and

"YOU CAN'T CATCH ME!"
[One of a group of conscientious shirkers, now at
Dartmoor, who have incensed the people of Devon by
their airs of self-congratulation.]   "*Daily Mail.*"
He who does not fight, but runs away,
May live to run as fast another day!

9 'DARTMOOR'S ARTFUL DODGERS . . . "YOU CAN'T CATCH
ME!"', *Daily Mail* (30 April 1917), p. 8.

pro-compulsionist Lord Northcliffe[65] encouraged such anxieties through his publications and was involved in creating a German spy scare from 1908 onwards. Despite an apparent lack of evidence, stories told of a network of trained German soldiers living in England, waiting for the cue to move.[66] In particular, Northcliffe's *Daily Mail* began to argue in often sensationalist terms that, if war with Germany was inevitable, England should be ready to meet any offensive or that a pre-emptive strike should be made.

Whether fiction or faction, these stories fed into and were used to encourage the sense that COs were enemy agents or that spies might pose as objectors, thereby not only increasing hatred for them and encouraging their outcast status but also supporting the idea that they were committing crimes against their country. As a result of these and other concerns, the secret state monitored COs and their supporters' activities.[67] Indeed, such suspicions were picked up in John Buchan's 1919 novel *Mr Standfast*.[68] Here, it transpires that the head of a network of German spies and agents is hiding within and exploiting a largely inoffensive and innocent pacifist community, which includes objectors.[69]

Such fears of the enemy within or of infiltration by foreign spies were perhaps best illustrated in the pro-war press. The *Daily Express* described objectors as traitors who were helping to stab the army in the back and as 'agents of the enemy', questioned whether the N-CF was financed with German money and referred to the 'GUY FAWKES PLOT OF THE NO-CONSCRIPTIONISTS'.[70] In short, such men, along with the organisations which supported them, were often assumed to be fighting for Germany.[71] Others also expressed such views, as CO Harold Blake recalled. The latter was astounded to hear a prison chaplain maintain that 'the efforts for peace being carried out in this country – including the resistance to military service on the part of conscientious objectors – were subsidised by German gold'.[72]

More specifically, the depiction of the CO in various contexts often portrayed him more generally as a 'criminal type' as described by some criminologists. For example, in continental Europe Caesar Lombroso focused upon the physiology of the male criminal, who was, in various respects, identified as a poor physical specimen.[73] Within early British criminology the influence of psychiatry was more in evidence with the 'classification system of morbid psychology' listing a number of conditions which criminals were said to often exhibit, although in this context '*the* criminal was not conceived as *a* psychological type'. These included 'insanity, moral insanity, degeneracy, feeble-mindedness'.[74] As this and previous chapters have suggested, these organic and psychological conditions were frequently associated with the objector, hence reinforcing the sense that, in terms of his deviance, he was a criminal as well as a degenerate type.

Thus, the objector was often depicted in terms that suggested he was a criminal, a 'blackguard' and a lawless man.[75] Moreover, as the observations of Dorothy Bing demonstrate, the fact that some COs actually were offenders (in refusing to respond to their call up papers or disobeying orders in the military) and a number ended up in military detention and civilian prisons, reinforced the general sense of their criminality and further encouraged their social ostracism.[76] Of course, it also meant that such men were incarcerated and thereby incapacitated within ordinary gaols, despite the fact that they were not guilty of an offence under the ordinary criminal law.

Criminality and punishment

If objectors were perceived of as (cultural and ideological) criminals, not least criminals of the worst kind (as their criminality was seen as being not merely ordinary but enacted against their gender and their country), then it followed that they deserved to be dealt with like offenders. Here, in line with criminal justice approaches to sentencing, their treatment, whether formally handed down or a matter of informal injustice, harshness or cruelty, had a variety of different aims. Most straightforwardly, the object was to take retribution or vengeance against the 'white-feathered crew' or to denounce them publicly. Alternatively, hardship was imposed with expiation in mind, so that objectors could make amends for their criminality through suffering. Otherwise the aim was to break or deter them from their stance or, at least, from their refusal to cooperate. More generally, the desired deterrent effect was aimed at men who might contemplate claiming conscience. On the other hand, harsh treatment could be seen as part of attempts to (re)masculinise, rehabilitate or cure objectors of their misplaced scruples. However, in some cases it seemed that the only way forward was to incapacitate the objector by removing him from society, through such methods as incarceration. Sometimes, of course, the motives for a particular treatment were mixed so that, for example, harshness could be aimed at inflicting retribution, as well as deterring both the individual concerned and others.

Punishment, in particular, was a common thread in attitudes towards COs and calls for retribution came in a variety of contexts. Thus, literary texts attacked the objector and called for him to be punished, as Harold Begbie's poem 'A Christian To A Quaker' illustrates. Each stanza castigates CO Quakers ('your cocoa nibs')[77] and suggests that such Friends deserve to be ill-treated and imprisoned or worse: 'So in you go (and may you die) / To two years hard'.[78] The press also sometimes expressed a desire for retribution. This is amply demonstrated by the *Illustrated Sunday Herald* which, having quoted one policeman charged with protecting objectors at the NC-F National Convention as saying that '[t]hey ain't worth powder and shot', observed that 'perhaps a few rounds *might* be spared'.[79] The Church too was not afraid to make such vehement and violent pronouncements about what objectors deserved. The Bishop of Exeter, Lord Rupert William Gascoyne Cecil, was particularly vehement in this regard, recommending punishment and suggesting that political objectors should be moved to 'that portion of England that is frequently visited by the enemy aeroplane'.[80]

Indeed, much of the ill-treatment of COs could be ascribed to the consequences of constructing objectors as criminal. For example, in the tribunals, the refusals to hear a claim, the outright rejection of an application, the failure to grant the level of exemption requested and the insults heaped upon objectors could all be seen not just as expressions of incomprehension and hatred but also as a tendency towards retribution. Thus, reports of the injustice that COs experienced at the hands of the tribunals led one contemporary observer to conclude that '[n]early all [tribunals] agreed in regarding conscience as an unpatriotic offence' because they felt that such deviance 'must be visited by penalties'.[81] Extreme examples of this tendency include the Chairman of Camberwell tribunal who told a CO applicant '[y]ou ought to be hanged. You ought to be shot'[82] and a Military Representative at Sheffield who informed the applicant that there was only one way to get absolute exemption from the tribunal and that was death.[83] Of course, such pronouncements were not necessarily only about expressing a desire for the ultimate punishment but might simultaneously be aimed at threatening and thereby deterring the applicant and others who might consider becoming COs.

Punishments in the military, along with the harsh conditions on the Home Office Scheme, reinforce this sense that objectors were being penalised for their stance or that attempts were being made to deter them from or even cure them of their perceived deviance. As soldiers, COs who refused to obey orders were not only subjected to officially recognised punishments, but were also particularly vulnerable to verbal abuse and beatings as well as unofficial forms of summary punishment. Here the aim was not only retribution and deterrence (both individual and general) but also, more specifically, to reform the man concerned by ensuring obedience and thereby turn him into a soldier. Indeed, this sentiment was oft expressed and initially, at least, seemed to be the view of many in the military.

More particularly, the assumption was that if these men could not be forced to aspire to be soldiers then at least they could be taught to resign themselves to their situation. Indeed, especially in the early days of conscription, the military response was often to assume that, genuine or not, objectors could and must be made to obey. Indeed, those who were forcibly enlisted were often presumed to be shirkers as the tribunals had failed to recognise them; although for some military men genuineness was not an issue as the idea of conscience was irrelevant. Consequently, in May of 1916 the military view was that:

> . . . once a man is handed over . . . to the military authorities as a soldier, it is not for the military authorities to consider the reasons such a man may have for refusing to do his work . . . the clear duty of every commanding officer [is] to do his best with the legitimate means at his disposal to make every man who is handed over to him an efficient soldier.[84]

Moreover, objector soldiers should, in the words of Wyndham Childs, who was responsible for COs in the army, 'be broken to discipline under the military machine', and thereby (re)trained to be men.[85] As a result, when stories of abuse in the military began to emerge, he was minded to do nothing, stating that 'as far as I am concerned, I have no intention whatever of making any investigation as to the treatment of members of this organisation [the N-CF]'.[86]

The means used to punish, deter and achieve conformity within the military were often brutal. In the extreme there was, of course, the death penalty, which was certainly threatened in many instances involving COs and was passed down but commuted in the case of a few men sent to the Front in France.[87] Other official penalties included Field Punishment No. 1, known as 'Crucifixion'. Although its practice varied, this classically involved standing a man next to an upright structure like a fence or a large wheel and attaching him to it by tying his wrists and ankles. This would be endured for an hour at a time, morning and evening. The punishment period was limited to a maximum 28 days and within this time a soldier had to have a break every fourth day.[88] Unofficial punishments and abuses were at least equally harsh and often inventive. Forrester, a CO taken to Wandsworth prison as a military detainee, describes the beating he received from soldiers when he refused to obey orders:

> Four of them set on me. One of them took hold of me by the back of the neck, nearly choking me, shook me, and dragged me along while the others punched and thumped and kicked me as hard as they knew how. They banged my head on the floor and the walls and threw me into a little cell . . . They told me to get my boots off, but I would not do so, and one of them deliberately punched me behind the ear, and all of them set on me again, and bruised me more. They at last cleared out and slammed the door, leaving me . . . on the floor exhausted.

Later, when the men returned and Forrester continued to refuse to obey, an officer 'allowed the other fellows to start the bruising again', until they had 'exhausted themselves'.[89]

There were reports of other severe cases of abuse. At Atwick Camp near Hull, Private John Gray was frogmarched, punched, stripped naked and, with a rope tied around his waist, he was pushed into a pond and dragged out again – this was repeated eight or nine times.[90] Whilst, at South Sea Camp, Cleethorpes, Private James Brightmore was kept in solitary confinement in a water-logged pit measuring five or ten feet deep and three feet in diameter.[91] Another CO conscript, George Beardsworth, describes the rough treatment and the violence used against him upon his arrival at Birkenhead Barracks. When he repeatedly refused to be ordered about, his body was forcibly made to obey orders. Amongst other things, he was manhandled, pushed, hit, punched, kicked, thrown over a gymnasium vaulting horse, repeatedly pushed into a water jump and dragged out and, while he lay on his back with a man's foot on his stomach, he had his arms and legs 'drilled' by other soldiers.[92] In addition, Clarence Henry Norman unsuccessfully sued

Lieutenant-colonel Reginald Brooke for allegedly putting him in a straitjacket, spitting in his face and attempting to force-feed him.[93]

Whilst some of the 'techniques' that were employed in attempts to break and make a soldier of a CO or enact punishment upon him were not dissimilar from the general 'horseplay' and realities of military discipline for the ordinary soldier,[94] there is some evidence to suggest that these 'punishments' were perhaps more severe in the case of objectors. Indeed, on 19 September 1916 a letter from the Army Council to all District Commanders notes that there had been reports of 'special treatment in the way of coercion'.[95] Arguably, this 'special treatment' of COs marked them out as being especially deviant in terms of the military but it was also an indication of how much their attitudes and behaviours differed from the career soldiers and volunteers that the authorities were used to training and disciplining. In this context, objectors were extraordinary criminals and deserved or required extraordinary tactics in order to punish, secure their obedience and deter others.

For the men on the Home Office Scheme conditions were sometimes severe and, despite their quasi-recognition, they too seemed to be being punished for their stance. Having visited Dyce Camp, MP Ramsay MacDonald reported back to the House of Commons, explaining that:

> These men simply felt that they were being punished, and that they were asked to do this because the state wished to punish them . . . If you are going to punish these men, punish them honestly.[96]

Indeed, some felt that objectors deserved and should accept hardship on the Scheme. Thus, Commander Wedgewood MP maintained that '[t]here must be some sign that a man who pleads conscience suffers for that conscience',[97] perhaps suggesting the need not just for punishment but also for expiation. Following on from this it is arguable that the Scheme carried both the ethos of criminal penalty and (sometimes) that of slave labour – although this was justified in policy terms by the notions of 'equality of service' or 'comparable hardship' with the soldier in the trenches.[98] Quarrying and road building were common employments for the men,[99] and often the work was so hard that even those who were fit, healthy and willing to toil could not cope with the ten hours' hard labour expected of them each day.[100] Consequently, expectations (along with the length of the working day) had to be cut, as the Brace Committee acknowledged.[101] Thus, at such places conditions were sometimes, as John Rae concludes, akin to a 'penal settlement'.[102] Nevertheless, when the Home Office Scheme was being set up some felt it was too lenient and one MP, Major Hunt, wanted the men to be carted off to Germany.[103]

Furthermore, for some objectors on the Scheme, who were released from civilian jail only to be transferred to prisons that were renamed Home Office Centres, even though the regime was more relaxed and their cell doors were not locked, their accommodation itself suggested that they were still criminals undergoing punishment. At Dartmoor Prison, renamed Princetown Work Camp, measures were taken to 'deprison' the environment, but the men were still being housed in a building constructed with penal purposes in mind and the work there carried the reminder of penal servitude, including as it did 'ordinary prison industries' as well as quarrying and land reclamation.[104] What is more, as unrest in local communities and pressure for a harsher regime in the camps increased and some of the objectors were perceived to be disruptive, the rules and discipline became more restrictive, more punitive and, ironically, more militaristic in character.[105] This tightening of the rules meant that objectors in such camps were incapacitated to a similar degree to those who remained in civilian prisons.

In the civilian work context too the treatment of objectors reflected a sense of their criminality. For example, there was an oft-expressed concern that, if they were not directly punished, then COs should at least not have an easy time and certainly should not benefit from their stance. Again atonement and deterrence were deemed appropriate. This was particularly evident in relation to those undertaking alternative work. Thus, the idea was to pick something particularly laborious or totally unsuited to an individual. When CO B.N. Langdon-Davies was put to work in a bakery by the Pelham Committee, one member explained the decision in the following terms: 'we think that you are so unsuited to the job that it is of national importance that you should do it'. Indeed, Langdon-Davies had suggested the bakery work because he had experience of the decisions of the Committee and felt that this was their approach. He recalls that he had come across cases where a schoolmaster had been forced to become a market gardener and a market gardener a schoolmaster, supposedly 'in the interests of national efficiency' – though there is more than a little flippancy here as objectors were generally directed away from employment in education.[106] However, communications between the Pelham Committee and the Central Tribunal would seem to suggest that the former adopted a less punitive stance, whilst the latter was concerned that the CO should suffer. The Central Tribunal was adamant, for example, that such men be put to work at least 50 miles from their homes.[107] Here the contents and tone of the documentation suggests that punishment and penance were key concerns of this body as regards conditional exemption. Also, there is a sense that such treatment might help deter both the individual involved and other men from seeing objection as an easy way to avoid the military.

Beyond this, many objectors were essentially economically penalised because of their stance. Those who lost their jobs were, amongst other things, being punished by their employers, fellow workers and members of the community who refused to deal with them. Those on the Home Office Scheme were granted some remuneration but this was limited, in part, so as not to provoke ill-feeling from soldiers and civilians but also because low pay was intended to be a form of punishment.[108] As a consequence, at Wakefield Centre James Primrose Malcolm Millar reported that objectors were paid only a penny a day.[109] Moreover, unlike the families of soldiers, the dependants of COs in this position were not generally offered separation allowances, creating potential hardship for parents, wives and children.[110] There were many who advocated this approach as they felt that what was needed was a 'form of arduous' as well as 'unremunerative public service'.[111]

As a result of this approach, COs were in many cases deprived of their status as breadwinners and protectors of their kinfolk as if they were criminals. They lost key elements of their manhood; namely, their independence, their earnings or career and their status as a male family member. Moreover, these consequences of their objection were unlikely to arouse many sympathies – they were seen as abdicating their male duty of assisting with the war as well as their familial role by professing their stance and this confirmed the popular view of them as less than men; they had brought their punishment upon themselves and were in this respect doubly unmanned by their stance.

After the war the sense of the criminality of COs and the consequent need for punishment, deterrence, expiation and incapacitation continued, albeit to a lesser and decreasing degree. The temporary disenfranchisement of all COs who had not served in the Non-Combatant Corps or could not satisfy the Central Tribunal that they had spent the war engaged in work of national importance was seen as both a punishment and a deterrent as well as a form of incapacitation by MPs.[112] Objectors had been deprived of this aspect of their citizenship at a time when other men and some women were gaining the vote for the first time[113] and, consequently, by implication they were no longer full Englishmen and were less deserving of the vote than some women. In addition, their delayed release from prison, the Home Office Scheme and work of national importance meant that their punishment continued and that, particularly in the case of those in gaol, they remained incapacitated. Indeed, strong views were expressed in relation to these absolutists in Cabinet discussions in 1919 – these were men who should not be released too soon.[114]

The various discriminatory practices against COs in employment to some extent continued after the war – they were still being penalised.[115] Thus, for some time after peace was declared their war record (or lack of a 'proper' one) was treated as if it were a criminal record.[116] What is more, those refuseniks who had (technically) been in the military received papers stating that they had been dishonourably discharged and warning them that any attempt to re-enlist would make them liable to two years' imprisonment.[117]

Conclusion

Objectors came to be seen and treated as representing dissonant and dissident identities, in terms of patriotism, gender, race and religion as well as in relation to ideologies of legality. Thus, they came to be seen as 'multiply deviant'[118] and were often considered and treated as harshly, if not worse than, the 'ordinary' criminal male. In this context it seemed that the legal recognition of objectors, whether in the rhetoric of statute or in the practice of the tribunals, made little difference to the way in which they were viewed, as these men were, by their stance alone, degenerates and outlaws. In consequence, although *some* objectors were technically minor offenders by failing to report under the Military Service Acts, *a number* became military criminals and *a few* were criminalised under the Defence of the Realm legislation, *all* objectors were subject to a form of 'informal criminalisation' and 'informal (in)justice' whereby they were seen as cultural and ideological criminals.[119] Ironically, as George Bernard

Shaw notes, 'the law to exempt him has resulted in his being punished more severely than other criminals'.[120] Beyond but linked to this notion of the criminality of objectors was a sense that they were dangerous men. Here, in various respects, they were viewed as posing a threat to the country and its people. This latter perception and the fears that were associated with it meant that during and after the war policy makers spent much time considering how best to deal with COs. In this context, however, it was not merely a question of seeking to punish, deter, rehabilitate or incapacitate them as criminals; far more was at stake. The next chapter examines the construction of objectors as dangerous and their treatment as a result.

Notes

1 On degeneracy and the various ideas linked with this concept see, for example: Greenslade, *Degeneracy, Culture and the Novel 1880–1940* (Cambridge: Cambridge University Press, 1994), especially ch. 1; Daniel Pick, *Faces of Degeneration: A European Disorder c. 1848–c. 1918* (Cambridge: Cambridge University Press, 1989); Steven Arata, *Fictions of Loss in the Victorian Fin-de-Siècle* (Cambridge: Cambridge University Press, 1996), especially ch. 1; Donald J. Childs, *Modernism and Eugenics: Woolf, Eliot and Yeats and the Culture of Degeneration* (Cambridge: Cambridge University Press, 2001); J. Edward Chamberlain and Sander L. Gilman (eds), *Degeneration: the Dark Side of Progress* (New York: Columbia University Press, 1985); Bill Luckin, 'Revisiting the idea of degeneration in urban Britain, 1830–1900', *Urban History*, 33:2 (2006), 234–52.

2 Or, as Nancy Stepan has argued 'the urban poor, prostitutes, criminals and the insane were being constructed as "degenerate types"'. 'Biology and degeneration: races and proper places', in Chamberlaine and Gilman (eds) *Degeneration*, p. 98.

3 For example, a journalist in 1895 castigated the 'shocking depravity of the English idle classes' and, in 1913 H.B. Gray expressed concern about the 'growth of luxury and desire for bodily comfort'. Anon., 'Sex-Mania', *Reynolds Newspaper*, 21 April 1895, p. 1; H.B. Gray, *The Public Schools and the Empire* (London: Williams and Norgate, 1913), pp. 11–12 – both are cited in Greenslade, *Degeneracy*, p. 30.

4 On the idea of 'white crisis', in particular, see further Alastair Bonnett, 'From white to Western: "racial decline" and the idea of the West in Britain, 1890–1930', *Journal of Historical Sociology*, 16: 3 (2003), 320–48.

5 Sir Francis Galton helped to popularise such ideas in the latter part of the nineteenth century. See, for example, *Hereditary Genius: An Inquiry Into its Laws and Consequences* (London: Macmillan, 1869).

6 For example, see John Atkinson Hobson, *Imperialism: A Study* (with an introduction by J. Townshend) (London: Unwin Hyman, facsimile of 3rd edn of 1938, 1988: first published 1902), pp. 136, 247–8, 366–7.

7 Frederic William Farrar, 1861, cited by James Walvin, 'Symbols of moral superiority: slavery, sport and the changing world order', in James Antony Mangan and James Walvin (eds) *Manliness and Morality: Middle-Class Masculinity in Britain and America 1800–1940* (Manchester: Manchester University Press, 1987), p. 251. Farrar uses similar arguments in 'Aptitudes of races', *Transactions of the Ethnological Society of London*, 5 (1867), 115–26, 116–23.

8 Thomas Henry Huxley, 'Emancipation – black and white' (1865), in *Collected Essays*, 9 volumes (London: Macmillan, 1893–1908), volume 3, p. 67.

9 Stepan, 'Biology and degeneration', p. 98.

10 Greenslade, *Degeneracy*, pp. 1–2.

11 Edwin Ray Lankester, *Degeneration: A Chapter in Darwinism* (London: Macmillan,1880).

12 Max Nordau, *Degeneration* (Lincoln, NE: University of Nebraska Press, 1993 – this translation originally published 1895), p. 1.

13 Other contemporary works include, for example, James Cantlie, *Degeneration Amongst Londoners* (London: Field and Tuer, 1885); Eugene Solomon Talbot, *Degeneracy: Its Causes, Signs and Results* (London: Scott, 1898).

14 For early twentieth-century examples in this genre see: Frederick J. Whishaw, *The Degenerate* (London: Everett & Co., 1909); Albert Wilson, *Unfinished Man: A Scientific Analysis of the Psychopath or Human Degenerate* (London: Greening & Co, 1910).

15 *Report of the Inter-Departmental Committee on Physical Deterioration* Cd. 2175, 1904. See further: Joanna Bourke, *Dismembering the Male: Men's Bodies, Britain and the Great War* (London: Reaktion, 1996), pp. 171–2; Greenslade, *Degeneracy*, p. 43; Jay Murray Winter, 'Military unfitness and civilian health in Britain during the First World War', *Journal of Contemporary History*, 15:2 (1980), 211–44; Richard Soloway, 'Counting the degenerates: the statistics of race deterioration in Edwardian England', *Journal of Contemporary History*, 17:1 (1982), 137–64.

16 Greenslade, *Degeneracy*, p. 31.

17 On decadence and its influence see, for example: Charles Bernheimer, *Decadent Subjects: The Idea of Decadence in Art, Literature,*

Philosophy, and Culture of the Fin de Siècle in Europe, ed. Thomas Jefferson Kline and Naomi Schor (London: Johns Hopkins University Press, 2001); Ian Fletcher (ed.), *Decadence in the 1890s* (London: Edward Arnold, 1979); Tracey Hill (ed.), *Decadence and Danger: Writing, History and the Fin de Siècle* (Bath: Sulis Press, 1997); Catherine Ruth Robbins, *Decadence and Sexual Politics in Three Fin-de-Siecle Writers: Oscar Wilde, Arthur Symons and Vernon Lee* (Warwick: University of Warwick Press, 1996). Further sources are suggested in Linda C. Dowling, *Aestheticism and Decadence: a Selective Annotated Bibliography* (New York: Garland, 1977).

18 Holbrook Jackson, *The 1890s* (London: Cresset Library, 1988 – first published 1913), pp. 77–8.

19 Wilde was beginning to represent unhealthy and unspeakable desires in men and the idea of effeminacy as a cultural term was changing; it was gradually recoded after the trial and was coming to denote a liminal category. (See Alan Sinfield, *The Wilde Century: Effeminacy, Oscar Wilde and the Queer Moment* (London: Cassell, 1994).

20 See further Greenslade, *Degeneracy*, p. 21; Sinfield, *The Wilde Century*; Elaine Showalter, *Sexual Anarchy: Gender and Culture at the Fin de Siècle* (London: Virago, 1992), ch. 9.

21 On the New Woman see, for example, Angelique Richardson and Chris Willis (eds), *The New Woman in Fiction and Fact: Fin-de-Siècle Feminisms* (Basingstoke: Palgrave, 2000). On links between and hostility towards decadence and the New Woman, see Linda Dowling, 'The Decadent and the New Woman in the 1890s', *Nineteenth-Century Fiction*, 33:4 (1979), 434–53.

22 Campaigns against extending the franchise in this manner often seemed to reflect concerns or suggest underlying fears about the various threats which voting women might, it was argued, pose. Similar worries were expressed or implied by those who opposed women's greater roles in other aspects of the public life. Examples of such anti-suffrage and related literature include: Admiral Frederick Augustus Maxse, *Woman Suffrage, the Counterfeit and the True: Reasons for Opposing Both* (London: W. Ridgway, 1877); Alexander MacCallum Scott, *The Physical Force Argument against Woman Suffrage* (London: National League for Opposing Woman Suffrage, 1912); Alexander MacCallum Scott, *Equal Pay for Equal Work. A Woman Suffrage Fallacy* (London: National League for Opposing Woman Suffrage, 1912). Images on posters and postcards reflected similar concerns about increased female power and the subjection of men to women. See, for instance, John Hassall, 'A Suffragette's Home' (poster) (London: National League for Opposing Woman Suffrage, 1900), Museum of London Picture Library, London, 740. Films also rehearsed similar themes – see Percy

Stow (director), *Milling the Militants* (produced by Clarendon Film Company), 1913. The film is included in a audio-visual documentary by Gordon Swire (*Rise Up, Women: The Suffragette Campaign in London!*, Museum of London, 1992). A print of the film is also at National Film and Television Archive, London. More generally, contemporary images and notions of the female as threatening are explored in Bram Dijkstra, *Idols of Perversity: Fantasies of Feminine Evil in Fin-de-Siècle Culture* (Oxford: Oxford University Press: 1986).

23 Michael J. Clarke, 'Morbid introspection', in William F. Bynum, Roy Porter and Michael Shepherd (eds), *The Anatomy of Madness: Essays in the History of Psychiatry*, vol. 3, *The Asylum and its Psychiatry* (London: Tavistock Publications, 1988), p. 72.

24 Psychiatrist Henry Maudsley quoted in Clarke, 'Morbid introspection', p. 72.

25 On this movement see, for example: Donald E. Hall (ed.), *Muscular Christianity: Embodying the Victorian Age* (Cambridge: Cambridge University Press, 1994); Norman Vance, *The Sinews of the Spirit: The Ideal of Christian Manliness in Victorian Literature and Religious Thought* (Cambridge: Cambridge University Press, 1985); William E. Winn, 'Tom Brown's schooldays and the development of "Muscular Christianity"', *Church History*, 29:1 (1960), 64–73.

26 On the work of the League see, for example, Denis Hayes, *Conscription Conflict: The Conflict of Ideas in the Struggle For and Against Military Conscription Between 1901 and 1939* (London: Sheppard Press, 1949), pp. 36–50; Ralph James Q. Adams and Philip P. Poirier, *The Conscription Controversy in Great Britain, 1900–1918* (London: Macmillan, 1987), pp. 10–48.

27 For example, see 'The Deterioration of the National Physique', *The Nineteenth Century and After*, 53 (1903) 797–805; *The Briton's First Duty: The Case For Conscription* (London: Grant Richards, 1901) – there were a number of other editions of this small volume, including a low-cost version (London: Army League and Imperial Defence Association, cheap edition, 1901); *The Advantages of Compulsory Service for Home Defence, together with a consideration of some of the objections which may be urged against it. A lecture, etc.* (London: J.J. Keliher & Co, 1902).

28 Notable amongst these was Italian positivist Caesar Lombroso. In particular see *Criminal Man*, trans. and ed. Mary Gibson and Nicole Hahn Rafter (Durham, NC: Duke University Press, 2006 – first published in Italian in 1876) and see further below. Lombroso along with William Ferrero identified similar trends amongst females: *The Female Offender* (London: Fisher Unwin, 1895).

29 For example, Earl Russell argued that 'modern humanitarian methods

preserve these wretched people alive, and incidentally give them the chance of reproducing and multiplying their kind'. Quoted in David Garland, *Punishment and Welfare: A History of Penal Strategies* (Aldershot: Gower House, 1985), p. 144.

30 'THE DIFFICULTIES OF THE WAR', *Lloyd's Weekly Newspaper* (28 January 1900), p. 12.

31 '"HA HA! YOU CAN'T CATCH US!" SAY THE DARTMOOR DO-NOTHINGS', *Daily Mail* (23 April 1917), p. 8; 'PRISONERS ABROAD AND "OBJECTORS" AT HOME – OFFICIAL AND EXCLUSIVE PICTURES', *Daily Mail* (24 April 1917), p. 8.

32 Home Office, 'The Home Office and Conscientious Objectors: A Report Prepared for the Committee of Imperial Defence 1919: Part I, The Brace Committee', p. 3 (subsequently 'Brace Committee').

33 On the links between the parasite, the vampire and degeneration see, for example, Greenslade, *Degeneracy*, pp. 18–19.

34 Images depicting the threat of the female parasite and vampire are explored in Dijkstra, *Idols of Perversity*. Of course, today the most well-known late-nineteenth-century literary text on the vampire is Bram Stoker's *Dracula (A Tale)* (London: A. Constable & Co., 1897). However, other contemporary publications feature the figure of the vampire or parasite. For example, see: Arthur Conan Doyle, *The Parasite* (London: A. Constable, 1894); Rudyard Kipling, *The Vampire, etc.* (New York: Critic Co., 1898); Florence Marryat, *The Blood of the Vampire (A Tale)* (London: Hutchinson & Co., 1897).

35 See, for example, Greenslade's discussion, *Degeneracy*, pp. 32–4.

36 Quoted by R.L. Outhwaite 5 HC 80, col. 2435, 16 March 1916.

37 Philip Snowden, *British Prussianism: The Scandal of the Tribunals* (Manchester: National Labour Press, 1916), p. 10.

38 *Ibid.*

39 '"CONSCIENTIOUS" SHIRKERS', *Daily Mail* (28 April 1917), p. 2.

40 'THE CONSCIENTIOUS OBJECTOR' *The Times* (8 April 1916).

41 '"I APPEAL UNTO CAESAR." THE DISABILITIES OF CONSCIENCE', *The Times* (4 September 1917), p. 4.

42 'Brace Committee', p. 9.

43 National Archives, London (hereafter NA), HO 45/10882, 'Memorandum concerning the treatment of conscientious objectors', July 1916. The aim was to prevent the over-punishment of COs whose health might suffer severely.

44 Quoted in Snowden, *British Prussianism*, p. 9, see also p. 8.

45 George Baker, *The Soul of a Skunk: The Autobiography of a Conscientious Objector* (London: Eric Partridge at the Scholartis Press, 1930), p. 170.

46 Snowden, *British Prussianism*, p. 8.

47 The illustration is headed 'AN "OBJECT" LESSON', Frank Holland, *John Bull* (4 May 1918), p. 5.

48 Reproduced in Jackson, *The 1890s*, p. 338.

49 Basil Thomson, *The Scene Changes* (London: Collins 1939), p. 222.

50 Cunninghame Graham, quoted in Cyril Pearce, *Comrades in Conscience: The Story of an English Community's Opposition to the Great War* (London: Francis Boutle, 2001), p. 126.

51 Michael MacDonagh, *In London During the Great War: The Diary of a Journalist* (London: Eyre and Spottiswoode, 1935), p. 100.

52 Although Quaker objections to the military had been recognised before, the term 'conscientious objection' and its use in the statute books in this context was new. On the history and legal reaction to various forms of conscientious objection see further: Constance Braithwaite, 'Legal problems of conscientious objection to various compulsions under British law', *Journal of the Friends Historic Society*, 52:1 (1968), 3–18; Constance Braithwaite, *Conscientious Objection to Compulsions Under the Law* (York: William Sessions, 1995).

53 See Military Service Act, 1916, s.1(2)(a) and War Office, 'Registration and Recruiting', August 1916, pp. 13–15. This was minor in the sense that disobedience was only punishable by a small fine. Andrew Ashworth argues that 'the maximum penalties attached to offences may also be taken to convey the relative seriousness of the types of offence'. *Principles of Criminal Law* (Oxford: Clarendon, 1991), p. 31.

54 For example, see the report of the case of Gilbert Norman Craven and his father John Wallace Craven – both of whom were convicted and fined. 'AN OBJECTOR'S FAMILY, FATHER FINED FOR HIDING HIS SON', *The Times* (31 October 1916), p. 5.

55 Defence of the Realm Act, 1914. This statute was subsequently amended and supplemented. Bertrand Russell was twice prosecuted under the Defence of the Realm Acts for his writings. Bertrand Russell, *Autobiography* (London: Unwin, 1978 – first published in two volumes, 1971) pp. 255–60; Ray Monk, *Bertrand Russell: The Spirit of Solitude* (London: Vintage, 1996), pp. 463–5, 520–4. See further Chapter 4 below.

56 See Nicola Lacey, 'Contingency and criminalisation', in Ian Loveland (ed.), *The Frontiers of Criminality* (London: Sweet and Maxwell, 1995), p. 14.

57 See further: Lois Bibbings, 'State reaction to conscientious objection', in Loveland (ed.), *The Frontiers of Criminality*; 'Images of manliness: the portrayal of soldiers and conscientious objectors in the Great War', *Social and Legal Studies*, 12:3 (2003), 335–58. In consequence,

proponents of a functionalist critique of criminal law (see Nicola Lacey, *State Punishment: Political Principles and Community Values* (London: Routledge, 1988), ch. 5) might sensibly conclude that the legitimate boundaries of their enquiries may extend not merely into the realm of ostensibly civil dispute resolution, but also into the minutiae of social, cultural and economic interaction.

58 *Daily Mail* (30 April 1917), p. 8. The full heading contrasts COs with fighting men – 'OUR WONDERFUL WOUNDED – DARTMOOR'S ARTFUL DODGERS – GUYNEMER'S 36TH'.

59 Henry Wood Nevinson 'The conscientious objector', *Atlantic Monthly*, 103:695 (November 1916), 686–94, 690.

60 Fenner Brockway, *Inside the Left: Thirty Years of Platform, Press, Prison and Parliament* (London: Allen and Unwin, 1942 – reissued in 1947), p. 69.

61 'COALITION AND CONSCIENCE', *Globe* (30 March 1916), p. 2.

62 For example, see: 'WHAT THE TRIBUNALS ARE DOING', *The Tribunal* (8 March 1916), p. 2; 'THE CASE AGAINST THE APPEAL TRIBUNALS: An Exhibition of Tolerance', *The Tribunal* (6 April 1916), p. 2.

63 More recently, in the 1980s Prime Minister Margaret Thatcher famously depicted striking miners using the phrase (Julian Haviland, 'Thatcher makes Falklands link – Attack on "enemy within"', *The Times* (20 July 1984), p. 1). On the use of this notion see further Penny Green, *The Enemy Without: Policing and Class Consciousness in the Miners' Strike* (Buckingham: Open University Press, 1990). In the Second World War, of course, such suspicions focused upon the idea of Fifth Columnists – see further Richard Thurlow, 'The evolution of the mythical British Fifth Column, 1939–46', *Twentieth Century British History*, 10:4 (1999), pp. 477–98.

64 Ignatius Frederick Clarke traces the development of this 'forecasts of war' genre from 1803 until the outbreak of war in 1914. In particular, see 'Forecasts of warfare in fiction 1803–1914', *Comparative Studies in Society and History*, 10:1 (1967) 1–25.

65 By this time Northcliffe's influence was impressive. In 1894 he acquired the *London Evening News*, in 1908 *The Times*. He founded the *Daily Mail* in 1896 and the *Daily Mirror* in 1903 and owned a number of other popular publications. On Northcliffe, see further: Reginald Pound and Geoffrey Harmsworth, *Northcliffe* (London: Cassell, 1959); Henry Hamilton Fyfe, *Northcliffe* (London: Allen and Unwin, 1930); Paul Ferris, *The House of Northcliffe: The Harmsworths of Fleet Street* (London: Weidenfeld and Nicolson, 1971).

66 Christopher Maurice Andrew, *Secret Service: The Making of the British Intelligence Community* (London: Heinemann, 1985), pp. 34–73.

67 The secret state's efforts in relation to objectors and their supporters is considered in the next chapter.

68 John Buchan, *Mr Standfast* (Ware: Wordsworth Classics, 1994 – first published London: Hodder & Stoughton, 1919).

69 *Ibid.*, chs 2 and 3.

70 'CONSCIENCE HUMBUG', *Daily Express* (10 April 1916), p. 4; 'SECRET MEETING OF PEACE CRANKS', *Daily Express* (7 April 1916), p. 5.

71 'THE ENEMY WITHIN OUR GATES', *Daily Express* (11 September 1914), p. 2. This article focused upon the Independent Labour Party.

72 Quoted in Felicity Goodall, *A Question of Conscience: Conscientious Objection in Two World Wars* (Stroud: Sutton Publishing Limited, 1997), p. 33.

73 See further David Garland, 'British criminology before 1935', *British Journal of Criminology*, 28:2 (1988), 1–17, 2 and Lombroso, *Criminal Man*.

74 Garland, 'British criminology', 3.

75 For example, see Snowden, *British Prussianism*, p. 12.

76 As Chapter 1 in this volume demonstrated, having a convict in the family was difficult for respectable people to deal with, not least because knowledge of this on the part of others could mean the isolation of a whole family. See, Dorothy Bing quoted in Caroline Moorehead, *Troublesome People: Enemies of War: 1916–1986* (London: Hamilton, 1987), pp. 30–1. Recordings of Bing's thoughts on the ostracism of COs' families and her own experiences are in the Imperial War Museum, London. (Department of Sound Records, 555/9, Reel 1, Dorothy Bing, 'British civilian pacifist in Croydon and London, GB, 1914–1945').

77 A reference to prominent Quakers' association with chocolate production.

78 Reproduced in David Roberts, *Minds at War: The Poetry and Experience of the First World War* (Burgess Hill: Saxon Books, 1996), pp. 199–200 (no date given).

79 Philip Page, 'CRY OF THE CONSCIENCE MEN: Objectors Play Part Of Martyrs', *Illustrated Sunday Herald* (9 April 1916), p. 2.

80 W. EXON., 'ANARCHIC DARTMOOR: A HOTBED OF MALCONTENTS' (letter), *The Times* (8 October 1917), p. 10.

81 Nevinson, 'The conscientious objector', 690.

82 Quoted in Stanley Bloomfield James, *The Men Who Dared: The Story of an Adventure* (London: C.W. Daniel, 1917), p. 15.

83 John W. Graham, *Conscription and Conscience: A History 1916–1919* (London: George Allen and Unwin, 1971 reprint – first published 1922), p. 72.

84 NA, CAB 37/147/35, 'Minutes of the Imperial War Cabinet, 1917 to 1918', 15 May 1916.

85 *Child's Notes for the Prime Minister on the History of Army Order X*, Asquith Papers 127, Bodleian Library, Oxford (quoted in John Rae, *Conscience and Politics: The British Government and the Conscientious Objector to Military Service 1916–1919* (London: Oxford University Press, 1970), p. 160).

86 NA, WO 32/2055/6923, quoted by Rae, *Conscience and Politics*, p. 140.

87 For example, see Harry E. Stanton's account, 'Will You March Too? 1916–1919', unpublished account of a CO's experiences (privately owned), volume 1, pp. 126–30.

88 War Office, *Manual of Military Law* (London: War Office, 1914), pp. 721–2.

89 Letter dated 12 May 1916, quoted in James, *The Men Who Dared*, p. 64.

90 The official view of the case is given in NA, WO 32/2055/1714. See also Graham, *Conscription and Conscience*, pp. 143–4.

91 The depth of the pit varies in the different accounts. NA, WO 32/2054/1654 includes official documents relating to the case. For further descriptions of such ill-treatment in the military see, for example, Graham, *Conscription and Conscience*, ch. 4.

92 Quoted in James, *The Men Who Dared*, pp. 27–31. The term 'drilled' here probably describes the soldiers moving his limbs to make his body march, stand to attention and so forth.

93 See: 'HIGH COURT OF JUSTICE. KING'S BENCH DIVISION, CONSCIENTIOUS OBJECTOR'S ACTION FOR ASSAULT. NORMAN V. BROOKE', *The Times* (27 July 1917), p. 4, (28 July 1917), p. 4, (31 July 1917), p. 2.

94 This was how some of the incidents of ill-treatment were initially described by the War Office. For example, see NA, Kitchener Papers 74/WS/73, report of meeting with Free Church leaders.

95 See J.I. Macpherson, Permanent Under Secretary, War Office 5 HC 96, col. 873, 23 July 1917.

96 5 HC 86, col. 802–815, 19 October 1916.

97 5 HC 86, col. 873, 19 October 1916.

98 For example, see Lord Salisbury's complaints to the Brace Committee, 'Brace Committee', p. 4. Salisbury was Chairman of the Central Tribunal.

99 For example, English CO Stanton gives an account of his experiences at 'Dyce Quarry Camp' in Scotland – 'Will You March Too?', volume 2, pp. 192–210.

100 For example see *ibid.*, pp. 196.

101 For example, see 'Brace Committee', p. 3.
102 Rae, *Conscription and Politics*, pp. 177–8.
103 5 HC 84, col. 1479, 25 July 1916.
104 'Brace Committee', p. 5.
105 See for example, Rae, *Conscription and Politics*, pp. 186–7. Indeed, in 1917 new and stricter Code of Rules for the work camps and the employment of objectors were introduced and these were amended and supplemented several times that year: *Committee on Employment of Conscientious Objectors: Rules*, Cd. 8550, Cd. 8627, Cd. 8627, Cd. 8884 (the latter, however, were not solely concerned with restricting COs and simultaneously introduced a more liberal approach to employment in 'exceptional' cases – see further Chapter 4 below).
106 B.N. Langdon-Davies, 'Alternative service' in Julian H. Bell (ed.), *We Did Not Fight 1914–1918: Experiences of War Resisters* (London: Cobden Sanderson, 1935), pp. 192–3. For the reluctance to employ COs in education see, for example, Friends Library, London, Temp MSS 835/8/1, Pelham Committee Papers (hereafter 'Pelham Committee Papers'), 5–6, minutes of Committee meetings (in T. Edmund Harvey: correspondence with COs from 1916 to 1920).
107 'Pelham Committee Papers', 'Preliminary List of Occupations'.
108 'Brace Committee', p. 2.
109 James Primrose Malcolm Millar, 'A socialist in war time', in Bell (ed.), *We Did Not Fight*, p. 243.
110 See *The C.O.'s Hansard*, No. 24, 29 March 1917, 299–300. This weekly publication was published by the N-CF. As the title suggests, it reprinted parliamentary debates which referred to objectors.
111 'A Policy for Conscientious Objectors', *The Times* (6 July 1916), p. 7.
112 S.9(2) Representation of The People Act, 1918. See NA, MH 47/3, Supplementary Report of the Central Tribunal, 1922. However, the disenfranchisement was not enforced rigorously (for discussions of the measure see 99 HC 5, cols 1135–1274, 20 November 1917 and G.P. Warner Terry, *The Representation of the People Acts, 1918–1928* (London: Knight, 1928), p. 44). As the state of war was not legally concluded until 31 August 1921, disenfranchisement technically should have lasted until 30 August 1926 (Statutory Rules and Orders 1921, No. 1276).
113 Not all men had the vote before the war and many were disenfranchised by their service abroad during the conflict, whilst the 1918 Act introduced the franchise for some women. See further, for example: Frederic A. Ogg 'The British Representation of the People Act', *The American Political Science Review*, 12:3 (1918), 498–503; Neal Blewett 'The franchise in the United Kingdom 1885–1918', *Past and Present*, 32:1 (1965), 27–56.

114 See NA, CAB 23/9/537(5), Imperial War Cabinet Minutes, meeting of 26 February 1919.

115 For example, see NA, CAB 23/4/298 (18), Imperial War Cabinet Minutes, 'Civil Service restrictions on employing and promoting COs', 14 December 1917.

116 See further, for example, in relation to employment 'EDUCATION AND PENALISATION' and 'AN APPEAL FOR £10,000', *The Tribunal* (12 June 1919), pp. 2, 4.

117 For example, see the accounts in Baker, *Soul of a Skunk*, pp. 259–60 and Brockway, *Inside the Left*, p. 119.

118 The idea of 'double deviance' comes from feminist criminology and is a widely used concept in gender scholarship on crime. Women convicted of crime are viewed as being doubly deviant and are thus liable to be punished more severely (contradicting the idea that women as suspects and convicts experience chivalry within the criminal justice system) because they disobey the law of the land *and* they fail to conform to the 'rules' of appropriate femininity (because women should not commit crimes as this is conceived as masculine behaviour). On this concept see, for example, Susan Edwards, *Women on Trial* (Manchester: Manchester University Press, 1984); Mary Eaton *Justice for Women?* (Milton Keynes: Open University Press, 1986); Loraine Gelsthorpe, *Sexism and the Female Offender: An Organisational Analysis* (Aldershot: Gower, 1989); Loraine Gelsthorpe and Nancy Loucks, 'Magistrates' explanations of sentencing decisions', in Carol Heddermann and Loraine Gelsthorpe (eds), *Understanding the Sentencing of Women*, Home Office Research Study 170 (London: Home Office, 1997); Anne Worrall, *Offending Women* (London: Routledge, 1990).

119 See further Bibbings, 'State reaction to conscientious objection'. In this paper I used the term 'informal criminalisation' but now feel that adding to this the notion of 'informal (in)justice' better encapsulates the treatment described.

120 George Bernard Shaw, 'Conscientious objection versus general strike', in *Everybody's Political What's What?* (London: Constable, 2nd edn, 1945), p. 305.

4

The 'national danger'[1]

As well as being perceived and portrayed as pathetic, unmanly and deviant specimens, conscientious objectors (COs) were often viewed and treated as dangerous men during the war years.[2] This chapter considers the idea of objectors as a menace, and focuses upon their treatment as a result. Here their dissent and, in some cases, dissidence often created an acute sense of anxiety, as it was assumed that they threatened to destabilise, undermine or even overthrow the Government, hence jeopardising the war effort. The text below examines some of the ways in which objectors were cast as a threat, and reflects upon efforts to deter men from adopting their course or sympathising with them. In this regard the chapter reconsiders some of the instances of harsh treatment noted previously, looks at efforts to monitor, censor and restrict COs and their supporters, and explores official concerns about the possible perils of persecuting objectors.

Dangerous men

Previous chapters have already suggested the notion of objectors as in various respects dangerous men. For example, the image of the objector as a criminal, as well as undermining his stance and encouraging his rejection, indicates that he was seen and constructed as posing a challenge to the order of society by his disobedience of its laws – actual, cultural and ideological. The notion of the objector as degenerate, decadent, parasitic or as an unman signified that he was a threat to the race, the nation and, indeed, the Empire.[3] Alternatively, by resisting and opposing the enthusiasm for the war, such men, along with the organisations which supported them, were often assumed to be plotting to bring down the state. Thus, the *Daily Sketch* campaigned against one such group, the Union of Democratic Control, telling its readers that 'to kill this conspiracy we must get hold of the arch-conspirator, E. D. Morel'.[4] More specifically, the fears that COs were pro-German or enemy spies suggested that they posed a very direct danger to the nation as did the idea that some objectors were socialists, anarchists or Bolsheviks, encouraging industrial unrest and planning revolution.

Indeed, it was the latter class of political objectors who were often most associated with danger. Within the pages of the *Daily Mail* these were 'bastard political agitators' who 'intended to give all the trouble they could and to work as little as possible'[5] and, in less colourful language, the Brace Committee felt that they 'would not work, but . . . could and would cause trouble'.[6] According to the Home Office, these were men who, unlike the devoutly religious objectors, were 'not in any sense genuinely conscientious and some of them [were] guilty of grave misconduct'. Instead they were perceived as being 'increasingly busy in their endeavours to induce their fellow citizens to defy the Government'.[7] Thus, even when the release of objectors was being discussed in the Cabinet following the armistice some argued that the militants in prison were 'blackguards' and 'revolutionaries' who should be held as long as possible in order not only to punish them but also to contain the threat that they apparently posed.[8]

But beyond this all objectors were often deemed to be menacing because if their stances towards fighting and the conflict spread then there was ultimately a danger that national stability and the war effort would break down. Consequently, COs and their supporters were a 'suspect community',[9] viewed with distrust and fear. These men and those who backed them, therefore, needed to be carefully suppressed, controlled and monitored. However, increasingly an extra element to the dangerousness of objectors was recognised; too much in the way of repression and cruelty could be counterproductive.

Containing and controlling conscientious objectors

A pervasive thread in the way in which COs were dealt with was the fear that if the anti-war movement, along with objectors and their supporters, were not treated and managed very carefully its ideas might flourish and, consequently, the numbers of those threatening

10 'A.E.' 'CONSCIENTIOUS OBJECTORS!', 1916.

conscription, the war effort and the nation itself could increase. In this context, fears that the conscientious contagion could proliferate indicate that the injustice, ill-treatment and cruelty towards objectors can be seen not only as the expression of hatred or as a consequence of their cultural and ideological criminality, but also, more specifically, as attempts to limit the danger they posed and prevent the 'conscience clause' from becoming a 'shirkers' charter'. Equally, the occasional ridicule of the CO not only suggests that these were unmen whose beliefs were flimsy and easy to overcome but also could be viewed as attempts to break such men and undermine their stance in the eyes of others. What is more, portraying objectors as outcast, pathetic, unmanly, suspect and deviant specimens could also be seen as a strategy adopted in order to help reduce their potential dangerousness by discouraging others from wishing to be associated with them or their ideas.

Thus, as was suggested in the context of deviancy in the last chapter, many of the policies adopted towards objectors can be seen variously as attempts to deter individual objectors or to cure (re)train and (re)masculinise them by teaching them to be men and making them into soldiers. In terms of the wider male community, the harsh treatment of objectors and the propaganda which attacked, disparaged and ridiculed them also sought to attempt to prevent the spread of objection, deviance and unmanliness by making the claim of conscience seem an unpopular and difficult path to choose. Moreover, the efforts to incapacitate some objectors by incarcerating them or preventing them from proselytising were also often aimed at restricting the spread of their ideas.

In the military too the idea of treating COs harshly in order to deter others was often cited. However, the cures for disobedience, which had worked with other men, were proving to be ineffective as far as determined objectors were concerned and thus the aim of general deterrence (as well as individual deterrence) was arguably failing. These men were, consequently, becoming both an embarrassment and a burden to the military. More significantly, the presence of COs who refused to obey any order in the training camps, barracks and in military detention was posing a particular threat. Objectors were bad for discipline and COs might spread their ideas to soldiers or encourage unrest in the ranks. Thus, there was a particular fear that soldiers exposed to objectors might be infected with the pacifist or socialist heresy. For example, in 1917 the Adjutant at Cleethorpes Camp, Captain MacBean, who was partially responsible for James Brightmore's stay in the pit, ordered that the CO be isolated from the other men as he posed 'a danger to discipline'.[10] Indeed, although the military initially tended to want as many men as possible and military representatives were directed to act accordingly in the tribunals, gradually objectors came to be viewed as a liability. When B.N. Langdon-Davies appeared before the local tribunal applying for conditional exemption on grounds of objection the Military Representative called objectors 'a national danger', adding that, for this reason, the military did not want him.[11] Moreover, when the Central Tribunal 'reviewed' the cases of incarcerated COs it also reflected similar fears, concluding that 'many of these men were of no use to the Army; their presence in military units was a hindrance to the performance of military duties'.[12]

In addition, it seemed that some of the more troublesome objectors were determined to stir up agitation amongst soldiers. It was, in part, as a result of such concerns that, before long, objectors were sent to serve out their sentences under court-martial in civilian jails.[13] However, a move to a civilian prison could not always guarantee that soldiers were shielded from these men. At Wandsworth one wing was used as a military detention barracks and the other as a civil prison housing, amongst others, over one hundred objectors sentenced by court-martial. Some of the more militant political COs went on strike against the prison regime, sought to incite military prisoners to mutiny and encouraged them to attack the sergeants in charge of them. As a result, a new governor was sent to restore order and discipline to the jail; the disruptive objectors had to be brought under control and prevented, in particular, from stirring up the soldiers.[14]

The creation of the Home Office Scheme was also, amongst other things, a means of removing objectors from the military and, thus, preventing soldiers' exposure to their dangerous influence[15] as, assuming these men co-operated, there was no risk of them being returned to the military. Moreover, it was thought that placing large groups together at work centres would prevent them from spreading their views to others. At the same time this was not to be portrayed as an easy route out of the military. As the last chapter noted, objectors were expected to give 'equality of service' or experience 'comparable hardship' to the soldier in the trenches in order, amongst other things, to discourage men from seeing objection as an easy option.[16] Thus, Nevil Macready at the War Office argued that COs under civilian control should be employed 'under conditions as severe as those of soldiers at the Front'.[17]

However, the political militants who were accused of deliberately stirring up trouble in the military and in prisons were also perceived to cause problems at the work centres. These men not only, according to Wyndham Childs at the War Office, resisted any attempt to make them co-operate but also 'were increasingly busy in their endeavours to induce their fellow citizens to defy the Government'.[18] Indeed, men on the Scheme were initially given a significant degree of freedom and this meant that new opportunities to preach their views both to each other and to local communities were suddenly available to them. Some even travelled to speak at meetings or produced and distributed anti-war literature, despite the fact that such activities were banned.[19]

In addition, the large numbers of men at some work camps became a matter of particular concern – John Rodker estimates there were over a thousand men at Dartmoor when he was there.[20] Following developments in Russia, the concentration of the militants at Princetown became a particular worry expressed by the local community and encouraged by the press. Thus, the Bishop of Exeter alleged that these men were plotting 'bloodshed' which would bring 'ruin, to England'.[21] Beyond this, holding objectors in large groups[22] around the country led to violence between them and the local inhabitants. Such unrest was not good for national cohesion, as order and stability were felt to be crucial to the maintenance of the war effort on the Home Front. These problems initially led to greater restrictions being imposed upon the men, including a ban on propaganda activities, and then to more radical action; the men were to be separated and dispersed around the country. As James Primrose Malcolm Millar suggests, this change in strategy was aimed at reducing the number of COs in one place as much as it was intended to get them to do the most useful work of national importance, which was the official explanation for what amounted to a complete reversal of policy.[23] But, paradoxically, the various attempts to scatter objectors also allowed them to spread their propaganda to new audiences, meaning that concerns about proselytising remained.[24]

Amid German successes in 1918 the concerns about the dissidence amongst political objectors became acute, and at the same time it was proposed that conscription be extended to Ireland. This prompted anxieties about Sinn Féin's reaction and the possibility of Irish nationalist COs increasing the objector problem, spreading dissent and assisting other objectors. Childs offered some radical recommendations in an attempt to scupper republican rebellion should the Military Service Acts' application be extended across the water. He proposed that:

> [I]t should immediately be made known that conscientious objectors who disobey a lawful command in such a way as to show a wilful defiance of authority (Section 9(I) of the Army Act) will be tried by General Court Martial and, if sentenced to death by that court, the sentence will be carried out if it appears that their objection is based on political and not religious grounds . . . If this proposal is adopted, it is no good disguising the fact that it will in certain cases mean shooting, and it should be recognised that Sinn Feiners will be shot as well as the anarchical atheists in this country . . .[25]

In fact conscription was not extended to Ireland, so this Minute was never implemented. However, there is evidence that Sinn Féiners and COs communicated in the prisons and that republican prisoners assisted objectors, so the suspicion that tactics would be shared and the authorities' problems increased was not without foundation.[26]

Beyond this, the fear that objection would spread if the treatment of COs was too soft arose in relation to every decision which was taken as to how to deal with objectors and in relation to each of the many shifts in policy. For example, Home Secretary Herbert Samuel had decided that when the men were transferred to civilian prisons discipline would be the same as for other prisoners, as any relaxation of the rules 'would tend to encourage the evasion of military service on a plea of conscientious objection'.[27] Equally, when the release of absolutists from prison was being discussed (in particular, the case of the prominent and well-connected CO Stephen Hobhouse), there was concern that 'the release of the first absolutist would be the beginning of the end'.[28] Later, Childs warned that 'the day that absolute exemption is granted to anybody whether his objection be based on religious or other grounds we are beaten'.[29]

Similarly, public announcements of concessions granted to objectors in the military were carefully considered and delayed if this was felt to make the objector route appear more attractive. Thus, there was a reluctance both to state categorically that no conscientious objectors should be shot without Cabinet approval and to publish 'Army Order X', which directed that court-martialled objectors should be transferred to civilian prisons. The broadcasting of these developments was delayed, as making these measures public before the closing date for applications for exemption in June 1916 seemed unwise.[30] At all costs men should be discouraged from claiming exemption on conscience grounds, so it was crucial that the consequences for objectors appeared to be severe.

Monitoring and censoring objectors

The construction of objectors, along with others who were anti-war and anti-conscription, as dangerous and, in particular, the fear that their particular brand of conscientiousness might spread also meant that there was a tendency to monitor, repress, censor and control them in civilian life. In particular, the No-Conscription Fellowship (N-CF or the Fellowship) was quickly perceived as a dangerous organisation by the state and the police. Even before the introduction of conscription it had attracted attention by campaigning against the Derby Scheme and attempting to recruit members. Indeed, in 1915 the Director of Public Prosecutions sent a summary of both the N-CF and the Union of Democratic Control's anti-war activities to the Attorney General,[31] and the police began to watch and report their activities around the country, ironically putting pressure upon the anti-conscription Home Secretary, Sir John Simon, to take action.[32] Once military compulsion came, efforts intensified on the part of both the N-CF and the authorities. In particular, elements within the War Office seem to have believed that those who were members or shadow officials had subversion in mind and aimed to destabilise the army from within.[33] Thus, Lord Kitchener saw the Fellowship as a 'growing and menacing body' and was especially unsympathetic towards political objectors.[34]

As this suggests, the N-CF attracted particular attention not only because of its work supporting, advising and coaching members for their tribunal appearances but also, more particularly, because it was often alleged that the organisation was both seeking to turn men into objectors and assisting shirkers to evade compulsion. For example, 'The Man in the Street', writing in the *Daily Sketch*, protested that the 'ineffable Clifford Allen' (Chairman of the N-CF) had been 'busy perverting the minds of the weak and uninstructed since the outbreak of the war'.[35] In similar tone in May 1916 Herbert Nield, the Chairman of Middlesex Appeal Tribunal, wrote to the Home Secretary complaining that:

> The No Conscription Fellowship is responsible for much of the trouble the Tribunals are having – as a rule the objectors are quite young men 18–22 and they appear to me to be carefully coached and induced to oppose the working of the Act. I venture to hope that you will have these men very carefully watched and that you will not hesitate to proceed against them directly you have proof of their activities.

The reply from Herbert Samuel confirmed that the Cabinet and the War Office shared these concerns but explained that there was a fine distinction between legal and illegal action in this context. In his view, whilst it was legitimate to help men to claim exemption on conscience grounds, inciting or advocating non-compliance with the law would constitute a criminal offence.[36]

Sometimes concern about anti-conscription activities led to more direct measures. In 1916 and 1917 the offices of the National Council Against Conscription, the N-CF and the Independent Labour Party were all raided by the police. On these occasions anti-conscription leaflets, posters and newspapers were confiscated.[37] In particular, the police sought to curtail the Fellowship's work by preventing the production of *The Tribunal*. In their efforts to achieve this they targeted the organisation's printing press, seized copy and sought to bring proceedings against individuals for producing a variety of leaflets that were deemed to be prejudicial to the war effort.[38]

Thus, the publications of the N-CF were viewed by many to be evidence of treason and treachery and were also considered dangerous as they might spread pacifist or socialist ideas. In consequence, many N-CF publications were seized or suppressed by the police and a number of individuals were prosecuted for undermining the war effort under the Defence of the Realm legislation and regulations.[39] Bertrand Russell, a shadow Chairman of the N-CF, was prosecuted twice for his writings in support of objectors and against conscription.[40] He was convicted and imprisoned on the second occasion for authoring a Fellowship leaflet.[41] In the summer of 1916 Edward Grubb, along with other N-CF organisers, was prosecuted for an N-CF leaflet that called for the repeal of conscription. According to his recollection, the authorities saw the statement that '[t]he Act has our determined *resistance*' as amounting to incitement to others to resist the Military Service Acts. They were convicted and fined £110 each with the alternative of two months' imprisonment, and their subsequent appeal was unsuccessful.[42]

Publishers also fell foul of the defence regulations. Thus, Rose Allatini's *Despised and Rejected*, with its inclusion of the wartime experiences of a number of objectors, became the subject of litigation.[43] Its publisher, C.W. Daniel, had previously been prosecuted for producing a pacifist pamphlet.[44] He was taken to court again for *Despised and Rejected* and charged with publishing material 'likely to prejudice the recruiting of persons to serve in His Majesty's Forces, and their training and discipline'; the positive portray of objectors in a work of fiction was felt to be dangerous. The legal action was successful and the book was banned.[45]

In addition, MI5, special branch and the various Ministerial intelligence units considered that the N-CF's and other such organisations' leading members and officials warranted their particular attention.[46] Reflecting public perceptions and propaganda, it was feared that these men and women, in particular, could be spies or revolutionaries, or that their organisations could become infiltrated and manipulated by enemy agents. Even if this was not the case they were still spreading information which could be considered detri-

mental to the war effort and which posed a sharp contrast to both
the official picture and the heavily censored jingoism of the press.
Consequently, N-CF officials were hounded by intelligence investigators and the police.[47] Fenner Brockway came to the security
services' attention both as editor of the *Labour Leader*, which was
publishing anti-war articles, and as Secretary of the N-CF. His intelligence file contains MI5 (formerly K division of the Secret Service
Bureau) papers and correspondence concerning fears about him and
his activities, along with cuttings about his frequent court-martials
as well as his anti-war and anti-conscription activities.[48]

Other measures were also used against prominent anti-
conscription speakers to prevent them disseminating their ideas.
Most notably, before his incarceration a travel ban was imposed
upon Bertrand Russell, who was active on the speaking circuit
around the country. The aim in this case was to prevent him from
visiting areas where his activities may, it was feared, have led to
industrial unrest.[49] Others campaigning for peace were similarly
pursed by the state.[50]

State surveillance also targeted the underground networks of
COs, pacifists and anti-war socialists around the country that
Sheila Rowbotham, Ray Challinor, Cyril Pearce and Ken Weller
have described.[51] For example, Derby was both the headquarters of
the N-CF[52] and the focus of the (Marxist) Socialist Labour Party's
opposition to the war. Speakers and activists formed a 'flying corps'
working locally and travelling the country to speak at meetings and
organise dissent. Such clandestine networks were feared because
they often focused upon stirring up unrest amongst workers. They
were also a cause for concern as they hid objectors who were on the
run and helped them flee the country. Thus, John S. Clarke, assisted
by local supporters, evaded capture by lying low at a farm whilst
working as a labourer and writing socialist articles.[53] Similarly, Alice
Wheeldon and her daughter Harriett (for a time local secretary of the
N-CF), who were socialist feminist opponents of the war, used their
home and business addresses in Derby as safe houses for objectors
and helped smuggle men to America.[54] They were part of a 'secret'
network, or rather a number of networks, which had centres in
various parts of Britain and supported the various facets of the anti-
war movement.[55] In Huddersfield too a consensus of Liberals and
the labour and socialism movement formed a community opposed
to the war and conscription, supporting objectors[56] and in Bristol

George Edward Barker was convicted of 'hiding and harbouring' men liable to military service in an underground chamber.[57]

Thus various departments of the state tried to keep tabs on pacifists, socialists and objectors around the country and their activities were monitored, as was their correspondence.[58] Indeed, all anti-war and anti-conscription groups were closely watched and the Home Office kept files on pacifist agitators and 'Anti-Recruiting and Peace Propaganda',[59] and the secret state monitored them just as they monitored the decadent establishments in London that were also viewed as potential nests of spies.[60] For example, investigators for the Ministry of Munitions intelligence unit reported the business interests of N-CF activists and sought to uncover funding roots and the means for distributing socialist and anti-war materials.[61] Indeed, the use of spies to mingle with objectors and their supporters or infiltrate organisations was not uncommon. Thus, in 1917 Beverley Nichols was sent by his unit in the Intelligence Department of the War Office to venues seen to be popular haunts for war resisters 'to act as a sort of agent provocateur to lure pacifist activists into trying to entice them to their cause'.[62]

The prosecution of Alice Wheeldon and her daughters, Harriett and Winnie, along with Alfred George for conspiracy to murder the Prime Minister (Lloyd George) and others, provides an extreme illustration of the work of the intelligence services. Two spies employed by an intelligence unit within the Ministry of Munitions, who acted as *agents provocateurs*, infiltrated Wheeldon's circle in late 1916 and a poison plot was 'discovered'.[63] The publicity associated with this case, of course, only served to confirm the more sinister suspicions about anti-war and anti-conscription activists' true intentions. Indeed, under cross-examination at trial amongst other things Alice admitted to sheltering COs, and much was made of the fact that her son was one.[64]

The perils of persecution

Although one means of preventing the spread of objection was assumed to be the harsh treatment of objectors, it soon became apparent that this approach could in itself hold dangers; if objectors were seen to be treated too harshly, public sympathy might be aroused for both their plight and their stance. Thus, whilst the cruelty towards objectors illustrates the perceived need for COs' lives not to be made too easy in order to discourage others from following them, some of the numerous changes in policy towards them demonstrate, amongst other things, the fear that persecuted objectors might attract the wrong kind of public attention. Indeed, there was concern that the non-recognition, injustice and abuse in the tribunals, the cruelty in the military, the severity of the prison regime and the rough conditions at some Home Office Centres threatened to alter public opinion.

In addition, harsh treatment might undermine the idea of liberal England. At this time this notion of the country was particularly important as it was often contrasted unfavourably with the image of an intolerant, militaristic Germany and used as a justification for the conflict. In this context, there was thus a tendency to treat objectors less harshly and to respond sympathetically to allegations of abuse. Indeed, the dangers of arousing sympathy for COs and their cause led to policy shifts that were aimed at improving the lot of objectors rather than merely punishing, deterring and denigrating them.

The dangers of the well-publicised cases involving the extreme ill-treatment of COs gradually became obvious to the military, as the following observation by Childs (who was in charge of matters of military discipline at the War Office) on some of the cases of abuse in the early days of conscription illustrates:

> This case [Brightmore's] and that of Private Gray and those of the five conscientious objectors sent to France have done more damage and produced more sympathy and support for the revolutionary and pacifist movements in this country than any other incident which has occurred in the past twelve months.[65]

Those on the side of the objectors also recognised this. For example, Bertrand Russell expressed his view in the following terms:

> I am convinced that from the beginning the policy of the Government has tended to produce some degree of sympathy for these people which would never have existed had they been treated in a different way . . . everybody knows that they are in fact being treated with hardship for conscience sake.[66]

Others in the military reflected a concern that harsh treatment might be counter-productive if it was widely publicised. In particular, harsh treatment experienced by the devoutly religious objectors was a problem for the authorities. Such men were respected, otherwise law-abiding citizens who aroused sympathies amongst the populous. Thus, General Smuts felt that the much publicised case of the well-connected Quaker Stephen Hobhouse was 'causing profound misgivings to thousands of good people who are by no means in favour of C.Os'.[67]

This kind of realisation prompted a series of policy changes and new instructions (although preventing public sympathy or support for objectors was often only one of a number of reasons for these shifts). Thus, criticism of the conduct of the tribunals led to clarifications of the law and new guidelines. For example, as early as 23 March 1916 a circular referred to allegations of the 'harsh cross-examination' of objectors and advised that, whilst questioning was necessary, 'it is desirable that enquiries should be made with tolerance and impartiality'.[68] Also, stories of the abuse of COs by the military occasioned the War Office to send out a letter on 19 September 1916 directing officers to stop ill-treatment and maintain ordinary regulations in relation to objectors.[69] Similarly, reports of the objectors shipped to France and threatened with execution eventually resulted in a clear restatement of policy and disquiet about objectors in military detention facing repeated court-martials led to their transfer to civilian prisons. Worries about sympathy for the objectors in prison led to the Home Office Scheme. Revelations about extreme cruelty and public complaints about abuse led to further changes in relation to COs on the Scheme. Thus, 'Exceptional Employment' was sanctioned by a Cabinet committee allowing men to work as individuals with private employers – with no mention of equal suffering in the new rules.[70] Concerns about the treatment of the religious absolutists in prison led to concessions that improved conditions for those men who complied with the regime[71] and a direction on the punishment of objectors in prisons addressed anxieties about the heath consequences of repeatedly punishing physically and/or mentally vulnerable men.[72]

In relation to all these changes in policy the need to get the right combination of harshness and leniency was a primary concern. There was, thus, a difficult balance to maintain in relation to the treatment of these men. In addition, the problem was compounded by the fact that COs, as well as the nature and extent of their objections and militancy, differed so greatly and because there was a need to have regard to the competing arguments of those who supported objectors and those who opposed them. The Home Office Report on the Brace Committee acknowledges some of these tensions:

> The men and their friends argued that they were genuine and therefore entitled to exemption and justified in not working enthusiastically and not behaving quietly under duress: the critics of the Conscientious Objectors argued that they were men who ought to be performing military service, instead of which they are being dealt with lightly by the Committee. . . . These two arguments resulted in constant pressure on the Committee to increase or to relax its disciplinary methods; and neither argument could be accepted as applying to the whole body of men.[73]

Moreover, the authorities' concerns were exacerbated by the fact that some objectors and their supporters and, in particular, the N-CF recognised that non-recognition and ill-treatment was useful to their cause. Even before conscription came into force the National Committee of the N-CF was of the view that:

> When members cannot accept the decisions of the Tribunals, and have to suffer, we shall have an unanswerable case to advance. We can show how our men faced every ordeal, and how those who failed to convince the Tribunals with words are now proving their sincerity by deeds.[74]

Indeed, its members were so briefed. Also, there were conscious efforts to publicise and exploit stories of brutality and suffering.[75] In particular, Clifford Allen saw the benefit in the ill-treatment and suffering of objectors. For example, at one stage of his imprisonment when he was on the punishment diet for refusing to work Allen talks of his declining health as possibly providing useful material for 'scandal propaganda'.[76] Moreover, in his correspondence smuggled out of prison he refers frequently to the need for and the best 'methods of pacifist propaganda'[77] and stresses that suffering for their stance would be 'a far more powerful propaganda than countless meetings'.[78] Thus, anti-conscriptionists and, in particular, the N-CF collected and sought to use examples of injustice and cruelty to their own advantage.[79] By so doing they both made themselves appear more dangerous to the state and made the authorities' task of managing objectors even more difficult.

In addition, there was particular concern about the suffering of objectors who were prominent in CO or wider circles and were already viewed by anti-conscriptionists as heroic figureheads for the cause. Communications between the Home Office, the War Office and the Law Society on the subject of James Scott Duckers, a solicitor and a CO, illustrate this point. The Law Society wished to make an example of Duckers by striking him off the roll of solicitors for calling the profession into disrepute by his unpatriotic stance. This organisation was, therefore, seeking the temporary release of Duckers from prison to enable them to proceed against him. However, the man in question was known to have supporters who would seek to publicise his case. It was decided (by the War and Home Offices) that the President of the Law Society was to be strongly discouraged from this course as it was felt that any disciplinary hearing would draw attention to the objector and might risk making him an even greater hero to the pacifist cause. Far better that he remain unpunished by his professional body, incarcerated and hidden.[80] Duckers, whose account of his early war experiences was published during the conflict, was probably totally unaware of these machinations.[81]

Preventing martyrdom

However, fears that stories of overly harsh treatment and suffering might spread sympathy for the CO and his stance were sometimes more specific. In particular, the authorities were exercised over the need to avoid the production of objector martyrs. Indeed, a prominent legal academic, Albert Venn Dicey, not only voiced concerns that COs might command popular sympathy but also that some might be martyred for their cause, and argued that reform should be instituted in order to diminish the *reality* or *appearance* of injustice to objectors.[82] This anxiety about martyrdom tended to be particularly acute in relation to those religious objectors who were most likely to occasion respect rather than hatred. Indeed, as already noted, their involvement in protest and passive disobedience, in some cases for the first time in their lives, was difficult for the state and the press to handle. A particular concern was how convincingly to portray these men as dishonourable when many were patently extremely honourable men whose stance during conscription merely demonstrated their consistent adherence to their principles. Whilst their refusal to assist the national effort along with their perceived unmanliness were firm bases upon which to demonise them, there were genuine concerns that these men should not receive too much attention and publicity lest they arouse sympathy. In the light of this, their possible martyrdom was a particular concern. As an absolutist writing from prison noted:

> No Government can face permanent imprisonment of admittedly good citizens. They would be a thorn in the flesh, or a nucleus always stimulating opposition which would ultimately prevail. Unconditional exemption would equally carry with it the seeds of ultimate, even if not immediate, destruction of conscription.[83]

The authorities' concerns about CO martyrdom are demonstrated, in particular, by the decision to stop force-feeding hunger-striking objectors when deaths became likely.[84] The temporary release from prison of men whose health was endangered by this form of protest and its treatment had a similar motive.[85] Similarly, a memorandum to local prisons, directing them to assess the health of objectors before subjecting them to repeated periods of punishment, was also aimed at preventing death. In addition, the concession that allowed for the release of unfit COs in prison and their transfer to the Army Reserve was, in part, a reaction to fears about martyrdom, as Lord Curzon noted in the House of Lords.[86]

As a result of these anxieties, the absolutists in prison were considered by some to have received better treatment than might otherwise have been the case, as Langdon-Davies recalls:

> . . . they were not permitted to be martyrs. For, to tell the truth, the authorities allowed there to be very few martyrs under the Military Service Acts. Whoever controlled the policy saw to it that the men who were ready and eager for martyrdom should not be allowed it, at all events if it were likely to be a spectacular kind.[87]

In similar vein, George Bernard Shaw refers to the well-connected Quaker Stephen Hobhouse as being the kind of man who the authorities would ensure was prevented from becoming a martyr.[88] Indeed, Hobhouse along with other prominent COs (for example, Clifford Allen) was released from prison on grounds of ill-health and placed on the Army Reserve.[89]

Conclusion

In a number of respects the CO was viewed, portrayed and treated as a dangerous man, and other men and women within the anti-conscription and anti-war movements were regarded and dealt with in a similar manner. In this context, objectors' dangerousness was conceptualised as a conspiracy against the state and the war effort. More fundamentally, they were seen as presenting a disturbing challenge to the dominant ideas underpinning support for the conflict. Consequently, some sought to break or cure COs, and there were efforts to prevent the 'conchie' contagion from spreading to others.

Indeed, throughout the period of conscription COs posed difficulties for the authorities which, in various guises, were forced to swiftly devise, then repeatedly reassess and alter their plans for the treatment of a very diverse and often difficult to handle group of men. In this context policy-makers were pushed and pulled in different directions. At some points they responded to complaints about objectors' ill-treatment or suffering and offered concessions, whilst at others they sought to toughen up the measures relating to COs. Thus, there were conflicting concerns about treating these men too harshly or too indulgently. These concerns, along with the need to promote national unity and quieten both those who argued for objectors and those who opposed them, meant that deciding upon how to deal with objectors was an especially challenging task.

Consequently, the objector problem was seen as a time-consuming and fraught distraction from the main business of the war and there was much frustration from those deciding on policy or dealing more directly with objectors, as one CO recalls: '[h]ow angry the authorities seemed with us; how they blustered, and how puzzled they were too'.[90] Indeed, impatience and frustration with the amount of time and effort objectors were taking up was sometimes expressed in Parliament.[91] In this construction of these men they, along with their supporters, were not only dangerous but also troublesome people.[92]

This notion of the objector as a menace is, of course, in keeping with the depictions of him already constructed and considered in *Telling Tales About Men*. Thus far he has been portrayed in negative terms as, for example, outcast, coward, parasite, unman, deviant, suspect and threat. However, other more positive constructions of objectors are also possible. This volume now turns to focus upon some of these conceptions of the CO. First the text picks up an implicit thread from the current chapter; namely, that objectors were by no means entirely alone and that they sometimes experienced sympathy and respect. Then, in the final tale-telling about First World War COs within this text, they are depicted as patriots and heroes.

Notes

1 A military representative's take on objectors, quoted by B.N. Langdon-Davies, 'Alternative service' in Julian H. Bell (ed.) *We Did Not Fight: 1914–18 Experiences of War Resisters* (London: Cobden-Saunderson, 1935), p. 191. See further below.

2 Theories of risk are not included in the analysis as they do not fit with either the interpretation of the CO's experience or his construction depicted here. On risk see, for example: Ulrich Beck, *Risk Society: Towards a New Modernity*, London, Sage 1992 (trans.); Anthony Giddens, 'Risk society: the context of British politics', in J. Franklin (ed.), *The Politics of Risk Society* (Cambridge, Polity Press, 1998); Michael Power, *The Risk Management of Everything: Rethinking the Politics of Uncertainty* (London: Demos, 2004), available free at www.demos.co.uk/files/riskmanagementofeverything.pdf (accessed July 2008).

3 For example, see Krishan Kumar, *The Making of English National Identity* (Cambridge: Cambridge University Press, 2003), pp. 198–9.

4 'The Man in the Street', *Daily Sketch* (1 December 1915), p. 3.

5 See report of Plymouth public meeting, 'From our special correspondent', 'CONSCIENTIOUS SHIRKERS. PLYMOUTH MEETING. A WOMAN'S POWERFUL INDICTMENT', *Daily Mail* (26 April 1917), p. 3. Whilst in this instance the words are ascribed to Mr J.Y. Woollcombe, the sentiment is by no means out of keeping with this paper's view.

6 Home Office, 'The Home Office and Conscientious Objectors: A Report Prepared for the Committee of Imperial Defence 1919: Part I, The Brace Committee', p. 3 (subsequently 'Brace Committee').

7 Home Office, 'The Home Office and Conscientious Objectors: A Report Prepared for the Committee of Imperial Defence 1919: Part II, Conscientious Objectors in Prison', p. 7 (subsequently 'Conscientious Objectors in Prison').

8 See, for example, National Archives, London (hereafter NA), CAB 23/9/537(5), 'Minutes of the Imperial War Cabinet, 1917 to 1918'.

9 See Paddy Hillyard, *Suspect Community: People's Experience of the Prevention of Terrorism Acts in Britain* (London: Pluto, 1993). Hillyard refers to the creation of a different suspect community, namely the Irish, and examines the criminalisation of Irish people living in Britain. In this context he shows how 'certain *categories of people* are drawn into the criminal justice system simply because of their status and irrespective of their behaviour' (p. 260).

10 Quoted in NA, WO 32/2054/1654, Major Fryer's second report on the allegations. The file includes further details of Brightmore's case.

11 Langdon-Davies, 'Alternative service', p. 191.

12 NA, MUN 5/52/300/72, Report of the Central Tribunal appointed under Military Service Act, 1916, February 1919, p. 23 (subsequently 'Report of the Central Tribunal').

13 This was as a result of a measure known as 'Army Order X': Army Order 179, 25 May 1916, reproduced in *The Tribunal* – 'NEW ARMY COUNCIL ORDER' (1 June 1916), p. 4.

14 See *Inquiry Held into the Allegations Made Against the Acting Governor of Wandsworth Prison*, Cd. 131, 1919 (known as the Richardson Report).

15 For example, see NA, CAB 37/147/35, Memorandum sent from Lt General Sir Nevil Macready, Adjutant General, to Lord Kitchener, Secretary of State at the War Office, 15 May 1916. This document recommends the removal of objectors from the military and their transfer to civilian control. In addition, the Central Tribunal justified its decision to release large numbers of men from prison by adopting the military view that 'many of these men were of no use to the Army; their presence in military units was a hindrance to the performance of military duties'. 'Report of the Central Tribunal', p. 23.

16 For example, see Lord Salisbury's complaints to the Brace Committee, 'Brace Committee', p. 4. Salisbury was Chairman of the Central Tribunal.

17 NA, CAB 37/147/35, Macready to Lord Kitchener, Secretary of State at the War Office, 15 May 1916.

18 NA, CAB 23/2/142, 'Minutes of War Cabinet meetings', 1917, quoted in John Rae, *Conscience and Politics: The British Government and the Conscientious Objector to Military Service 1916–1919* (London: Oxford University Press, 1970), p. 89.

19 Initially the view was taken that only vague rules were needed as released men would co-operate: see 'Brace Committee', p. 2. However, following reports of such proselytising in 1917, the revised Code of Rules for the Scheme re-emphasised this ban on public propaganda 'whether by making speeches, taking part in processions or demonstrations, or otherwise'. *Committee on Employment of Conscientious Objectors: Rules*, Cd. 8550, 1917.

20 John Rodker, 'Twenty years after', in Bell (ed.) *We Did Not Fight*, p. 289.

21 W. EXON, 'ANARCHIC DARTMOOR. A HOTBED OF MALCONTENTS' (letter), *The Times* (8 October 1917), p. 10.

22 This policy was adopted in order to demonstrate that these men were treated like soldiers and, therefore, were put to work together. See 'Brace Committee', p. 3.

23 James Primrose Malcolm Millar, 'A socialist in war time', in Bell (ed.) *We Did Not Fight*, p. 253.

24 For example, see Stephen Hobhouse, 'Fourteen months service with the colours', in Bell (ed.) *We Did Not Fight*, p. 170.

25 NA, WO 32/2055/6923, Childs, 23 April 1918.

26 For example, when in prison Brockway received a smuggled note: '. . . What can we do for you? De Valera, Milroy and sixteen other Irish rebels are interned. We are Irishmen and can do anything you want – except get you out. Have your reply ready for "Trusty" when he calls tomorrow. Cheerio!' (Archibald Fenner Brockway, *Inside the Left: Thirty Years of Platform, Press, Prison and Parliament* (London: Allen and Unwin, 1942), p. 113).

27 'Conscientious Objectors in Prison', p. 1.

28 WO 32/2051/3302, Childs, 18 June 1917.

29 Royal Archives, Windsor Castle, 5910/2, Childs to Lieutenant Colonel Clive Wigram, Private Secretary to George V, 17 September 1917, quoted in Rae, *Conscience and Politics*, p. 215.

30 Rae, *Conscience and Politics*, pp. 153–4.

31 A copy is included in NA, HO 45/10786/297549/10, Home Office file on the wartime publications of the Independent Labour Party, 1915–17 (this includes documentation from the N-CF).

32 For example, see 5 HC 75, col. 520, 2 November 1915.

33 For example, see NA, Kitchener Papers, 30/57/74 (former reference WS/72).

34 *Ibid.*, WS/73.

35 The Man in the Street, 'WAR-OR SLAVERY' *Daily Sketch* (16 March 1916), p. 5.

36 NA, HO 45/10801/307402, Conscientious objectors: note on Kitchener's interview with a deputation, 1 June 1916.

37 For example, see the report of a raid on the headquarters of the N-CF at Merton House, Sainsbury court, 'POLICE RAID ON N.C.F. OFFICES', *The Times* (6 June 1916), p. 5.

38 NA, HO 45/10801/307402, 'WAR: Anti-conscription campaigns by various bodies', 1916–17. This file holds details of raids, newspaper stories and some of the materials confiscated. See also David John Mitchell, *Women on the Warpath: The Story of the Women of the First World War* (London: Jonathan Cape, 1966), pp. 331–46.

39 The original 1914 Act was repeatedly supplemented and amended.

40 For a report of the first case see '"NO CONSCRIPTION" LEAFLET. MR BERTRAND RUSSELL FINED £100', *The Times* (6 June 1916), p. 5.

41 See: Bertrand Russell, *Autobiography* (London: Unwin, 1978 – first published in two volumes, 1971) pp. 255–60; Ray Monk, *Bertrand Russell: The Spirit of Solitude* (London: Vintage, 1996), pp. 463–5, 520–4; 'MR. BERTRAND RUSSELL SENTENCED: MISCHIEVIOUS

WORDS IN AN ARTICLE: INSULT TO THE U.S. ARMY', *The Times*
(11 February 1918), p. 2; 'MR. BERTRAND RUSSELL'S APPEAL.
MITIGATION OF SENTENCE', *The Times* (2 May 1918), p. 2.

42 Edward Grubb, 'War resistance', in Bell (ed.) *We Did Not Fight*,
pp. 148–9.

43 A.T. Fitzroy, *Despised and Rejected* (London: Gay Men Press Publishers
Ltd, 1988 – first published London: C.W. Daniel Ltd, 1918). Fitzroy
was a pseudonym used by Rose Allatini.

44 See Jonathan Cutbill, 'Introduction' in *Ibid.*, 1988, p. 4.

45 See: *ibid.*, pp. 1, 4–5, 11; Claire M. Tylee, *The Great War and
Women's Consciousness: Images of Militarism and Womenhood in
Women's Writings, 1914–64* (London: Macmillan, 1990), p. 121.
The Times carried reports of the case: '"A PERNICIOUS BOOK."
PUBLISHERS CHARGED UNDER DEFENCE REGULATIONS' (27
September 1918), p. 3; '"DESPISED AND REJECTED." PUBLISHER
OF PACIFIST NOVEL FINED' (11 October 1918), p. 5.

46 On the history of the secret state see Tony Bunyan, *The History and
Practice of the Political Police in Britain* (London: Quartet Books,
1977). A brief general official history is also available at MI5's website
www.mi5.gov.uk/output/Page66.html (accessed July 2008).

47 See John W. Graham, *Conscription and Conscience: A History 1916–
1919* (London: George Allen and Unwin, 1922, reprinted 1971),
pp. 190–204.

48 See NA, KV 2/1917, 1 January 1916–31 December 1917.

49 Thomas C. Kennedy, *The Hound of Conscience: A History of the
No-Conscription Fellowship* (Fayetteville: University of Arkansas Press,
1981), p. 130; Monk, *Bertrand Russell*, pp. 471–7, 481–2; Bertrand
Russell, *Autobiography* (London: Unwin, 1978 – first published in two
volumes, 1971), pp. 256, 300.

50 For example, see founder of the Union of Democratic Control, Sir
Norman Angell, 'War and peace, 1914', in Bell (ed.) *We Did Not Fight*,
p. 48.

51 Sheila Rowbotham, *Friends of Alice Wheeldon* (London: Pluto, 1986),
pp. 38–9; Raymond Challinor, *The Origins of British Bolshevism*
(London: Croom Helm, 1977), pp. 42–3; Cyril Pearce, *Comrades in
Conscience: The Story of an English Community's Opposition to the
Great War* (London: Francis Boutle, 2001); Ken Weller, *'Don't be a
Soldier!': The Radical Anti-War Movement in North London, 1914–
1918* (London: Journeyman Press, 1985), pp. 49–51;.

52 Brockway, *Inside the Left*, pp. 26, 66–8.

53 Raymond Challinor, *John S. Clarke: Parliamentarian and Lion Tamer*
(London: Pluto Press, 1977), p. 244.

54 See Rowbotham, *Friends of Alice Wheeldon*, p. 38.

55 *Ibid.*

56 See Pearce, *Comrades in Conscience.*

57 'The "FUNK-HOLE." DUG-OUT FOR SHIRKERS IN A WELL', *The Times* (15 March 1917), p. 5.

58 See, for example, Pearce, *Comrades in Conscience*, pp. 205–7; Rowbotham, *Friends of Alice Wheeldon*, pp. 40–8.

59 NA, KV1, 'The Security Service: First World War Historical Reports and Other Papers'.

60 Homosexuality was often a cause of concern, not least because of assumed associations with Germanness. For example, see Philip Hoare, *Wilde's Last Stand: Decadence, Conspiracy and the First World War* (London: Duckworth, 1997), pp. 26–7.

61 For example, see Rowbotham, *Friends of Alice Wheeldon*, p. 37.

62 Bryan Connon, *Beverley Nichols* (London: Constable, 1991), pp. 54–5.

63 See Rowbotham, *Friends of Alice Wheeldon*, pp. 48–52. The text goes on to describe the trial: see pp. 52–6. The official papers are in NA, CRIM 1/166, 'Defendant: Wheeldon, Alice Wheeldon, Harriett Ann Mason, Winnie Mason, Alfred George. Charge: Conspiracy to murder the Prime Minister and other people', February 1917.

64 'THE POISON PLOT CHARGE. MRS. WHEELDON IN THE WITNESS-BOX. STRYCHNINE "FOR DOGS."', *The Times* (8 March 1917), p. 3. This paper followed the arrests and trial closely (as did others). See, for example: 'GRAVE CONSPIRACY CHARGE. FOUR PERSONS IN COURT. ALLEGED PLOT TO KILL MR. LLOYD GEORGE. CHEMIST'S ASSISTANT AMONG THE ACCUSED' (1 February 1917), p. 9; 'THE POISON PLOT CHARGE. ATTORNEY-GENERAL'S STATEMENT. SECRET AGENTS' DISCOVERIES' AND 'ALLEGED POISON PLOT. SECRET AGENTS' DISCOVERIES' (5 February 1917), pp. 4, 9; 'THE POISON PLOT CHARGES. TRIAL AT THE OLD BAILEY. SECRET AGENT'S EVIDENCE' (7 March 1917), p. 3.

65 NA, WO 32/2054/1654, Childs, 17 August 1917. His view expressed here was that all soldiers including COs should be treated 'in accordance with the law' and not victimised. Brightmore and Gray's cases are described in the previous chapter.

66 Quoted in Monk, *Bertrand Russell*, p. 395.

67 NA, WO 32/2051/3319, J.C. Smuts, 1 December 1917.

68 NA, MH 47/142, R.70.

69 See J.I. Macpherson, Permanent Under Secretary, War Office 5 HC 96, col. 873, 23 July 1917.

70 *Committee on Employment of Conscientious Objectors: Rules*, Cd. 8884, 1917.

71 Rule 243A, see NA, CAB 23/4/257(3), 24 October 1917.

72 NA, HO 45/10882, 'Memorandum concerning the treatment of conscientious objectors', July 1916.

73 'Brace Committee', p. 9.

74 Friends Library, London, MS VOL 149, No-Conscription Fellowship: duplicated papers, 1914–1919, N-CF letter to members, 31 January 1916.

75 *Ibid.*

76 Letter to Catherine Marshall from Winchester Prison, July 1917, quoted in Martin Gilbert, *Plough My Own Furrow: The Story of Lord Allen of Hurtwood as Told through his Writings and Correspondence* (London: Longman, 1965), p. 86.

77 For example, see diary entry 17 August, 1918, quoted in Gilbert, *Plough My Own Furrow*, pp. 121–2, 121.

78 Allen quoted in Gilbert, *Plough My Own Furrow*, p. 37.

79 The central aim of many objectors and their supporters was to bring down conscription, challenge militarism and the war. However, there was disquiet from some who felt that the publishing of examples of suffering was sometimes merely being used to improve the objectors' or a particular objector's lot. This caused concern that the N-CF was becoming an organisation for the 'prevention of cruelty to C.O.s'. See Kennedy, *The Hound of Conscience*, p. 203 and ch. 10 generally.

80 Official correspondence relating to Duckers is in NA, HO 45/10808/311118–4, see especially 25 April 1917.

81 James Scott Duckers, *Handed Over: The Prison Experiences of Mr. J. Scott Duckers, Solicitor of Chancery Lane, Under the Military Service Act, Written by himself. With Foreword by T. Edmund Harvey* (London: C.W. Daniel, 1917).

82 Albert Venn Dicey, 'The conscientious objector', *Nineteenth Century*, 83:492 (1918), 357–73, 358, 360.

83 Friends Service Committee, *The Absolutists' Objection: A Statement and an Appeal to the Conscience of the Nation* (London: Pelican, May 1917), p. 13.

84 'Conscientious Objectors in Prison', p. 6.

85 Under the Prisoners (Temporary Discharge for Ill-Health) Act, 1913.

86 See Lord Curzon, 5 HL 27, col.53–6, 4 December 1917.

87 Langdon-Davies, 'Alternative service', p. 188.

88 Letter headed 'C.O.'s AND PERPETUAL HARD LABOUR', *Manchester Guardian* (12 June 1917), p. 4.

89 See: NA, WO 32/2051/3319, Memorandum of meeting between Lord Derby (Secretary of State for War) and Lord Curzon (a member of the War Cabinet), Childs and Sir George Cave (Home Secretary), 19 November 1917 and Derby to Curzon, 20 November 1917; Lord Curzon 5 HL 27, col. 53–6, 4 December 1917. For the story of

Hobhouse's release (and mention of Allen's) see, for example, Rae, *Conscience and Politics*, pp. 201–27.

90 Rodker, 'Twenty years after', p. 287.

91 For example, see the debates on the Home Office Scheme: 5 HC 86, col. 802–39, 19 October 1916.

92 In the context of this chapter the phrase 'troublesome people' is used in a negative sense. However, it has been used in a more positive way in relation to those who oppose war. See Caroline Moorehead, *Troublesome People: Enemies of War: 1916–1986* (London: Hamilton, 1987). This title is drawn from George Bernard Shaw: '[a]fter all, we have to admit that it is always the troublesome people who force us to remedy the abuses that we lazily let slide.' *What I Really Wrote About the War* (London: Constable, 1930), p. 247.

5

Conscientious objectors

This chapter explores constructions of conscientious objectors (COs) as *conscientious* and, consequently, honourable men who followed the dictates of their beliefs. Here they embody admirable qualities and their self-discipline and commitment are applauded in similar ways to that of the idealised image of the conscientious military man. Thus, far from being despised and rejected or seen as deviant and a threat, in this chapter's depiction of objectors they are supported, viewed as comrades, treated with compassion and understanding, as well as sometimes being revered and respected. Whilst such responses were most common from their own ranks along with those who backed them or at least sympathised with their situation, they also came from less likely sources.

In addition, the CO's conscientiousness in his objection meant that he stood out from many men and women who lacked enthusiasm for the war and the military – not least because their motives, unlike his, were often far from laudable. Thus, not everyone shared in the supposed fervour for the war and desire for soldiering depicted earlier in this text. For example, men refused to enlist or, by a variety of means, sought to avoid conscription in the interests of selfishness and self-preservation. Similarly, even those men who did enlist or attest did not always do so for the most admirable of reasons and men who were conscripted could be far from happy about their position. Moreover, other men and women who laboured towards the war effort did so for reasons of profit and self-advancement rather than self-sacrifice and patriotism.

Such narratives about the conflict present a very different image of the wartime mood from that portrayed earlier in this text. Indeed, they challenge the idea of mass support for the war which was portrayed in and formed a backdrop to previous chapters.

Instead, here the idea is that, for example, far from welcoming the war and rejoicing, many felt fear and panic even in early August 1914 and that subsequently people became disillusioned and weary of it, laboured to avoid hardship or make the best of the adversity they experienced and, in some cases, sought to create some benefit from it.[1]

So, in this construction of the war it was not only pacifists and other opponents of war who opposed or regretted the conflict or felt fear when the declaration of war came. Indeed, people could experience a whole range of conflicting emotions and thoughts about the war simultaneously or over a period of time. Thus, many who might have initially welcomed the war became weary of it as the weeks, months and years dragged. So, as the war that was meant to be swift and victorious dragged on, initial enthusiasm, where it existed, was hard to maintain. For example, in his consideration of the labour movement James Hinton argues that 'patriotism was neither a very stable attitude (moments of patriotic fervour alternated with moments of war weariness and militant protest among the same group of workers)'.[2] Thus, in some histories of the First World War, war enthusiasm was not entirely the order of the day, far from everyone was rushing to be a part of the great adventure, support for the conflict was patchy, and even where fervour for the war existed it fluctuated.[3]

As this chapter shows, CO accounts of their wartime experiences and of the mood within the country also provide some support for this idea of lack of enthusiasm and war weariness. Indeed, this perspective has been developed by Cyril Pearce, who rejects the 'old consensus' view or 'war enthusiasm' thesis in relation to objectors, suggesting instead that at least some objectors were embraced by their communities who shared their dislike for war and conscription.[4] Thus, these men were far from being despised outcasts.

This chapter begins by considering comradeship and support for objectors along with examples of sympathy, compassion and respect towards them. It then juxtaposes this construction of the conscientious CO with the less than admirable motives and behaviour of others who, for example, sought to avoid the military or, at least in part, contributed to the war effort for self-serving reasons. Thus, the analysis situates constructions of COs within a narrative which rejects or is at least sceptical of the idea of popular fervour for the conflict and the supposed rush to join in.

Of support, comradeship, compassion and respect

Most obviously, support for objectors came from those who shared their cause. Thus, as this text has previously suggested, anti-war groups and informal networks around the country provided assistance, as did some of the families and friends of COs. For example, the Derby underground that Alice Wheeldon was involved in was just one example of the pockets of support around the country.[5] More significantly, Cyril Pearce's *Comrades in Conscience* describes a community largely unenthusiastic about the war and tolerant or supportive of war resisters in Huddersfield. Indeed, he challenges the view that objectors were 'individuals making a stand for the principle of the individual's freedom', arguing that the Huddersfield evidence suggests that, in some contexts at least, COs 'represented and spoke for a collective or group consciousness'. Hence, in his construction of COs, to their supporters 'they were as much "Our Boys" fighting for the cause as were those who had taken the Khaki'.[6]

The No-Conscription Fellowship (hereafter N-CF or the Fellowship) played an important role in this context. As the only organisation specifically focusing upon opposition to conscription, it assisted many COs. Amongst other things, it enlisted prison visitors to provide outside contact for men incarcerated and gathered information for families, for the organisation's records as well as for propaganda purposes. Also the Fellowship provided assistance and hardship funds for COs' families and it offered both practical help and ideological support through its publications.[7]

Support also came through the publications of the pacifist, radical socialist and pacifist religious press. In particular, the pages of *The Tribunal*, *The Labour Leader* and *The Friend* give accounts of the progress of objectors and of events in Parliament, expressing a unity of purpose and a comradeship in adversity. The labour movement also sometimes provided encouragement to their objector members and, as a result, in some tribunal hearings the public gallery was filled with supporters. This was particularly true in areas with a strong socialist movement where spectators reportedly cheered applicants on and sang 'The Red Flag'. The local press often carried stories about such displays of support, although their accounts were generally far from favourable.[8] However, the socialist press coverage was generally more approving and celebratory. Thus, *The Worker* reported 'EXCITING INCIDENTS' at Huddersfield

11 G.P. Micklewright, 'C.O. IN PRISON: THE IDEAL'. Friends Library, London, Picture Collection, 86/AL 9.

Tribunal when an application by a well-known socialist was heard. The story records that a large number of CO applications were being considered on the day in question and 'the public attended in large numbers'. 'An air of excitement was noticeable from the outset' but when the applicant, Arthur Gardiner, was called 'the excitement found expression in a startling outburst of cheering'. A lively discussion then ensued between the tribunal, the military representative, the applicant and members of the public as to whether the latter should or could be excluded from the tribunal because of the disruption they were causing.[9]

Some of the most prominent objectors also had their own bands of supporters who attended tribunal and court hearings. Such shows of encouragement, attracting publicity as they did, tended to alarm the authorities, as happened in the case of James Scott Duckers. When he appeared at Malborough Magistrates' Court before being handed over to the military he was, according to the press, 'applauded by a large number of his supporters' and received between thirty and forty letters and telegrams. Following his conviction for failing to report, there were cries of 'Shame' and a disturbance broke out resulting in one arrest.[10]

More fundamentally, as Pearce's comments along with the title of his book, *Comrades in Conscience*, suggest, COs supported each other. Indeed, the comradeship and camaraderie of objectors was often described by these men in glowing terms. What is more, as Bertrand Russell notes, fear of what patriots would do to a known pacifist during the war 'led one to prefer the company of pacifists' so that '[g]radually a pacifist herd was formed'. The difference this brought was great '[w]hen we were all together we felt warm and cosy, and forgot what an insignificant little minority we were'.[11] Following a prolonged period in solitary confinement Fenner Brockway, N-CF Secretary, also wrote of the relationship between objectors: 'I cannot describe to you the wonderful sense of comradeship there is among the COs in prison', noting also that '[w]e are not allowed to speak to each other, but the unity we do feel does not need expression in speech'.[12]

Such intramasculine comradeship, most usually associated at the time with soldiers,[13] was heightened by objectors' social and physical isolation and was fostered by a range of clandestine activities. Most notably, in prison successful attempts to get around the hated silence rule included the creation of complicated tapping codes to communicate between cells. Other men used ventriloquism to confuse warders or concocted other means to surreptitiously 'speak'.[14] In Winchester Clifford Allen (N-CF Chairman) managed to play 'piped chess' with Duckers five cells away by tapping the hot-water pipes.[15] In addition, in some gaols objectors managed to put together underground magazines or 'newspapers', which were circulated between captives. These were handwritten on whatever paper was available (often thin and brittle sheets of lavatory paper) with pencils smuggled into the prisons. 'Publications' such as the *Court Martial*, *Winchester Whisper*, *Walton Leader*, *Canterbury Clinker* and *Joyland Journal* included a wide range of contributions – poems, short stories, sensational serials, jokes, studies in ethics, philosophy and psychology, illustrations and cartoons.[16] The production and perusing of these slim volumes not only helped ease the sense of monotony and introduced a sense of intrigue but also helped boost camaraderie and served as a means of communication between COs.

Sympathetic members of COs' families also stood behind them, sometimes agreeing with their stance. For example, Dorothy Bing's support for her brother Harold has been depicted in previous chapters.[17] Understanding and a degree of respect was even possible within families which included both soldier and objector members. Stephen Hobhouse had three brothers serving in the military. He recalls that they were 'able mutually to respect each other's convictions' and his mother came round to accept, if not support, his position, having been at first 'strongly opposed to my conduct'.[18] In addition, his mother campaigned to secure Stephen's release from prison, lending her name to the pamphlet *I Appeal unto Caesar*, an account of the absolutists, in order to highlight the plight of these men.[19]

Even beyond their own circles, objectors experienced sympathetic and fair treatment and were esteemed. For example, in the tribunals objectors could experience fairness and understanding as well as injustice and abuse. Indeed, John Rae, with his more establishment version of events, disputes the extent to which objector applicants experienced ill-treatment in front of these bodies, thereby challenging the picture which some authors have painted of the tribunals as almost uniformly unjust.[20] In keeping with this more favourable portrait of these bodies, *The Friend* recognised that '[m]any Tribunals have been most considerate and patient'.[21] Similarly, as Rae notes, two MPs who sought to expose the injustice of these bodies, Philip Snowden and R.L. Outhwaite, recognised that 'many' tribunals had 'tried to do their duty sincerely, and had been most anxious to administer the Act in a fair and judicious way',[22] and the N-CF itself considered Guilford Local Tribunal to be conducted on model lines.[23]

Objectors' accounts of their experiences also support the view that some tribunals could be fair. Wilfred Ernest Littleboy experienced two very different Chairmen at his local tribunal in Birmingham. At the first hearing the future Prime Minister, Neville Chamberlain, was sympathetic and granted an adjournment to allow Littleboy time to consider whether he was prepared to accept alternative work. However, when the applicant returned to the Tribunal he was faced with a Chairman with a much 'more rigid' attitude.[24] In addition, the appeal tribunals tended to present a very different style from the local bodies, presided over as they were by at least one member with legal training. Thus, Harold Frederick Bing notes the differences between his first instance and appeal hearings. At the local level his case was swiftly dismissed without a full hearing; on appeal the proceedings were 'quite fair and legal', the judge was familiar with the grounds of application, allowed Bing and his father to speak and granted 'rather a lengthy hearing'.[25] Harry E. Stanton also describes his appeal tribunal hearing as being fair[26] as does British Israelite Theodore Price, who sensed a 'decorum and order' to the proceedings.[27]

Also in the military, alongside the examples of minor cruelty and more extreme abuse, there could be sympathy and fair treatment. Certainly some camps were better than others and some soldiers could feel understanding for the CO. Moreover, as we saw in the last chapter, treatment improved as revelations of cruelty emerged and the military was warned to treat objectors better. Thus, objectors record the compassion and courtesy of soldiers.[28] Duckers writes of his experience of military detention, describing the Commandant and Sergeant-Major as being 'anxious to see that there was no treatment of which we could reasonably complain', and recounting how he felt that, as a consequence, 'on the whole we [COs] were treated a good deal more civilly than the soldier prisoners'. He adds that 'I never had the slightest discourtesy from any private soldier either in London or afterwards'.[29] In contrast, he reports witnessing instances of warders brutally knocking about non-CO prisoners.[30] Indeed, at one point whilst detained at Scotland Yard he (and he alone amongst the military detainees) was even allowed to receive a visit from his father.[31] Duckers also records that soldiers were often friendly to him and sometimes showed respect for his courage and stoicism. His book includes an account of his time at the Rifle Brigade Camp in Minster when he experienced one of a number of moments of good-hearted camaraderie with the men. The ranks cheered him and '[t]he soldier who called for the cheers said, "We should all do like Scott Duckers if we thought we could stick it out!"'[32] He also notes the solidarity of ordinary (non-CO) soldier-prisoners in military detention, who were mostly deserters and absentees:

> [they] gave us their heartiest sympathy. They did not understand the grounds for our objection very clearly . . . but they quite applauded our resistance to the authorities.[33]

Officers too could also show support for objectors. Max Plowman, who resigned his commission when he developed anti-war sentiments, felt for objectors and maintained that '[t]he soldier in the trenches understands the position of the CO in prison'.[34]

Both *The Friend*, the Quaker journal, and *The Tribunal* recognised that much kindness was experienced by objectors in the military and that most of the punishments used against objectors were those which all soldiers were subject to under military law, the former noting that '[o]ver and over again military officers have shown kindness and forebearance in these awkward circumstances'.[35] Indeed, as early as May 1916 the N-CF's organ observes that, with some notable exceptions, treatment had improved so that '[i]n many cases we find officers and men expressing sympathy with their [COs'] views, and in most cases their sincerity is acknowledged'.[36] In Parliament those who took up the objectors' case agreed that instances of extreme abuse were rare.[37] Thus, accounts of soldiers' respect for and sympathy with objectors suggest a very different conception of objectors from that propounded in earlier chapters within this volume.

Understanding between the soldier and the objector was also evident outside the military. James Primrose Malcolm Millar records that by summer 1917 the warders at Wakefield Home Office Centre (formerly the gaol) had been replaced by badly wounded soldiers. Millar, who was housed there at the time, guesses that the authorities might have thought that such men would give COs a particularly rough time. But the authorities were mistaken if this was their purpose as, whilst the prison warders had been 'trained to brutality and lack of consideration for prisoners' feelings', it was an entirely different matter in the case of the ex-soldiers:

> They were not unduly impressed by the fat gentlemen who sat on tribunals and insisted on other men, mainly young men, going and fighting for them. Besides that, their experiences had jerked their minds out of a rut and they were prepared to listen to argument.[38]

Even within the War Office the objector was by no means universally hated. Wyndham Childs, who as head of the Directorate of Personal Services was responsible for the treatment of COs in the army,[39] had mixed feelings in relation to these men. As Rae points out, Childs distinguished between the movement and individual objectors. Indeed, the latter was to describe his ambivalence in the following terms:

> I used to find myself torn between conflicting emotions – contempt for the Conscientious Objector in the main, and intense sympathy which I could not keep within bounds when I came across specific cases of Conscientious Objectors who were brutally treated, as I am sorry to say was sometimes the case.[40]

Thus, sympathy with or understanding for the COs' plight as well as respect for their stance could come from the most unlikely of sources. Such reactions frequently took the form of an outcry at instances of unfairness against objectors. Soldiers, MPs and others, often grudgingly, but occasionally wholeheartedly, praised the CO. However, such expressions of sympathy for objectors were often measured and limited to a particular category of such men. Harold Tennant, who was Permanent Under Secretary at the War Office (June 1915–July 1916) and an MP not usually particularly well disposed towards objectors who hindered his work, felt the need to slightly begrudgingly recognise the sacrifices some such men made:

> While the conscientious objector has not made my path easier . . . I'm afraid I cannot, for my part, withhold my – I do not want to use too strong a word – but certainly my respect for persons who on religious grounds will undergo privation and even persecution rather than do violence to their conscience.[41]

Also, Herbert Samuel, who replaced Sir John Simon as Home Secretary, described objectors as 'men who unquestionably, by common consent, are men of the highest character, and in other matters good citizens'.[42]

So amongst the calls for COs to be punished for their refusals to fight or to be forced into conformity, there were other voices that sometimes raised themselves above the supposed roar of jingoism, calling instead for leniency, compassion and respect. At one stage, even the staunchly pro-war recruiter Emmeline Pankhurst was moved to voice her concerns and call for clemency.[43] Some sections of the mainstream press, along with liberal and left-wing publications, also carried calls for unfair or cruel practices to end. The *Daily Chronicle*, alerted to the unfair treatment of COs by Philip Snowden's House of Commons speech of 22 March 1916, maintained that 'no one can read the tremendous array of recruiting injustices . . . without realising that we are here in face of a very grave scandal indeed'.[44] In a similar vein, in the House of Lords both Lord Parmoor and the then Archbishop of Canterbury, Randall Thomas Davidson, complained at the use of successive terms of imprisonment for essentially the same offence of disobedience of military orders, and quoted authority stating that this would not happen. They also praised the sincerity and good behaviour of conscientious men.[45] Parmoor referred to such men's motivations as being 'a matter of honest sincere conviction' and pointed out that 'men of considerable education, men who have done some of the best social work in the East-End of London and in other poor districts' suffered in consequence.[46] Likewise, Davidson, spoke of men whose 'honesty is undoubted, men whose high character is unchallenged'. The latter said this despite the fact that he opposed their stance and, indeed, felt the need on this occasion to be clear that he had 'no sympathy with the convictions that these men hold', finding them 'intolerable and inconsistent with the ordinary working of a civilised community'.[47] Thus, the very mainstream Christianity which could castigate both COs and their stance could also see objectors as genuine and intensely devout men who were deserving of fair and respectful treatment.

In addition, despite the fact that it might appear unlikely, John Buchan, author of *The Thirty-Nine Steps* along with other popular patriotic adventure stories and a prominent establishment figure (having served in the War and Foreign Offices, the Intelligence Corps, the Propaganda Department and the Department of Information),[48] became concerned about the CO's treatment. After the armistice

Buchan was party to an appeal for the release of the objectors still in prison which drew attention to both their treatment as criminals and their genuineness:

> . . . 700 of whom have served terms of two years or more, whereas two years is the maximum punishment allowed for ordinary criminals either under our civil or military code. As a result of recent inquiries, it was found that a majority of these men are sincerely convinced that they have acted under the demands of their conscience and in accordance with deep moral or religious convictions. We urge that men in prison under these conditions should not be kept there during the period of national rejoicing, and that our country should not show itself slow at such a time to carry through an act of just mercy.

Buchan also felt that:

> [t]he genuine conscientious objector was, in many cases, denied even his legal rights, and a number of sincere and honourable, if abnormal, beings were subjected to a persecution which could be justified on no conceivable grounds of law, ethics, or public policy.[49]

Thus, the various outcries at the harsh treatment of objectors illustrated that their plight could sometimes arouse compassion. Unsurprisingly, the expression of such sentiment was most likely where the men concerned were respectable and, in particular, devoutly religious. Indeed, beyond the ranks of COs' supporters and sympathisers, it is the Christian, rather than political, COs with whom this image of honour and respect can be most associated; with their law-abiding, upstanding and God-fearing image they were harder to see either as figures of hate or as a national danger, although where they were perceived to have taken things to extremes they were sometimes conceived of as cranks. In addition, they were more likely to be assumed to be genuine, so were less likely to be ill-treated. Of all denominations, it was the Quaker COs, with their long association with pacifism,[50] who tended to be the most well-treated and esteemed, as John Rae notes.[51] Thus, Childs recognised that long-term membership of an organisation like the Friends could not be faked and that these were after all, by definition, honourable men of peace.[52]

As Rae notes, the well-known and well-connected Quaker objector Stephen Hobhouse perhaps provides the best example of this compassion for religious objectors.[53] Thus, the Archbishop of Canterbury, Randall Davidson, felt that 'Stephen Hobhouse is of course the most conspicuous instance of a really fine fellow who is, or has been, suffering in mind and body on account of "crankiness" which is in no sense mischievious in itself.'[54] Even the official report on conscientious objectors in prison describes him as 'a Conscientious Objector of the most genuine type'[55] and Lord Derby wrote of him:

> I do not think there is the least doubt in his case that he is a genuine Conscientious Objector – one of the few – and personally I should be glad to liberate him. . .[56]

Similarly, Herbert Fisher, then Permanent Under Secretary to the Local Government Board (which was in charge of the tribunals) felt that:

> It is absurd to suppose that Stephen Hobhouse for instance is not a conscientious objector, seeing as he has been ready to undergo a long term of imprisonment rather than submit to Military discipline.[57]

Thus, Hobhouse seemingly represented a 'good' or 'worthy' CO. He was not altogether alone in this status. For example, a report in *The Times* describes the work of COs in the Non-Combatant Corps in France. According to the story these were men who were 'doing honest work of a useful character quite contentedly', they were described as 'doing their best to acquit themselves with credit', '[t]heir conduct was exemplary' and a 'large percentage' were reported to be 'total abstainers as well as non-smokers'.[58] Fiction also depicted this version of the objector. John Buchan's *Mr Standfast*, published in 1919, includes a sympathetic account of Lancelot Wake, an objector.[59] Here Wake is a 'conscientious' CO who seeks to assist his country and the war effort through non-combatant work.

In this context of concern, understanding and respect for the CO, the various changes in policy as well as the directions to the tribunals and the military to improve their treatment towards objectors can, at least in part, be seen as having been motivated by sympathy with the plight of objectors. Certainly those pressing for greater fairness and compassion were showing that, in their view, some of these men, at least, were worthy of more than loathing and rejection.

Unconscientiousness and the war

In contrast to this depiction of COs as conscientious, many other men and women failed to behave as admirably during the war.

Indeed, so-called 'revisionist' scholarship such as Niall Ferguson's *The Pity of War* has suggested that the idea of war enthusiasm and the desirability of the soldier (described in Chapters 1 and 2) seem to be contradicted by evidence of behaviours such as shirking, cowardice and profiteering, along with a general sense of war weariness.[60] For example, by no means all men actually desired the military. Indeed, many men were even strangely resistant to the many tactics of the recruitment drives and the pressure from concerned citizens who handed out white feathers not just to COs but 'to all young men who [were] not in uniform'.[61] They failed to be lured by the promise of heroism and adventure and resisted the urge to act patriotically by sacrificing their liberty for their country. Instead, they seemingly preferred the comforts of home.

Indeed, although the statistical evidence could be said to show that vast numbers of men enlisted in the military during 1914 and 1915, most men remained at home[62] There was also a pervasive and growing perception that many men aside from those claiming to be COs were shirking their responsibility, benefiting from their cowardice and prolonging the war.[63] The various recruitment drives and attempts to get shirkers to come forward demonstrate this. These utilised a range of tactics to seek to entice, cajole, threaten or even embarrass men into the military. A notable example was Savile Lumley's 1915 poster, 'Daddy What did <u>YOU</u> do in the Great War?', which sought to shame men into coming forward (page 178 below).[64] The press also reflected the idea that too many slackers were refusing to join up. In November 1914 Owen Seamen's poem 'To The Shirker: A Last Appeal' was published in *Punch*. It bids men to do their duty by enlisting of their free will; threatening the introduction of compulsion should they fail to come forward.[65]

This notion that many able men were failing to come forward became increasingly widespread as 1915 progressed. The results of the National Register of August 1915 were to reinforce this perception that a vast number of men were failing to do the manly thing. This workers' census was heralded in the (pro-conscription) press as revealing the scandal that in the London area alone an estimated 750,000 young unmarried men had yet to join up.[66]

Moreover, the Derby Scheme was launched in the autumn of 1915, apparently in part as a result of the concerns about the number of able men failing to enlist.[67] Although presented as a final effort to 'galvanise the voluntary system into renewed vigour',[68]

12 Savile Lumley, 'Daddy, What did YOU do in the Great War?', 1915.
Imperial War Museum, PST 2763, 0311.

this justification along with much publicised concerns about the National Register statistics seemed only to confirm the lack of enthusiasm for the war and the perception that men were failing in apparently large numbers to do what was supposedly natural in terms of manliness and patriotism. Indeed, Paul Fussell sees the Scheme as 'a genteel form of conscription'.[69]

More significantly, the introduction of compulsion in itself seemed to contradict the notion of mass enthusiasm for the war and of an inherently patriotic, courageous and self-sacrificing English manhood which propaganda, the recruitment drives and the pro-war press were simultaneously propounding. Indeed, for most of the war the method of recruitment was conscription rather than volunteerism and most men who served in the military in the First World War were consequently compelled to do so.[70]

Thus, COs were not the only men who failed to join up during the period of voluntarism and other men also sought to evade both the Derby Scheme and conscription. Such men had a variety of motives for their (in)actions in this regard and attempted a number of methods to achieve their aim. Indeed, most were probably looking out for their own interests. Some were (understandably) afraid and concerned for their families' welfare or worried about their businesses and careers. For instance, there was particular resistance to going to war from married men who argued that they had responsibilities on the Home Front which they could not easily leave behind and should not be expected to abandon – at least until all single men were fighting.[71]

There were many methods of avoiding the military which men attempted, sometimes with some success. Under the Derby Scheme, men who had been refused as unfit sold their documentation to others who were prepared to pay handsomely (reports suggest the figure of £15) for the proof that they had tried to become soldiers but were officially excused.[72] When compulsion was introduced many men of all classes resisted the military in their own varied ways and this was well known. Indeed, T. Edmund Harvey refers to the thousands of ways of getting out of the military.[73] Some men attempted to disguise their maleness by posing as women in order to evade detection. Thus, Alfred Goodman Dunn was caught by a detective who, becoming suspicious, discovered the woman before him was in fact a man in disguise when he pulled 'her' hair and found it was a wig.[74] Others attempted to avoid service by claiming that their papers had been lost, that they were skilled workers replacing men who had volunteered for war or made blatantly spurious claims in the tribunals in order to postpone or avoid compulsion, arguing business or family hardship or essential employment.[75] A *Punch* cartoon of 12 July 1916 reflects an awareness that such attempts to evade conscription were being made. A seemingly well-off besuited businessman sits before a tribunal, the conversation given below the image reads as follows:

> I'm not asking to be let off – I'm asking for more time. I've got a lot of contracts to finish.
> How long will they take?
> Oh about three years – or the duration of the war.[76]

Other men used influence or connections to gain work of national importance or exemption. For example, one tribunal Chairman stood down from the bench so that his application could be decided by his colleagues. They then granted the applicant, T.R. Stubbins, his exemption without any discussion.[77] The Chairman of Market Boswell Tribunal, having just rejected an application on conscience grounds, stating that he hoped there would be no more of his kind, proceeded to exempt the whole of the local hunt.[78] Further, men sought out what they hoped would be a safe job. Thus, as CO B.N. Langdon-Davies notes, 'funk holes were occupied in Whitehall and down mines'.[79] Some men resorted to feigning illness or infirmity or even sought to acquire an injury. Such war 'malingering' to avoid service involved a whole range of techniques and tricks.[80] A cartoon from the period by John Hassall shows men visiting an establishment which advertises 'Bones broken while you wait'. Of the men emerging onto the street one is on crutches with one leg in a cast and another has his arm in a sling.[81] In addition, men lied or took other extreme measures in their attempts to evade the military. On 21 April 1916 *The Times* reported one case where a man posed as his father in order to claim that he ran a business essential to the war effort and another where the young man claiming to be a socialist CO set forward his position then proceeded to prove his 'earnestness' by stabbing his hand with a knife.[82]

Unsurprisingly, the government was particularly concerned with identifying, pursuing and securing those who were trying to avoid conscription (for whatever reason). Thus, when it became clear that some men had fled to Ireland to evade the Military Service

Acts attempts were made to recover these men. Posters were issued and a system of medical examinations and recruitment was set up. It was intended that those who failed to come forward would be prosecuted and forcibly handed over.[83] The police carried out a number of raids at railway stations, sports matches and theatres in order to detect men who were avoiding service.[84] There were also plans to 'comb out' hunting and racing establishments for people evading military service[85] and concerns about men enrolling as war work volunteers in order to avoid the call-up.[86] The official files also include cases of attempted bribery of the authorities and of the doping of potential recruits in order to feign illness.[87]

In July 1917 *The Times* reported on such less than honourable activities. Under the headings 'CONSCRIPTION AND CRIME', 'DEVICES TO ESCAPE SERVICE' and 'METHODS OF DETECTION', the paper comments upon the 'new rascality' and details instances of 'conspiracy to avoid conscription'. The article highlights such practices as 'personation and forgery', 'traffic' in rejection or discharge certificates, along with malingering and the use of drugs to fake unfitness. 'Simulated, or even artificially induced, symptoms of tuberculosis, synovitis, and debility', starvation and sleep deprivation are also cited as methods by which to achieve rejection by the military. The piece concludes in strong and sinister terms:

> Master minds are, and have been at work. Every degree of rascality has been suspected and proved. Even to-day every kind of chicanery is resorted to by the coward. The fight against crime goes on unceasingly, and day by day new and strange records are added to the dossier. . . . That side of the recruiting problem the public should know.[88]

Additionally, some shirkers attempted to use the 'conscience clause' as a means to evade the military. Thus there were stories of 'alleged cowards and shirkers' posing as COs and objectors themselves recognised this. Langdon-Davies recounts how these rumours were being discussed in all quarters and considers, with some sympathy, whether there were such men:

> That they existed I have no doubt. That only a bestial foolish type of man could be free from fear of war's horrors is to me obvious. . . .

Of those men which objectors themselves judged to be counterfeit, there was an artist who came to consult the National Council for Civil Liberties. He asked whether the conscription legislation provided for 'a man who would not mind pressing a button to kill a man at a distance, but who could not reconcile it with his conscience to use a bayonet or see the enemy'.[89]

By 1918 a new potential route to avoid the military became well known. Theoretically, men who claimed to be conscientious objectors but ended up in the military could now be transferred to civilian prison, apply to the Central Tribunal and, if successful, be granted recognition and put on the Home Office Scheme. At this time the number of men claiming to be COs and recognised as such increased. Whilst many of these might have been genuine, the Central Tribunal was understandably sceptical. In its Report it noted that some, at least, 'did not scruple to allege such objections as a last resort to avoid combatant service'.[90] Thus, in 1918 conscientious objection became an easier option for those wishing to avoid fighting and it arguably became particularly attractive to young men who at this stage in the war had been removed from reserved occupations to boost recruiting figures.[91]

However, even volunteering for service did not necessarily entail that the individual man was motivated or solely motivated by the most praiseworthy or conscientious of reasons. As George Bernard Shaw notes, men enlisted for a variety of motives:

> Men flock to the colours by instinct, by romantic desire for adventure, by the determination not, as Wagner put it, 'to let their lives be governed by fear of the end,' by simple destitution through unemployment, by rancour and pugnacity excited by the inventions of the press, by a sense of duty inculcated in platform orations which would not stand half an hour's discussion, by the incitements and taunts of elderly noncombatants and maidens with a taste for mischief, and by the verses of poets jumping at the cheapest chance in their underpaid profession.[92]

For example, Robert Graves volunteered because of his horror at the German violation of Belgian neutrality, but also admitted that it allowed him to find a way to delay going to Oxford – which he dreaded.[93] Isaac Rosenberg initially felt that more men for the army meant more war and described himself as having no patriotic convictions. Weeks later he enlisted, recording that 'I could not get the work I thought I might so I have joined this Bantam Battalion'.[94] Similarly, others have recognised that unemployment and poor wages were an incentive for working men. Thus, Niall Ferguson argues that 'one reason so many men volunteered in the first weeks of the war was that unemployment soared because of the economic crisis the war had unleashed'.[95] In addition, David Silbey examines the various motives of working-class volunteers, concluding that such things as escaping the drudgery of daily life, leaving behind the powerlessness they experienced at work and in the home or improving their financial position were important factors in men's decisions to join up.[96]

Attestation under the Derby Scheme provides a good illustration of the other motives which might lie behind a man coming forward. Although it appeared successful in its goal of gently encouraging more men to come forward,[97] it effectively bribed them to do so. It allowed men to 'attest' (profess a willingness to join up at some future date if required to do so and even then a man could apply for a postponement) rather than to enlist and offered payment for this (men were paid 2s. 9d.). Indeed, some men even exploited the system by attesting at a number of recruiting stations and collecting their reward several times over. In addition, when conscription became a certainty the Scheme offered some reluctant men a final opportunity to be categorised as selfless volunteers rather than reluctant conscripts, thus there was a final flurry of attesting.[98]

Also, men who accepted conscription were not necessarily that enthusiastic about their position. Indeed, they could be resistant or ambivalent to military service. Bet-El quotes one conscript who awaited the 'dreaded' call up, fought it, failed and gave himself up. Another felt himself a patriot but his religious conviction made fighting 'abhorrent'; nevertheless, he answered the call when it came.[99] Working men could also sometimes be reluctant conscripts. Official policy and concessions secured by the unions tended to protect skilled labour from conscription but not the unskilled men. As a result, the latter class would find themselves in the military, whilst their comrades remained safe at home. In Sheffield this created friction and led to the circulation of the following verse amongst wounded soldiers and unskilled engineers:

Don't send me in the Army, George,
I'm in the ASE.
Take all the bloody labourers,
But for God's sake don't take me.
You want me for a soldier?
Well, that can never be –
A man of my ability
And in the ASE[100]

Such bitterness hardly reflects any great enthusiasm for the military.

Beyond this, men outside the military also demonstrated uncon-scientiousness in their lack of enthusiasm for the conflict and their motives for assisting the war effort. For, example, enthusiasm and patriotic fervour were by no means the primary motivation of many who were assisting the war effort. Unsurprisingly, some men sought to benefit from the war. Thus, workers sometimes attempted to put the national crisis to good use by calling for better wages and terms of employment and even those who backed the war did not 'necessarily rule out radical social demands'.[101] Indeed, continued resistance to the war and wartime working conditions by socialist groups and trade unions was a feature of manufacturing areas, with industrial unrest a recurrent concern for the government as strikes were not uncommon during the war.[102] As a result, the secret state (the police and various intelligence units) monitored the trade union movement just as it monitored opponents of the war and conscrip-tion.[103]

A *Punch* cartoon of 1915 shows that there was concern at this kind of labour unrest and, by depicting such activism as unpatri-otic, it seeks to deter it. Entitled 'Soldiers All' it depicts a wounded soldier and a workman standing in front of a factory. The soldier is speaking and the caption reads '[w]hat'ld you think o' me, mate, if I struck for extra pay in the middle of an action? Well, that's what *you've* been doing.'[104] Profiteers also turned the war to their advan-tage and, unsurprisingly, propaganda encouraged hatred of them. For example, an anti-conscription cartoon from 1915 shows an extremely overweight man picking a worker's pocket. The former, a 'War Profiteer' says 'Ah if these ruffians pause to object to me picking their pockets at such a moment as this the country will have to conscript the unpatriotic shirkers'.[105] In particular, factory workers were concerned about profiteering bosses as they feared that owners undertaking government contracts would exploit their employees and the war effort.[106]

Women who assisted in the war effort could, of course, also be motivated by self-interest, rather than solely by war fever and self-less patriotism. Working in previously male employment could be lucrative. Indeed, many left other jobs in order to earn more in war work. However, joining the military was not so popular. Despite poster campaigns, press releases, cinema displays, meetings and recruiting events, women were often reluctant to join up. This was probably, at least in part, because of the conditions offered rather than apathy. Although army wages were reasonable by the standards of the time, it was the package that was uninviting, including, for instance, no career prospects and no compensation for loss of security. Whilst these factors were less likely to put off the very young, more experienced women were not so happy to move. In addition, other fields were far more lucrative. Workers in the munitions industry were fairly remunerated, enjoyed a greater degree of autonomy and were still contributing to the war effort.[107] Thus, it is not surprising that Doron Lamm's study of the Women's Army Auxiliary Corps reveals that it was only following a massive wave of female unemployment that the Corps size expanded significantly. Consequently, many women turned to this organisation only when the supply of more financially worthwhile and attractive war work dried up.[108] Additionally, the women who formed the Women Police and the Women Patrols were, to some extent, seeking to turn wartime concerns to their own advantage. They were creating a new field of female work that might survive the war and gain a more official status.[109]

More generally, working in previously male preserves and contributing to the war effort was attractive because it could provide a new-found freedom. Women could wear trousers, shorter skirts and makeup, smoke in public and dine in restaurants without a male chaperone.[110] Thus, contrary to the image of woman as patriots, loyal helpers and workers, self-interest also motivated the female population during the war.

Beyond this, dealing with dissent on the Home Front was a major task for the Government during the war. Indeed, the need for the successful management of the domestic sphere in this context was of crucial importance. Thus, far from the vision of war enthusiasm presented elsewhere in the present volume, various forms of disaffection and dissidence apart from the challenges posed by COs were a continuing problem for the state during the war.[111]

Conclusion

This construction of objectors poses a stark contrast to the idea that they were the hated Ismaelitish, criminal, unmanly and dangerous figures which have previously been depicted in this text. Instead, in the accounts presented above they were viewed with respect and

13 Statue of Archibald Fenner Brockway (Baron Brockway),
Red Lion Square, London.

appreciated as upstanding men. These images of the CO also compare favourably with the far from admirable actions of many who, contrary to the idea of war fervour, failed to be a part of the war effort, actively sought to avoid the military or acted from motives which had more to do with self-interest than commitment to their country or any of the other contemporary ideas and ideals which supported the narratives of mass support and enthusiasm for the war.

Moreover, this sense of the decency and conscientiousness of some of these objectors continued and arguably grew in the years and decades after the war. Several became peers and others took up positions of responsibility and trust. Most prominently, Clifford Allen became Lord Allen of Hurtwood and Fenner Brockway went on to be a Labour MP and in 1964 accepted a life peerage, becoming Baron Brockway.[112] Subsequently, the latter was honoured by a statue in Red Lion Square, London (reproduced on p. 186).

Having looked at the construction of the CO as a conscientious, honourable and admirable man with his own band of comrades and supporters, the text now moves on to pursue the notion that the dichotomy of the CO versus the soldier can be represented in different ways. In this next narrative about objectors, far from being cowardly traitors they are portrayed as patriots and as brave, intrepid, noble heroes, whilst the shinning image of the soldier is depicted as being tarnished.

Notes

1 For example, Niall Ferguson's *The Pity of War* adopts this line, directly disputing the 'Myth of War Enthusiasm' ((London: Allen Lane, 1998), ch. 7). Whilst accepting that there was clearly some initial excitement, he argues that this has been greatly over-emphasised and, at the same time, that other reactions to the war have tended to be concealed. Thus, he contends that to describe the moods of the crowds in London on 3 and 4 August 1914 in terms of 'enthusiasm' or 'euphoria' is 'misleading' as '[u]nder the circumstances, feelings of anxiety, panic and even millenarian religiosity were equally common popular responses to the outbreak of war' (p. 177). For a brief discussion of the 'war enthusiasm' thesis and such 'revisionist' takes upon it see above Chapter 1, footnote 3.

2 James Hinton, *Labour and Socialism: A History of the British Labour Movement, 1867–1974* (Brighton: Wheatsheaf books, 1983), p. 56.

3 This notion of lack of enthusiasm and war weariness, of course, was not only posited as existing amongst the civilian population; those in the military have also been depicted as feeling disenchanted, worn down and frustrated. In this context, for example, it has been noted that soldiers complained of boredom, went absent without leave, went on strike, shirked military discipline and malingered. (See further Chapter 6 below.)

4 Cyril Pearce, *Comrades in Conscience: The Story of an English Community's Opposition to the Great War* (London: Francis Boutle, 2001), pp. 23–5. See further below.

5 See further Sheila Rowbotham, *Friends of Alice Wheeldon* (London: Pluto, 1986), pp. 39–40.

6 *Ibid.*, p. 184.

7 For fuller accounts of the N-CF's work see, for example: No-Conscription Fellowship, *The No-Conscription Fellowship: A Souvenir of its Work During the Years 1914–1919* (London: No-Conscription Fellowship, 1920); Thomas C. Kennedy, *The Hound of Conscience: A History of the No-Conscription Fellowship* (Fayetteville: University of Arkansas Press, 1981). In addition, the Fellowship's records and papers give a sense of the scope of its endeavours: see, for example, Friends Library, London, MS VOL 149, No-Conscription Fellowship: duplicated papers, 1914–1919.

8 For example, see *Glasgow Herald* (16 March 1916) and *Leeds Mercury* (24 March 1916), cited in John Rae, *Conscience and Politics: The British Government and the Conscientious Objector to Military Service 1916–1919* (London: Oxford University Press, 1970), p. 99.

9 'EXCITING INCIDENTS', *The Worker* (2 March, 1916), reproduced in Pearce, *Comrades in Conscience*, pp. 247–8.

10 'STOP-THE-WAR MAN PASSED INTO ARMY: SOLICITOR ESCORTED FROM COURT BY TWO GUARDSMEN', *Daily Chronicle* (19 April 1916), p. 8. See also James Scott Duckers, *Handed Over: The Prison Experiences of Mr. J. Scott Duckers, Solicitor of Chancery Lane, Under the Military Service Act, Written by himself. With Foreword by T. Edmund Harvey* (London: C.W. Daniel, 1917), pp. 20–1.

11 Bertrand Russell, 'Some psychological difficulties of pacifism', in Julian H. Bell (ed.), *We Did Not Fight 1914–1918: Experiences of War Resisters* (London: Cobden Sanderson, 1935), p. 330.

12 Quoted in Stanley Bloomfield James, *The Men Who Dared: The Story of an Adventure* (London: C.W. Daniel, 1917), p. 46.

13 Although this association has been subject to challenge, see Joanna Bourke, *Dismembering the Male: Men's Bodies, Britain and the Great War* (London: Reaktion, 1996), ch. 3.

14 David Boulton, *Objection Overruled* (London: MacGibbon and Kee, 1967), pp. 226–7, 228.

15 *Ibid.*, p. 226.

16 See, for example, Boulton's description of these materials, *ibid.*, pp. 228–30.

17 Imperial War Museum, London (hereafter IWM), Sound Collection,

555/9, Reels 1–8, Dorothy Bing ('British civilian pacifist in Croydon and London, GB, 1914–1945').

18 Stephen Hobhouse, 'Fourteen months service with the colours', in Bell (ed.), *We Did Not Fight*, p. 172.

19 Mrs Henry (Margaret) Hobhouse, '*I Appeal unto Caesar': the case of the conscientious objector (with introduction by Professor Gilbert Murray and notes by the Earl of Selborne, Lord Parmoor, Lord Hugh Cecil, M. P., and Lord Henry Bentinck, M. P.)* (London: Allen and Unwin, 1917). Although this was published under her name it has been argued that, in fact, the author was none other than Bertrand Russell (see Ray Monk, *Bertrand Russell: The Spirit of Solitude* (London: Vintage, 1996), p. 499).

20 Rae, *Conscience and Politics*, p. 131.

21 'SOME IMPRESSIONS OF THE TRIBUNALS', *The Friend* (5 May 1916), p. 306.

22 See *Conscience and Politics*, p. 109; 5 HC 82, col. 1044, 11 May 1916; 5 HC 82, col. 1046, 11 May 1916.

23 'WHAT THE TRIBUNALS ARE DOING', *The Tribunal* (8 March 1916), p. 2.

24 IWM, Sound Collection, 485/6, Reel 2, Wilfred Ernest Littleboy ('British civilian absolutist conscientious objector imprisoned in Warwick Barracks, Wormwood Scrubs and Dorchester Prisons, GB, 1917–1919').

25 *Ibid.*, 358/11, Reel 2, Harold Frederick Bing ('British civilian absolutist conscientious objector imprisoned in Kingston Barracks, Wormwood Scrubs and Winchester Prisons, GB, 1916–1919').

26 Harry E. Stanton, 'Will You March Too? 1916–1919', unpublished account of a CO's experiences (privately owned), volume 1, p. 10.

27 Theodore Price, *Crucifiers and Crucified* (Alvechurch: The Author, 1917), p. 29. His commitment to the British Israelite movement is, for example, indicated on the dedication page to this slim volume.

28 See, for example, Hobhouse, 'Fourteen months service with the colours', pp. 169–70.

29 Duckers, *Handed Over*, p. 35.

30 See, for example, *ibid.*, p. 112.

31 *Ibid.*, pp. 36–7.

32 *Ibid.*, p. 151.

33 *Ibid.*, p. 113.

34 Max Plowman, *Bridge Into the Future: Letters of Max Plowman*, ed. Dorothy Lloyd Plowman (London: Andrew Dakers, 1944), p. 104.

35 'THE BEGINNINGS OF PERSECUTION', *The Friend* (19 May 1916), pp. 349–50.

36 'MAY DAY, 1916 – AND OVER 100 ANTI-MILITARISTS IN THE DETENTION CELLS!', *The Tribunal* (4 May 1916), p. 2.

37 See: Arnold Rowntree 5 HC 82, Col. 2633, 30 May 1916; Philip Snowden 5 HC 82, 2658, 30 May 1916.

38 James Primrose Malcolm Millar, 'A socialist in war time' in Bell (ed.), *We Did Not Fight*, p. 251.

39 The Directorate was known as AG3(CO). See National Archives, London (hereafter NA), WO 32/2051–5.

40 Rae, *Conscience and Politics*, p. 138; Major-General Sir Borlase Elward Wyndham Childs, KCMG, *Episodes and Reflections: Being Some Records From the Life of Major-General Sir Wyndham Childs* (London: Cassell and Co., 1930), p. 152.

41 See Caroline Moorehead, *Troublesome People: Enemies of War: 1916–1986* (London: Hamilton, 1987), p. 53.

42 5 HC 78, col. 451, 19 January 1916.

43 Moorehead, *Troublesome People*, p. 51.

44 'Root Difficulties in Recruiting', *Daily Chronicle* (24 March 1916), p. 4.

45 Reported in *The C.O.'s Hansard*, 32 (14 June 1917), pp. 385–91 and 36 (12 July 1917), p. 392.

46 *Ibid.*, pp. 387, 388.

47 *Ibid.*, p. 391.

48 By 1916 Buchan had worked in both the War and Foreign Office. He was a Major in the Intelligence Corps and compiled summaries of the fighting for the Press and the Propaganda Department. When Lloyd George became Prime Minister, Buchan was asked to draft proposals for a new Department of Information which would take over the work of the War Propaganda Bureau. Set up in 1917, its role was to unify all foreign propaganda activities and war-related materials. Buchan was appointed Director of Information, with direct responsibility to Lloyd George. See: Janet A. Smith, *John Buchan* (London: Rupert Hart-Davis, 1965), pp. 197–8, 200; David Roberts, *Minds at War: The Poetry and Experience of the First World War* (Burgess Hill: Saxon, 1996), p. 59.

49 Quoted in Smith, *John Buchan*, p. 260.

50 On the history of Quakers' association with pacifism see, in particular, Peter Brock, *The Quaker Peace Testimony 1660 to 1914* (York: Sessions Books Trust, 1990).

51 See Rae, *Conscience and Politics*, pp. 72–3.

52 See Childs, *Episodes and Reflections*, p. 148 and NA, WO 32/2055/6923.

53 Rae, *Conscience and Politics*, pp. 73, see further 207–16.

54 Davidson to Milner (then a member of the War Cabinet, subsequently to become Secretary of State for War) 21 May 1917, quoted in George

Kennedy Allen Bell, *Randall Davidson, Archbishop of Canterbury*, volume 2 (London: Oxford University Press, 1935), pp. 821–2.

55 Home Office, 'The Home Office and Conscientious Objectors: A Report Prepared for the Committee of Imperial Defence 1919: Part II, Conscientious Objectors in Prison', p. 2.

56 NA, CAB 24/23/1799, Derby's remarks to the Cabinet, 21 August 1917.

57 Fisher writing to Lord Milner (at that time a member of Lloyd George's War Cabinet), 30 May 1917, cited by Rae, *Conscience and Politics*, p. 212.

58 'THE CONSCIENTIOUS OBJECTOR. WORK IN FRANCE. A CONTENTED FORCE DOING USEFUL WORK', *The Times* (19 May 1916), p. 7.

59 John Buchan, *Mr Standfast* (Ware: Wordsworth Classics, 1919 – reissued in 1994).

60 Ferguson, *The Pity of War*, ch. 7.

61 George Bernard Shaw, quoted in Virginia Woolf, *Three Guineas* (New York: Harcourt, 1938), p. 182.

62 See, for example, Trudi Tate's discussion of this in terms of gender and the fiction and historiography of the Great War in *Women, Men and the Great War: An Anthology of Stories* (Manchester: Manchester University Press, 1995), Introduction and, in particular, p. 5.

63 This was fervently encouraged by pro-conscriptionists. For example, see Denis Hayes, *Conscription Conflict: The Conflict of Ideas in the Struggle For and Against Military Conscription Between 1901 and 1939* (London: Sheppard Press, 1949), pp. 36–50.

64 IWM PST 2763, 0311.

65 Owen Seamen, 'To The Shirker: A Last Appeal', *Punch* (11 November 1914), reproduced in Roberts, *Minds at War*, p. 197.

66 'SINGLE MEN FIRST: A CHANGE FOR THE BETTER', *Daily Mail* (18 October 1915), p. 4.

67 See Earl of Derby, KG, Director-General of Recruiting, *Report on Recruiting*, Cd. 8149, 1916.

68 David Lloyd George, *War Memoirs of David Lloyd George*, vol. 1 (London: Odhams, 1938, first issued 1933), p. 434.

69 Paul Fussell, *The Great War and Modern Memory* (Oxford: Oxford University Press, 25th anniversary edn, 2000 – first published 1975), p. 11.

70 War Office, *Statistics of the Military Effort of the British Empire During the Great War 1914–1920* (London: War Office, 1922), p. 364. Despite this, the iconic image of the soldier both during the war and to some extent subsequently remained the volunteer, and (unsurprisingly) propaganda reinforced this notion. Indeed, seemingly all men in the

military acquired the status of the altruistic brave man once they donned a uniform. Ilana R. Bet-El refers to this fixation upon the volunteer and consequent eschewing of those men who had no choice but to serve as the 'Myth of the Volunteer'. Bet-El, 'Men and soldiers: British conscripts, concepts of masculinity, and the Great War', in Billie Melman (ed.), *Borderlines: Genders and Identities in War and Peace 1870–1930* (London: Routledge, 1998). See further Bet-El, *Conscripts: Lost Legions of the Great War* (Stroud: Sutton: 1999). For a discussion of Great War myths see John Terraine, *The Smoke and the Fire: Myths and Anti-Myths of War, 1861–1945* (London: Sidgwick and Jackson, 1980), ch. 5.

71 For example, see Lloyd George's description of their arguments and influence. *War Memoirs*, vol. 1, p. 438, see generally pp. 437–9

72 See NA, MH 47/144, General Geddes, 'Report of the Select Committee on Military Service', 1917.

73 T. Edmund Harvey, 'Foreword' to Duckers, *Handed Over*.

74 'CONSCIENTIOUS OBJECTOR DRESSED AS A WOMAN', *The Times* (1 September 1917), p. 3.

75 See, for example, Rae, *Conscience and Politics*, pp. 111–12.

76 *Punch* (12 July 1916), p. 51.

77 The case became the subject of a judicial review on another procedural matter and – although the High Court felt that, if challenged, such a decision could not stand – the Court of Appeal failed to even acknowledge the issue. See further *R v Lincolnshire Appeal Tribunal; Ex parte Stubbins* [1917] 115 Law Times 513.

78 Philip Snowden, *British Prussianism: The Scandal of the Tribunals* (Manchester: National Labour Press, 1916), p. 9.

79 B.N. Langdon-Davies, 'Alternative service', in Bell (ed.) *We Did Not Fight*, p. 189.

80 See Bourke, *Dismembering the Male*, pp. 81–2.

81 Reproduced in *ibid.*, p. 82.

82 The brief reports are given under the heading to the previous story, 'RECRUIT IN A BLANKET', p. 2.

83 See NA, NATS 1/909 'Army Reservists normally resident in Great Britain who have proceeded to Ireland in order to evade military service', 1918 and NA, NATS 1/935, 'Men of military age escaping to Ireland to evade call up', 1917–18.

84 Several such raids are reported in 'NEW PRESS GANG. SMALL RESULT OF MUCH EFFORT. ONE MAN SECURED AT MARYLEBONE', *The Times* (12 September 1916), p. 5.

85 See NA, NATS 1/964, '"Comb Out" of hunting and racing establishments of persons evading military service: exemption to be granted only in the case of men physically unfit, or holding Certificates of Exemption from Tribunals', 1915–18.

86 See NA, NATS 1/975, 'Discharged men of military age holding Exemption Certificates in previous occupations enrolling as War Work Volunteers to evade National Service when their contracts have ended', 1918.

87 See NA, NATS 1, 'Files relating to policy or to matters of permanent interest dealt with by the Trade Exemptions, Medical, Labour Supply, Finance and Organisation, Recruiting and Recording Departments of the Ministry of National Service', 1914–20.

88 *The Times* (9 July 1917), p. 4.

89 Langdon-Davies, 'Alternative service', p. 189.

90 NA, MUN 5/52/300/72, Report of the Central Tribunal appointed under Military Service Act, 1916, February 1919, pp. 26–7.

91 See Rae, *Conscience and Politics*, pp. 68–79.

92 George Bernard Shaw, 'Common Sense About the War', *New York Times* (22 November 1914), p. 14.

93 See Bet-El, 'Men and soldiers', p. 77.

94 Quoted in *ibid.*, p. 77.

95 See Ferguson, *The Pity of War*, p. 444.

96 David Silbey *The British Working Class and Enthusiasm for War* (London: Frank Cass, 2005), chs 5, 6; chs 4–7 examine the range of motivations.

97 For the figures (and their interpretation by Derby as a cause for concern) see NA, CAB 37/139/26, Lord Derby 'Memorandum on recruiting', 13 December 1915.

98 For the details of the Scheme and concerns about its operation see Derby, *Report on Recruiting*, 1916.

99 Bet-El, 'Men and soldiers', p. 77.

100 Quoted in Rowbotham, *Friends of Alice Wheeldon*, p. 42.

101 Hinton, *Labour and Socialism*, p. 56.

102 See, for example, Andrew Rothstein, *The Soldier Strikes of 1919* (London: Macmillan, 1980), pp. 7–10.

103 For example, see Pearce, *Comrades in Conscience*, pp. 205–7.

104 'B.P.', 'Soldiers All', *Punch* (10 March 1915), reproduced in Bourke, *Dismembering the Male*, p. 106.

105 Will Dyson, reproduced in Boulton, *Objection Overruled*, p. 128.

106 For example, see Lloyd George, *War Memoirs*, p. 804; Pearce, *Comrades in Conscience*, p. 209.

107 Doron Lamm, 'Emily goes to war: explaining the recruitment to the Women's Army Auxiliary Corps in World War I', in Billie Melman (ed.), *Borderlines: Genders and Identities in War and Peace 1870–1930* (London: Routledge, 1998), pp. 383–4.

108 See *ibid.*

109 See Angela Woollacott, '"Khaki Fever" and its control: gender,

class, age and sexual morality on the British Homefront in the First World War', *Journal of Contemporary History* 29:2 (1994) 325–47, 334.

110 See Bonnie S. Anderson, and Judith P. Zinsser, *A History of Their Own: Women in Europe from Prehistory to the Present*, vol. II (New York: Harper and Row, 1988), pp. 201–3.

111 For a recent contribution to the literature on domestic dissent see Brock Millman, *Managing Domestic Dissent in First World War Britain* (London: Frank Cass, 2000). The latter's arguments in relation to the government role have, however, provoked some controversy. See, for example, Jon Lawrence's review, *Twentieth Century British History*, 14:1 (2003), 86–8.

112 See further Rae, *Conscience and Politics*, p. 238.

6

Patriots and heroes

Just as conscientious objectors (COs) could experience fair treatment, sympathy and respect they were also seen and saw themselves as patriots and heroes. For a variety of reasons some objectors and their supporters, along with others who were anti-war, viewed their stance as in their country's best interests and, consequently, conceived of them as fighting for the good of the nation. For others, who objected to compulsion itself, objectors were defending a very English tradition by refusing to be enlisted. Also, there were those who were hardly inclined to sympathise with COs but nevertheless took a degree of patriotic pride in their existence, viewing them as quintessentially English. Beyond this, the bravery of the CO was recognised in a variety of contexts and sometimes they were seen as Christian heroes or religious martyrs.

This chapter begins by depicting the objector as patriot and hero and constructing resonances between the ideal of the soldier and the CO. The text then moves on to consider the idea that, in various ways, the soldier was failing to live up to his uniform. The narrative below, therefore, proffers a different configuration of the dichotomy of the soldier versus the CO than that previously constructed. Here the former's image fails to accord with that of the exemplary military man. Moreover, far from being a shirker and a coward, the objector is portrayed as embodying the very characteristics supposedly epitomised by the soldier.

A 'nobler patriotism'[1]

Of our fellow-countrymen who once hated us, I would beg only that they will believe us when we say we acted as we did because we loved our country.[2]

Far from being traitors or spies, some objectors saw themselves as intensely patriotic men, fighting for their country. Their explanations for their beliefs were founded in a deep and fervent love of their country and all that they felt it stood for. In these visions of patriotism what is generally being described is the 'nobler patriotism' of which W.P. Byles spoke in 1904:

> It is the duty of all peace reformers to try to generate, by word, act and vote, a new patriotism; and the duty especially lies heavily upon us women to nourish a nobler patriotism.[3]

Thus, whilst the conception of patriotism depicted in propaganda and the jingoistic press dictated that all should support their country unquestioningly in difficult times, others interpreted the interests of the country very differently. The latter approach had its roots in the later part of the nineteenth century, when a new ideology developed from Evangelical, radical, pacifist and feminist thinking. This version of pacifist patriotism tended to stress that loyalty and duty should be directed at what was morally best for one's nation (in this analysis, peace) rather than adopting a blind allegiance to official policy.[4] As a result, patriotic objectors could find that they were very much in opposition to conventional ideas about what a love for one's country should entail. For example, there were those who saw the Great War as the crime and couched their opposition to it in patriotic terms,[5] reflecting peace advocate Priscilla Peckover's view that '[i]t is the truest form of patriotism to do our utmost to save our country from the crime and shame of an unjust war.'[6]

Hence, although many COs rejected the very notion of loyalty to a country (preferring, for example, loyalty to God or international socialism),[7] some of these men professed a deep devotion to their country or even proclaimed themselves to be true patriots.[8] For example, George Baker's autobiographical account, *The Soul of a Skunk: The Autobiography of a Conscientious Objector*, describes his experiences as a socialist objector: 'this is a story of a man who, then not much more than a boy, during the Great War did his bit for England as a pacifist in prison'. He continues:

> I . . . am a pacifist . . . a patriot. I love my country, and its heroic poor who are the salt of its English earth. I delight in this rich English tongue, in the loveliness of its poetry and in the comeliness of its prose.[9]

In the penultimate chapter in this volume he writes that he 'was not necessarily less a lover of England than Tommy who went to the double ditch of death for the sake of a more conventional patriotism' as his was a 'patriotism for peace'.[10] So here we have the supposedly unpatriotic CO celebrating his allegiance to and love of his country and, as a socialist, all its workers.

Patriotism was important even for objectors who felt that they had to temper it to their more deeply held views or beliefs or put their stance towards the war above notions of allegiance to country. In Baker's words, many had a 'spiritual battle to fight' as the 'sensibility of our patriotism warred with the sense of our pacifism'.[11] Similarly Willie Campbell, whilst not rejecting patriotism out of hand, feels that 'Christianity is a higher ideal than mere patriotism'. His faith and its teachings had to take precedence over his country when a conflict arose. Nevertheless, he recognises that 'love of country & of home & dear ones is very strong . . . one feels irresistibly drawn to protect home & country at all costs & even in spite of Christian idea [sic].'[12]

Those who saw war as variously dysgenic rather than regenerative or illegal sometimes also viewed their objection in patriotism terms; in this context avoiding war was in the country's best interests. Here COs were couching their patriotism in terms of a range of pre-existing ideas. Indeed, both before and after August 1914 some political, pacifist and feminist opponents of war argued that, rather than being a blessing and offering regeneration, war was by no means a boon. In addition, some in the women's movement felt that war was the result of masculine urges that needed to be curbed and tempered for the good of the nation. Moreover, as violence was an inherent male characteristic it needed to be limited by women's involvement in politics or cured through female instruction. Thus, Mrs Mabel Annie Saint Clair Stobart, argues that war was unnatural, that conflicts were fought for 'paltry purposes' and ought to be prevented. She also feels that 'wars would never be suppressed by men alone'. The 'woman's movement' was the 'antidote' to this 'poison':

> The more 'natural ' it seems for man to fight his fellow-man, in order to acquire supremacy, the more urgent it is for society to intervene . . . But society has hitherto been controlled by men only . . .[13]

Ironically, Suffragette Christabel Pankhurst expressed such anti-war views before August 1914, although, as Chapter 2 demonstrated, once the declaration was issued she swiftly changed her view (recognising the political currency which joining in could bring) and took up recruiting.[14] In June 1914 she felt that:

> Warfare as developed by men had become a horror unspeakable . . . Not only soldiers . . . [suffer]: non-combatants die, too . . . [this] is the tragic result of the unnatural system of government by men only.[15]

COs drew upon such ideas. In particular, there were clear links between feminist pacifism and the No-Conscription Fellowship (hereafter N-CF or the Fellowship). For example, the influence of Catherine Marshall, former female Suffragist and Parliamentary Secretary of the National Union for Women's Suffrage, upon the Fellowship was significant; when the key players were arrested she took over the running of the organisation and her views were shared both by some objectors and their supporters.[16]

Others who opposed war prior to 1914 included Sir Norman Angell, founder of the Union of Democratic Control. Along with other peace campaigners, he argues that war was not beneficial for the participant states. More specifically he maintains in *The Great Illusion: A Study of the Relation of Military Power to National Advantage* that, because of modern military technology and economic interdependence, the world had 'passed out of that stage in development in which it is possible for one civilised group to advance its well-being by the military domination of another'.[17] Objectors who adopted or were influenced by such views included Harry E. Stanton. Although a Friend from birth, he sought other justifications for resisting conscription in order to establish whether fighting or not fighting would be the 'truest service to the State'.[18]

Moreover, even those who rejected the patriotism which supported war and hatred of the enemy still often described their love of their country and a need to support it. Edward Grubb, Treasurer of the N-CF, recalled the position of pacifist Quakers like himself: 'We felt the need to serve the community, if a way opened for us to do so, in public life; we wished to be loyal to our own country and to humanity.'[19] In addition, Stephen Hobhouse contrasts the schoolboy patriotism which led him to join the Officer Training Corps at both Eton and Oxford University with a new outlook which he espoused subsequently, having been exposed to the views of other family members and the works of Tolstoy. Leaving his 'conventional patriotism' as well as his Anglicanism behind, in 1908 he resolved 'to do my small part to save my country' by working for international peace.[20]

Objectors commenting upon their experiences were also keen to highlight the patriotism that caused men to stand out. Notably, Clifford Allen, Chairman of the N-CF, reflects upon his wartime experiences when released from prison on health grounds in January 1918:

> I am glad – unashamedly glad that this sea-girth is my native country
> . . . I want my country to be the greatest amongst the nations of the
> world – great by virtue of its loyalty to freedom and tolerance . . . We
> C.O.s must somehow make it clear to our fellow countrymen that it
> was our very love of country that made us choose prison rather than
> see her sported and bound by conscription.[21]

In a similar tone, John Graham dedicates his 1922 book, *Conscription and Conscience*, 'with affectionate reverence to the young men who in the dark days of the war kept the faith and stood by their country and mankind with a courage that did not fail'.[22] Bertrand Russell's description of members of the N-CF in April 1916 was more poetic, stating that if Blake or Shelley were alive they would have joined their number and that 'Like Blake, they had seen a vision; they wished to "build Jerusalem in England's green and pleasant land"'.[23]

Sometimes even the mainstream press commented upon the patriotism of those objectors who assisted with the war effort. In particular, men who accepted service in the Non-Combatant Corps were more easily conceived of as citizens who adhered to their pacifist views but also demonstrated a love for their country. Thus in 1916 a report in *The Times* notes with approval the willing labours of this Battalion in France, observing that they should be seen 'as men who are rendering what service they conscientiously can to their country in her need, just like any other patriotic Britons.'[24]

In addition, the existence and suffering of genuine objectors was occasionally viewed as a source of national pride by unlikely commentators. Such sentiments could even, for example, be voiced by military men. Most notably Commander Wedgewood MP declared that:

> I think I am prouder of my country than I was before, because it has
> produced people who have sufficient conscientious scruples to enable
> them to face a long term of imprisonment rather than upset their

consciences. It is something to be proud of even to produce martyrs of this sort as well as martyrs on the battlefield.[25]

Beyond this, English objectors and their supporters were often keen to state that they were defending Englishness/Britishness.[26] One dominant thread in this patriotic self-construction related to the arguments mounted against military conscription itself. Here it was contended that COs, like soldiers, were fighting Germany, as the English military tradition was one of voluntarism rather than the dreaded Prussian militarism. Thus, men who adopted this stance on recruitment often saw themselves as defending English liberalism and freedom.

By the early twentieth century England had two very different traditions of recruitment; namely, a professional core supplemented by either compulsion or voluntarism.[27] It was the latter approach that had been adopted in most recent times and was celebrated by some contemporary commentators including some objectors as both the truly English, liberal way and the antithesis of the despised Prussian militarism.[28] Thus, even before the war many portrayed voluntarism as the English tradition and resisted the stridently pro-conscriptionist arguments of the National Service League as being foreign, unnecessary and unrepresentative. Indeed, compulsion was 'an idea which in most Edwardian nostrils stank of Continental militarism'.[29] Fundamentally, it was felt that men should be left to choose whether to enlist and the assumption was, of course, that the majority would do so willingly if needed.

Moreover, this voluntary tradition was both a reason for and an illustration of England's greatness as the following verse suggests:

Go Tell the world of Conscripts
That Britain's Britain still;
Go tell the world of Conscripts
Our watchword's Freedom still.
So let aggression's forc'd array
Fill those it may with fears,
We'll answer their conscription with
A Million Volunteers.[30]

Thus, voluntarism was often depicted as a source of great pride for the nation and something that had been instilled in many a boy through schools and boys' organisations. Therefore (as this text has previously argued in the context of enthusiasm for the war and the soldier hero ideal), men and boys came forward, in part, because they had been taught that this was the English and manly thing to do.

In the last days of voluntarism, those who actively opposed conscription and sympathised with or supported objectors included prominent figures in Government. Most notably, Sir John Simon, who resigned as Home Secretary because of the introduction of conscription, felt this move to be unacceptable: 'the real issue is whether we are to begin an immense change in the fundamental structure of our society'.[31] Such a shift in his eyes would encompass far too great a sacrifice of individual liberty. In addition, as Simon saw it, the principle of voluntary enlistment was part of the 'birthright' of the English people.[32] Thus, supporters of military conscription were not only 'infecting themselves with false doctrine' but they were also forgetting or casting aside the 'real truth' that 'military organisation by force is the very system which this country is united to destroy'; namely the despised Prussian militarism.[33] Similarly, MP and supporter of objectors Arnold Rowntree appealed for the rejection of conscription in terms of Englishness. He asked the House 'to leave still the masters of their own souls, and to do nothing to destroy the fabric of England's appeal to the conscience of the world'.[34]

COs who either based their objection on a rejection of compulsion as un-English or cited this as one of a number of reasons for their stand included George Baker. In his view objectors were making a 'very English stand for the great English principle of the Liberty of conscience'.[35] The N-CF adopted a similar position, citing this as a fundamental reason for its creation; indeed, this was often seen as a common and unifying purpose in an organisation whose membership was extremely diverse in terms of their perspectives on the state, war and fighting. Thus, for example, when the Military Service Act passed the organisation wrote to members stating that their objective was now to bring about 'the removal of Conscription from the life of this country of free traditions'.[36]

'The men who dared'

By facing popular contempt and ridicule, ill-treatment in the barracks, long imprisonment, and in thirty-six cases the shock of the death sentences, these men have proved their convictions genuine. They have shown themselves possessed of a moral courage at least equal to the common soldier's, and far greater than most of us educated people could show.[37]

If standing out as an objector and maintaining this stance meant facing ostracism, hatred, abuse and ill-treatment and entailed being seen as a shirker, coward, unmanly, deviant and dangerous it is, of course, arguable that doing so took heroism and strength of conviction. For example, 22-year-old William (Willie) Campbell's letter to his parents in November 1915 illustrates that making the decision to stand out as a CO could require courage.[38] At the time of writing he is in his first year of Divinity at New College, Edinburgh (then a Free Church college), studying for the ministry. Willie describes the turmoil he is experiencing and writes of the 'revolution of feeling and mind' that he has been going through, adding that '[e]ven yet I feel in a whirl & nothing else has been occupying my thoughts, so I can write of nothing else.'[39] As the letter progresses it becomes increasingly clear that he is particularly concerned that his parents will think him 'misguided' and consider that he has taken 'a completely wrong view of things'.[40]

The decision to be an objector also meant resisting war enthusiasm and propaganda. Clifford Allen, writing in the 1930s (by which time he was Lord Allen of Hurtwood), recalled the difficulty that those who 'felt it necessary to resist the emotion and passion which swept over the nation' experienced.[41] Similarly, objector B.N. Langdon-Davies remembers that '[i]t was hard to resist the view that Germany represented the rule of force and that the war was a crusade against it'. He continues:

> Only those who have done it know how difficult it is to keep level-headed in the orgy of emotionalism and the dissolution of mentality which is known as war fever. There were moments when I wanted to join the herd.[42]

Thus, at a time when everybody seemed to be rushing to join up or at least seeking to find a means of joining in, men whose consciences led them to resist the flow stood outside the great adventure, despite 'the clamour of the Press, the outcry of the platform and the eloquence of the pulpit'.[43] Consequently, as former shadow Chair of the N-CF, Bertrand Russell, was to note after the conflict, the biggest problem experienced by those who resisted the war in different ways was to resist and continue to resist the 'wiles of the herd instinct':

> . . . the greatest difficulty was the purely psychological one of resisting mass suggestion, of which the force becomes terrific when the whole

nation is in a state of violent collective excitement. As much effort was required to avoid sharing this excitement as would have been needed to stand out against the extreme of hunger or sexual passion, and there was the same feeling of going against instinct.[44]

Adopting this view, Stanley Bloomfield James celebrates the fortitude that COs needed to stand against the crowd, resisting war fever and mafficking:

And when the war came and relatives and friends and popular feeling were all pulling him in one direction some sacred instinct held him back. To have joined the crowd then would have been easy, but it would have meant the loss of what had made his life worth living. . . . [when he] [a]rrived at that decision some strange power within him was released. He became another man. He had joined the army of dedicated men and women through whose travail God's Kingdom comes.[45]

In addition, for many objectors not only did their views on soldiering have to be formed in the midst of all this war fever but decisions needed to be taken and resolutions made swiftly. Lord Allen of Hurtwood recalled that once war was declared:

Taken unawares, and without preparation, all of us between the ages of nineteen and thirty-five, had to make up our minds as to what we honestly meant by patriotism and Socialism, what our attitude to peace and war really was, and what significance we attached to the word 'liberty'. Moreover, we had to do all this, faced by the issue of life and death.[46]

The last sentence highlights the consequences that might face a soldier on the battlefield and, some believed, an objector. Similarly, James Primrose Malcolm Millar writes of the dangers that objectors believed they faced: '[w]hen the C.O.s decided to be C.O.s and refused to join the army or obey military authority, they quite well knew that their refusal might be followed by the death penalty'[47] and, indeed, a few were sentenced to death, although these penalties were commuted.[48]

However, as Langdon-Davies notes, it was arguable that the greatest courage was displayed by the men who went first, without support, not knowing what would happen to them and fearing that once in the military they might be called upon to give their lives for their beliefs.[49] In fact, this uncertainty as to what lay ahead was the major difficulty which men faced when deciding to take the path of conscience. As James observes '[t]hese men are quite conscious of the desperate nature of the struggle in which they are engaged . . .'[50] and, once in military hands, '[w]ho would know if he were done away with?'[51] James Scott Duckers's description of his preparations for imminent arrest reveals this sense of uncertainty as to the nature of the sacrifice he would be called to make. Having refused to obey his call-up papers, he put his affairs in order, arranged for his office to be closed and his business to be wound up. He then sent a copy of his correspondence to his friend J.M. Hogge, MP, 'with the request that if and when I fell into the hands of the military authorities he would, for the benefit of my relatives, try and find out what had become of me'.[52]

As a result of these difficulties, COs were often seen as heroes by their fellows, their supporters and sympathisers.[53] As demonstrated in the previous chapter, some objectors, like Duckers, gained a degree of celebrity and an heroic status amongst a band of followers. Similarly, when Clifford Allen came before Battersea Tribunal the 'hundreds who came to hear his case were unable to gain admission' and there was much cheering.[54] The reaction he received led the Chairman to remark '[a] bit of a hero isn't he', to which one of his colleagues responded '[h]e is the leader of the gang'.[55] Similarly, when he was due to be released from prison having completed his first term of imprisonment a crowd of well-wishers gathered at the gates.[56] In jail too he was a celebrity amongst his fellows. For example, one objector recalled the 'thrill' of finding out that Allen was in the same prison.[57] Thus, to some COs Clifford Allen was 'a well-loved and revered name'.[58]

Indeed, the depiction of COs as heroes was common and could be seen, in part, as propaganda for their cause and also as a defence of their manliness. In his Introduction to *We Did Not Fight*, Julian H. Bell reflects this construction of COs as brave, noting 'that pacifists and conscientious objectors were not cowards I think these narratives make clear', and he argues that the objectors and others who resisted the war left behind them 'a magnificent tradition of personal integrity and intellectual courage'.[59] However, he reserves his greatest praise for those who remained in prison:

> In many ways the attitude of the idealist and absolutist conscientious objector, prepared to endure anything rather than surrender his convictions, is more satisfactory: there is something most moving in such courage and nobility of character.[60]

Unsurprisingly the N-CF sought to cast the objector in a heroic light. The organisation had decided at its first National Convention in November 1915 to produce its own propaganda.[61] Thus, *The Tribunal* and the various pamphlets not only sought to provide support, assistance and information to COs but also to reach out and influence popular opinion. Portraying objectors and their supporters as heroic, self-sacrificing and, therefore, not unlike the soldier in their determination to do what they thought right, whatever the cost, was not only good for the morale of the Fellowship's members but might also influence opinion about conscription and the war.

In addition, Arthur Marwick's description of the N-CF's ability to continue its work, despite the various attempts by the state to disable or quash it, as 'a breathtakingly efficient conspiracy against the organised might of the state'[62] suggests a very different conception of the Fellowship itself from that previously described. Here the efforts of the shadow operation, in particular, are recast as hazardous, intrepid and courageous. Indeed, George Baker describes the N-CF's continued publication of *The Tribunal* throughout the war in the following terms: 'the romance of . . . [*The Tribunal*'s] continued printing, publishing and distributing would make an exceedingly fine detective thriller, with the C.I.D. as the villain of the piece.'[63]

Other sources also configured the objector as courageous. *The Men Who Dared: The Story of an Adventure*, by James and published in 1917, represents one such narrative. In this text these men's sacrifices and experiences are celebrated in an often dramatic, breathless style. Indeed, the book's very title challenges the dominant conceptions of the objector in its representation of these men as swashbuckling heroes who undertook daredevil deeds:

> . . . Brute Force became the Dictator of Europe. Militarism with its hectoring tyranny, its destructive mania, its disregard for individual liberty and life . . . violated the world-consciousness. The very pulpits rang with appeals to arm and kill. . . . But the powers of spiritual and moral resistance that are latent in mankind found at last expression. With desperate courage, a handful of men and women stood out against the Thing that was destroying the nations. . . . These men are quite conscious of the desperate nature of the struggle in which they are engaged, but they are none the less certain that there can be but one result. . . .[64]

In this book, First World War COs were out to save the world.

This then is an heroic adventure narrative, albeit one involving exploits of a character very different from that of the soldier or spy. Moreover, James refers to the way of the CO as a 'Crusade', suggesting the image of objectors as knights of old.[65] Others also made such allusions. Everett, one of the first objectors to experience imprisonment and, therefore, in the vanguard, refers to his experiences as being 'a great religious adventure'.[66]

In the fiction of the First World War there are also examples of COs depicted as heroes. Such writings posed a particularly sharp contrast to those authors, like Barrie, who produced literature as establishment propaganda, sometimes at the state's bidding. For example, published on the 22 May 1918, Rose Allatini's *Despised and Rejected*, amongst other things, focuses upon a circle of objectors. The work portrays such men as being far from cowardly. Indeed, towards the book's close, Antoinette, the heroine, maintains that '[you] can't call a man who's ready to go to prison for his convictions a weakling or a coward'.[67]

John Buchan's *Mr Standfast*, published in 1919, was another example of fiction that went against the flood of jingoistic hatred of objectors in its portrayal of Lancelot Wake.[68] Wake is a brave man who, as a non-combatant on the Western Front, willingly volunteers for a mission he cannot survive and dies heroically when his task is fulfilled, thereby symbolising pacifist martyrdom on the battlefield. The main character of this, the third in a series of six John Hannay novels, wishes he has Wake in his battalion and calls him a hero when the objector saves his life.[69] Reflecting upon Wake's death, Hannay feels that:

> If the best were to be taken, he would be chosen first, for he was a big man . . . The thought of him made me very humble . . . he had . . . reached a courage which was forever beyond me. He was the Faithful among us pilgrims, who had finished his journey before the rest.[70]

As Buchan's biographer, Janet A. Smith, comments, '[d]ifferent kinds of bravery are displayed in Mr Standfast'.[71] However, the novel is by no means a wholehearted celebration of all COs. Here it is the objector who directly assists the war effort and dies as a consequence that is celebrated; he epitomises the 'good' or, perhaps, the 'conscientious' CO. Wake is doubly conscientious because he not only obeys his conscience and objects but also because, by assisting with the war, showing bravery at the Front and dying for his country, he is viewed as honourable, responsible, moral and upright. Indeed, Wake embodies a type of objector whom supporters of the war were least unhappy to recognise. This construction of the heroic objector is reminiscent of Asquith's reassurances in introducing the first Military Service Bill and its 'conscience clause'. He portrayed COs as brave men, prepared to serve and willing to risk their lives alongside fighting soldiers but not prepared to take life, adding 'but [they] were quite willing to perform many other military duties'. Further, he noted that some COs (who had, for example, gone to the Front with the Friends Ambulance Unit) were already doing this 'with the greatest bravery and courage, exposing themselves to the very same risks as those who go into the trenches to man the guns and use the rifles'.[72]

Buchan's positive portrayal of Wake was also a welcome relief for some of his readers who had grown tired of the castigation of objectors and could see them as heroes. For example, a United Free Kirk Minister in Fife was grateful to Buchan:

> for the sympathy and understanding with which you have sketched Lancelot Wake. . . . Next to the men who died I honour the real objector and only feel that the one perfectly abominable thing is that he should grumble at his own sufferings or in any way comport himself as other than a different kind of soldier in a fight as grim and wounding; and your Lancelot Wake seems this sort and is, I fancy, more typical than the mean fellow the general press has depicted.

In this response to *Mr Standfast* again we see the valiant and steadfast CO as a soldier, albeit of a different type. The Minister continues, describing objectors as 'hanging on to something immensely true and heroic' and 'all the more so that it is unhonoured'. In a similar vein, another reader, who had been in the Friends Ambulance Unit in France, compares Wake with himself and concludes that unfortunately he 'never had either Wake's courage or his fanaticism'.[73] In such comments again Wake is cast as the model CO, the embodiment of an heroic, intrepid, if unconventional, manhood of which Britain could be proud. Without actually being a combatant, he inhabits the battlefield and volunteers for a suicide mission but refuses to the last to bear arms or fight.

Beyond this, even those who were generally opposed to the CO stance could sometimes see the heroism of some of these men's actions. Indeed, prominent military men sometimes recognised the courage of these men. As was noted above, Commander Wedgewood MP described the bravery of those who chose to suffer imprisonment rather than go against their consciences, and paid tribute to 'martyrs of this sort [COs in prison] as well as martyrs on the battlefield'.[74] However, perhaps one of the best illustrations of the official recognition of the bravery of men who were supposedly cowards and shirkers was provided by France's decision to award the Croix de Guerre to some members of the Friends Ambulance Unit for their work at the Front. Here, then, we have objectors who went to the war unarmed and were decorated as war heroes for their courage under fire.[75]

Moreover, despite the authorities' fears, just like the fallen soldiers, a few objectors other than the fictional Wake came to be seen and portrayed as martyrs by their supporters. Certainly those who died during the war on the Home Office Scheme or in prison were granted this status by the N-CF. The first CO to perish was Walter Roberts. He passed away while at Dyce Camp in September 1916. Although his death was apparently from natural causes, his life ended in harsh conditions, which could not have improved his health. He was seen by the N-CF as the first victim of state persecution. *The Tribunal* published a valediction celebrating his struggle:

[a]nd now the struggle of this brave bearer of the banner of Peace is over. His body rests beside those of many noble men at Hawarden . . . To all of us his life and death must be an inspiration . . .[76]

The text uses the same 'high' diction that Paul Fussell has noted in relation to war and the military man.[77] Thus, here, and in accounts like the aforementioned *The Men Who Dared*, those who supported the objector were seeking to create heroes and martyrs and, in order to do so, utilised the language used to celebrate the warrior. Given the desire to celebrate a CO life, the use of dominant forms to praise the dead was unsurprising; they were what was available. Moreover, this approach was strategically important as it might have suggested an air of legitimacy to both the CO cause and objector manhood.

For Christian objectors and their supporters the image of their heroism and martyrdom was often depicted in religious terms. It emphasised, for example, parallels with the persecution of biblical figures, of Christians in other ages or the Christian chivalric imagery which was also associated with the soldier. Thus, again drawing upon the same imagery as propaganda, the press and pro-war writers and artists, materials produced by objectors and their supporters often used religious imagery or allusions to describe the heroism of these men. For example, James compares the plight of objectors in the military to the Old Testament story of Daniel and the fiery furnace.[78] Perhaps Stephen Hobhouse was the best example of a man who came to be perceived in this light. As the previous chapter began to suggest, he was viewed, even by some less than sympathetic to the CO cause, as the quintessential genuine objector; an intensely religious man, a Quaker, respectable, well educated (at Eton and Balliol) and as a man who was willing to suffer like the Christians of old.

Some Christian groups had more specific narratives which saw them as on the side of God and aided by heavenly figures. Thus, the Seventh Day Adventists COs had their own version of the Angel of Mons story. When some of their number were held overnight in an underground military cell a man in khaki brought them tea and biscuits. The next morning they asked to be able to thank him but could find no evidence of his existence. One account concluded 'that an angel donned khaki on this occasion and was sent of God to minister to His hungry children'.[79]

Moreover, objectors were sometimes seen as Christ-like figures, for Jesus too would have refused to fight:

> Look! Christ in khaki, out in France thrusting his bayonet into the body of a German workman. See! The Son of God with a machine gun ... No! No! That picture is an impossible one and *we all know it*. [Emphasis in the original][80]

A short story written by Eva Gore-Booth portrays objectors as disciples of Christ. The tale catalogues the injustices of the tribunal system by depicting one such body at work.[81] It ends with a clergyman member questioning an applicant on conscience grounds who is, just like those who have gone before him, refused exemption. But in the visionary close to the story the identity of this applicant is revealed: 'it is Someone I have been hoping all my life to meet – people said He would come again, but, indeed, I never thought to find Him here'.[82] Others saw the religious COs as saintly men. For example, James described the objector as bearing a symbolic testament of his beliefs:

It is only those whose spiritual explorations result, as did those of Francis of Assisi, in some kind of bodily stigmata who can be credited with adventuring the whole man.

The Conscientious Objector's enterprise is mainly of a spiritual and moral character. But he has not failed the physical test. He bears on his body the stigmatic of Peace.[83]

Here the CO is portrayed as bearing the stigmata of Christ. Thus, supporters of objectors sought to claim this image, with its deep significance, for themselves.

Further, for Christian COs their ill-treatment in society, the tribunals, the military and, in particular, the use of Field Punishment No. 1 ('Crucifixion') in the army was a poignant reminder of their beliefs and perhaps served as a reinforcement of the rightness of their path. Max Plowman notes the ill-advised imagery suggested by this punishment: '[w]ouldn't the army do well to avoid punishments which remind men of the Crucifixion?'[84] Imprisonment also drew parallels with biblical stories. For example, as Baker observes, once in civilian prisons they had literally '[f]allen among thieves' and like Christ on the cross, they were placed in cells between thieves and murderers.[85] Moreover, many saw the tribunal and court martial hearings that they faced as providing an opportunity to bear witness to their faith. Indeed, John Rae suggests that most Quakers who refused the tribunal decision were probably doing so to witness against conscription.[86] For James the tribunal hearing involved the public 'profession of faith before those who openly mocked that faith' which he sees not only a means to weed out 'slackers' but as an 'initiation', as '[a] conviction for which one has to endure public scorn becomes doubly precious'.[87] He goes further arguing that

When Tribunals arraigned the Conscientious Objectors before them they initiated them into the Church of saints and martyrs, prophets and reformers. When Militarism laid sacrilegious hands on these youths it ordained them to the apostolate of Human Brotherhood.[88]

In addition, sometimes the portrayal of the heroic religious objector utilised the image of the Christian soldier; however, these were warriors who would not fight – at least in the conventional sense of violence and warfare. Thus, Maude Royden emphasises the image of objectors as Christian soldiers battling for a different cause:

This warfare is the most heroic of all, and heroism will always move mankind. . . . Well, I tell you that there is a mightier heroism still – the heroism not of the sword, but the cross; the adventure not of war but of peace. For which is the braver man when all is said – the man who believes in armaments, or the man who stakes everything in an idea? Who is the greater adventurer – he who goes against the enemy with swords and guns, or he who goes with naked hands?[89]

The soldierly CO

The pacifist is fighting too, but on another front. The warrior and the pacifist correspond to different types, fighting for different reasons.[90]

As this narrative along with the above quotation begins to suggest, objectors were not always viewed as being the antithesis of the idealised soldier and the characteristics he was supposed to embody. Examining the issue of motivation can further disrupt the supposedly oppositional manliness/unmanliness of the soldier and the objector. The brave CO, like the exemplary volunteer, was acting upon his conscience and doing his duty by following his beliefs, whilst the conscript was merely doing what he was told. Thus, as recruitment propaganda was keen to emphasise:

[a] free man enlisting will carry with him all his days the honourable pride of having done so. The conscript will get no credit either from his conscience or from public opinion for his forced services.[91]

Thus, both volunteers and COs stood for active rather than passive manliness; volunteers came forward, objectors refused to come forward. Both made their own choices, whilst conscripts merely obeyed state compulsion; their passive patriotism only became active because of conscription.[92] Ilana R. Bet-El notes this distinction between conscripts and volunteers, observing that the way in which men wrote about their entry into the military could often reflect passive acceptance and resignation versus a more active account. For example, two men's diary entries provide illustrations of the manner in which some conscripts greeted their papers:

Received calling up notice from Croydon Recruiting Office.
In the December of the year 1916, I reached the age of 18. In the following March I was duly enlisted.

Although, as Bet-El observes, neither all volunteers nor all conscripts had the same responses to or understanding of what they were doing or why, there is a tendency for volunteers, like objectors, to describe taking a positive decision to join up, whilst conscripts tend merely to record their obedience.[93] In addition, in the cases of both volunteers and COs their decisions to act were often seen as a rite of passage or initiation; for young men joining up was a means of becoming a man and for objectors, religious and political alike, objection could be a means of achieving masculinity as well as a profession of faith or conviction.[94]

The N-CF often promoted the similarities between the volunteer and the CO, although, whilst it was recognised that both suffered, the greater hardship and dangers faced by the former were carefully acknowledged. Thus, in one pamphlet the call to arms was phrased as follows: 'let the example of those who have gone out at great sacrifice in response to what they felt to be their highest duty, inspire us to follow . . . the call of conscience . . . with the same enthusiasm and devotion.[95] Indeed, the Fellowship's aim was to 'sacrifice as much in the cause of the World's peace as our fellows are sacrificing in the cause of the nation's war'.[96] Similarly, in April 1916 Clifford Allen, Chairman of the N-CF, acknowledged the common suffering of the soldier and the objector:

> We, representing thousands of men who cannot participate in warfare and are subject to the Military Service Act, unite in comradeship with those of our number who are already suffering for conscience sake in prison or the hands of the military. We appreciate the spirit of sacrifice which actuates those who are suffering on the battlefield, and in that spirit we renew our determination, whatever the penalties awaiting us, to undertake no service which for us is wrong . . .'[97]

The N-CF, as well as individual objectors and their supporters, also often used military terminology and the language of war to describe their cause. James writes of the solidarity of all those who 'fought the good fight' and quotes John Hubert Bert Brocklesby, one of the objectors sentenced to death in France, who is proud to be one of 'the noble army' who are 'engaged in the most glorious struggle that has ever been fought – bar NONE'.[98] Similarly, George Thomas writes of 'that other army, the army of anti-militarists in guard-rooms, prison, and work-centre'.[99] Even after the war such militaristic language persisted. Thus, particularly in the immediate aftermath of the war, there was a tendency to celebrate the triumphant victory of objectors in standing out throughout the conflict. Allen at the end of November 1919 at an N-CF meeting at Devonshire House made a victory speech stating that:

[w]e are proud, to have broken the power of the military authority
... We have defeated it; we will defeat it again if conscription should
be continued.[100]

In a similar vein, Bertrand Russell describes the N-CF triumph at a
reunion:

[the Fellowship] has been completely victorious in its stand for
freedom not to kill or to take part in killing . . . You have won a
victory for the sense of human worth, for the realisation of the value
of each individual soul.[101]

Military unmanliness

In contrast to these positive constructions of the objector, the
portrait of the soldier can be depicted very differently to the admirable and brave manly ideal represented elsewhere in this volume.
Indeed, in this version of the war story merely wearing a uniform
was not enough to ensure that men in the military would live up
to the cultural image of the soldier, and degeneracy, dishonour
and cowardice lurked beneath many a khaki coat. Thus, once
men found themselves in military hands their manliness was by no
means assured. For example, the numbers of men who were judged
to be unfit for service or fit only for limited duties was a matter
of concern to the authorities. These men heightened the anxieties
about racial decline and, more specifically, physical degeneration
that had previously been highlighted in the Boer War[102] (and were
often associated with the CO). As a result, in 1919 the Ministry
of National Service reported that 'War is a stern taskmaster . . . It
has compelled us to take stock of the health and physique of our
manhood; this stock-taking has brought us face to face with ugly
facts'.[103] As recruiters and medical examiners became increasingly
desperate for men and relaxed the physical criteria for fitness,
these problems could be seen in the military. One officer recalled
that:

Whether Volunteers, Derbyites or Conscripts, the average physique
was good enough, but the total included an astonishing number of
men whose narrow or misshapen chests, and other deformities or
defects, unfitted them to stay the more exacting requirements of
service in the field . . . Route marching, not routine tours of trench
duty, made recurring casualties of these men.[104]

Indeed, as a result of the unfitness of large numbers of military men, many spent their war performing non-combatant duties, sometimes alongside objectors in the Non-Combatant Corps. Some remained at home because they were deemed incapable of work overseas and others who were passed for military service 'had to be sent back' or, in extreme cases, discharged.[105]

There was also official evidence of the sexual inversion (again suggesting degeneracy as well as decadence) with which COs were sometimes associated. Samuel Hynes cites army statistics which record that, between 1914 and 1919, 22 officers and 270 other ranks were court-martialed for gross indecency.[106] Yet soldiers were meant to epitomise exemplary manliness and war was supposed to purge degeneracy, decadence and inversion and so improve the race.

Moreover, contrary to evolutionist and Darwinian ideas about war as a project of (re)masculinisation, it soon became evident that, although some men were 'improved' by war,[107] it was often the fittest of the race and those who were intensely patriotic who were dying or returning from the conflict physically and psychologically wounded. In fact, it is in this context and in relation to Great War soldiers that the term 'unmen', employed previously in this text to refer to representations of the objector, was originally used. Thus, as Sandra M. Gilbert notes, 'Paradoxically, . . . the war to which so many men had gone in hope of becoming heroes ended up emasculating them'; they had become '*un*men'.[108]

The dysgenic vision favoured by some opponents of war seemed to resonate with this evidence. Despite this it was still widely assumed that soldiering along with war improved men and could weed out or 'cure' the physically unfit along with shirkers and COs, hence improving the race. Thus, medical examiners frequently passed men whose physical abilities were at least doubtful in the belief that the military would soon (re)masculinise them[109] and, although some men in the military noticed an improvement in both their physique and their health arising from their training, war was not so kind to many men's bodies (and minds).[110]

Indeed, the existence of so-called 'shell-shock' or 'soldier's heart' provides another disruption of the dominant images of the supposedly glorious military man; according to official figures around 200,000 men were affected.[111] The condition, once it was identified, was initially suppressed by the authorities in the interests of preserving discipline at the Front, preventing false claims and hiding the psychological harms of war.[112] Subsequently, it became politically expedient to accept the reality that shell-shock was an illness rather than a sign of war resistance, moral degeneracy or cowardice.[113] However, the existence of this neurosis could be said to suggest the mental fragility of manhood. Indeed, it has been conceived of as one of the feminising effects of war, as a form of resistance to the war and as a male protest against dominant notions of manliness.[114] Thus, war, the 'most masculine of enterprises', represented the 'apocalypse of masculinism', feminising soldiers through the experience of shell-shock.[115] Men, it seemed, rather than thriving on warfare, had actually caught the 'female malady', hysteria, in the trenches. Their reason and manliness were softened rather than proved and toughened by fighting; they were degenerating.[116] Yet, on the Home Front during the war the image of the *un*man was popularly associated with the civilian and CO man rather than the soldier.

Also, men at the Front, far from enjoying the adventure that they had been promised, resisted service and sometimes damaged their bodies in order to escape the intolerable conditions. Joanna Bourke discusses the many ways of shirking and malingering including self-injury, deliberate infection or feigned illnesses.[117] She quotes one frontline malingerer, who had repeatedly been absent without leave, then tried feigning madness and finally got himself run over. Describing his efforts he explains:

I started to scheme, how the hell can I work my ticket and get out of this bloody war . . . I admit I am a coward, a bloody, bleeding coward, and I want to be a live Coward than a dead blasted Hero [sic].[118]

Indeed, soldiers shirked their duties or refused to comply in numerous ways, committing offences against military law, disobeying orders, going on strike, mutinying or deserting.[119] As a consequence, many suffered the kinds of official and unofficial punishments experienced by objectors in attempts to cure them or deter others. In addition, soldiers who refused to behave as soldiers were, like the CO in the military, a danger to discipline and also, should their stories become widely known, to the perception of the war at home.

Even misconduct of the most serious kinds was not that uncommon. Thus, although official figures state that around 300 men were shot following court martial, they also suggest that this represented around 10 percent of the death sentences passed. Further, studies

have concluded that many more men faced charges that potentially carried a capital sentence. These gaps between the actual and
potential use of the death penalty are, in part, explained by the fact
that capital punishment was seen as providing a deterrent to other
military men but its widespread use was discouraged; its use for all
capital offences might have sparked mutiny and would have implied
that many Englishmen at the Front were not heroes.[120]

Furthermore, as some of the poetry of the Great War illustrates,
soldiers could have doubts about the war and the way it was being
conducted, yet they were generally portrayed at home as being
proudly at the front line of the national effort. Of the doubters, officers were best placed to register their views. Siegfried Sassoon's story
is well known. He made a public protest about the 'errors' and 'insin-
cerities' which were resulting in loss of life and injury,[121] seeing this
as 'an act of wilful defiance of military authority'. In consequence,
he was placed in a military hospital where he could cause less trouble
and his stance could be put down to shell-shock, although subsequently he returned to the Front to be with his men.[122]

There were other officers who changed their views about war
or the Great War and resigned their commissions. These men were
court-martialled and discharged or were sent before a tribunal,
whereas men in the ranks who expressed such a change of heart
were more likely to be punished and at the Front were liable to be
shot. Max Plowman followed the former course, citing conscientious objection as his motivation.[123] In contrast, Lieutenant H.S.
Buss was permitted to return home and apply for exemption on the
grounds of conscientious objection.[124]

Other soldiers also doubted the rightness of the conflict. One of
the most famous of these, Wilfred Owen, wrote the following:

> I am more and more a Christian as I walk the unchristian ways of
> Christendom . . . Passivity at any price! Suffer dishonour and disgrace;
> but never resort to arms. Be bullied, be outraged, be killed; but do not
> kill . . . I think pulpit professionals are ignoring it [this principle] very
> skilfully and successfully indeed . . .
> Am I not myself a conscientious objector with a very seared con-
> science?
> Christ is literally in no man's land.[125]

He adds that men on all sides hear Christ's voice, concluding, in
words similar to CO Willie Campbell, that 'pure Christianity will
not fit in with pure patriotism'.

As the above discussion suggests, soldiers' experiences were often very far removed from the stories widely circulated at home. Tony Ashworth has also described a reality that was very different from the tales of heroism at the Front. He argues that troops on the Western Front operated a 'live and let live' system, seeking to limit danger.[126] Indeed, even when there was evidence of bravery, contrary to popular knowledge, the military sometimes actually sought to discourage it; courageous acts were by no means a universal good in military terms. For example, Field Marshall Sir Douglas Haig records a conversation with the King on 4 December 1914. The monarch suggested that the Victoria Cross should be awarded to men who carried the wounded out of battle. Haig was forced to explain that this was not such a good idea and that he had in fact already taken steps to stop this kind of act becoming too widespread in order to avoid further loss of life or injury:

> As a matter of fact we have to take special precautions during a battle to post police, to prevent more unwounded men than are necessary from accompanying a wounded man back from the firing line![127]

In addition, soldiers' lives were often characterised by extreme depravity, horror, fear and sometimes boredom, rather than by the honourable deeds which they had been promised. In consequence, both the war and trench life have been argued to have had a feminising effect upon soldiers. For example, being a soldier removed the ability for the lower ranks to control their lives and trench life in some ways arguably domesticated them – not least as they had to undertake tasks, such as darning, laundry and tea-making, which had feminine associations. The result was a femininity and an enforced passivity which again posits the image of the soldier rather than the CO as an unman.[128]

Beyond this, other dissonant ideas inhabit and taint the idealised image of the First World War soldier. Both during the war and subsequently much has been made of the comradeship of soldiers and the importance of the strong bonds between fighting men. However, men in the military have sometimes refuted such claims as Joanna Bourke argues.[129] Indeed, new soldiers came from vastly different backgrounds and sometimes had little common ground.[130] In addition, conscripts were by no means universally welcomed by the military. Officers had already had a hard task of training enthusiastic but inexperienced volunteers. Once conscription began the

training camps had to cope with reluctant men from a wide variety
of backgrounds. Moreover, as these were men who had failed to
come forward they were likely, at least initially, to be unpopular
with regulars and volunteers. As David Lloyd George notes:

> The army in the field felt strongly that those at home who would not
> come out otherwise should be fetched, and while . . . the conscripts
> might at first have to put up with a certain measure of chaff and
> ragging, this would soon pass, and the difference in their conditions
> of enlistment be forgotten.[131]

In this context the portrait of the support, camaraderie and close
comradeship between objectors which was described in the previous chapter can be placed in sharp contrast to this view of the
differences and distances between soldiers.

Also, it was not only objectors who found the apparently jingoistic mood of the country difficult to understand and deal with
and, consequently, felt themselves to be outsiders. For soldiers, who
were meant to embody an idealised patriotic manliness, the fervour
and enthusiasm for war which they sometimes witnessed at home
could seem strange. As the discussion above has briefly suggested,
their experiences were very different from those presented to the
public. Indeed, the conflict was distorted and glamorised to such
an extent that Robert Graves, home from the Front having been
injured, commented that:

> England was strange to a returning soldier, he could not understand
> the war madness that ran about everywhere looking for a pseudo
> military outlet.[132]

In addition, military men could have a particular scepticism for
the press:

> Don't believe the stories which you see in the papers about troops
> asking as a special privilege not to be relieved. We stick it, at all costs
> if necessary, as long as ordered, but everyone's glad to hand over to
> someone else. Any anyone who says he enjoys this kind of thing is
> either a liar or a madman.[133]

Thus, some warrior men, for a whole variety of reasons and in a
number of different ways, patently failed to conform to the image
constructed for them. But, of course, while men in the military
were likely to be all too aware of these realities, they were, as far
as possible, hidden from those on the Home Front. The need to

maintain both morale and the image of the soldier meant that information needed to be policed. Indeed, just as positive portrayals of the objector and anti-conscription propaganda were suppressed or feared, so too were negative depictions of the soldier. Such censorship was never going to be entirely successful. However, stories of unmen in the military tended not to gain widespread publicity during the war, given the tight control over the press, publishers and printers. However, Rose Macaulay's 1916 novel *Non-Combatants and Others* reveals that those on the Home Front were not all totally unaware of the unmanhood of some soldiers.[134] The book describes the less than noble army record and death of the heroine's brother, who 'went all to bits and lost his pluck', tried to get himself injured then, having failed, fatally shot himself. The true tale of his death had been hidden from his sibling but is accidentally revealed to her.[135]

Such silencings of less than honourable stories was partially motivated by a wish to protect relatives, but it was also important if morale was to be maintained. Thus, families were told tales of valour, reputations remained unsullied and campaign medals were awarded to those who died an 'honourable' death on a battlefield. In some cases the reality was somewhat different and the public story of a soldier's death could mask all number of unfortunate, mundane and less than heroic ends such as an unreported suicide, alcohol poisoning, drowning in mud, or the outcome of an accident.[136]

Conclusion

In this the final tale-telling about First World War COs the objector is depicted as acting in the interests of his country and sometimes he is a man for the nation to feel pride in. This portrayal of the CO as patriot poses a stark contrast to the image of the traitor seeking the nation's downfall through revolution or German conquest presented earlier in this text. In addition, here the objector is constructed as courageous in facing uncertainty and adversity. Sometimes, indeed, he was depicted as a saintly religious figure, as a Christian soldier fighting for God or as a martyr suffering for his beliefs. In contrast, very different depictions of the military man are proffered from those sketched elsewhere in this text. Thus, in this chapter it appears that the CO embodies the iconic characteristics of the military man, whereas the image of the soldier is besmirched by cowardice, unconscientiousness and unmanliness. Such celebratory accounts of the objector are reflected in

14 Conscientious Objector Stone, Tavistock Square, London. The main text reads 'TO ALL THOSE WHO HAVE ESTABLISHED AND ARE MAINTAINING THE RIGHT TO REFUSE TO KILL. Their foresight and courage give us hope.'

subsequent remembrances of such men. Illustrations of this are provided by the Conscientious Objector Stone in Tavistock Square, London, which was dedicated on 15 May 1994, and by the fact that this date is now designated International Conscientious Objectors' Day.

Notes

1 W.P. Byles in Universal Peace Congress, 1904, p. 117, quoted in Heloise Brown, *'The Truest Form of Patriotism' Pacifist Feminism in Britain, 1870–1902* (Manchester: Manchester University Press, 2003), p. 183.

2 Clifford Allen, Chair of the No-Conscription Fellowship, 'Preface', in John W. Graham, *Conscription and Conscience: A History 1916–1919* (London: George Allen and Unwin, 1922, reprinted 1971), p. 23.

3 *Ibid.*

4 See, for example, Brown, *'The Truest Form of Patriotism'*, especially pp. 8, 179–83. See further Sandi E. Cooper, *Patriotic Pacifism:*

Waging War on War in Europe, 1815–1914 (Oxford: Oxford University Press, 1991).

5 However, unsurprisingly, 'military thinkers' tended to steer away from this idea. See John Gooch, *The Prospect of War: Studies in British Defence Policy 1847–1942* (London: Frank Cass, 1981), p. 40.

6 Priscilla Peckover, *Peace and Goodwill: A Sequel to the Olive Leaf* (16 October 1899), p. 97, cited in Brown, 'The Truest Form of Patriotism', p. 1.

7 For example, socialist and atheist objector Arthur Gardiner told the Local Tribunal 'I have no country', *The Worker* (25 March 1916), quoted in Cyril Pearce, *Comrades in Conscience: The Story of an English Community's Opposition to the Great War* (London: Francis Boutle, 2001), p. 253.

8 Indeed, the tendency for socialists and internationists to see themselves as patriots and to consciously seek to portray themselves as such was by no means a new phenomenon. For example, see Krishan Kumar, *The Making of English National Identity* (Cambridge: Cambridge University Press, 2003), pp. 213–15.

9 George Baker, *The Soul of a Skunk: The Autobiography of a Conscientious Objector* (London: Eric Partridge at the Scholartis Press, 1930), p. x.

10 *Ibid.*, pp. 270, 273.

11 *Ibid.*, p. 173.

12 Letter from William Campbell to his parents, dated November 1915, privately owned, pp. 3–4.

13 Mabel Annie Saint Clair Stobart, *The Flaming Sword in Serbia and Elsewhere* (London: Hodder & Stoughton, 1916), pp. 315–16. See also, Stobart, *War and Women: From Experience in the Balkans and Elsewhere . . . With a preface by Viscount Esher* (London: Bell & Sons, London, 1913).

14 Once war began and she had elected to change her view it was Germany that was the masculine nation, with France and Belgium cast in her eyes as non-violent feminine victims. Her pro-war stance is illustrated, for example, by her calls for men to join up – for example see Pankhurst, quoted in Andio Linklater, *An Unhusbanded Life: Charlotte Despard, Suffragette, Socialist and Sinn Féiner* (London: Hutchinson 1980), p. 177. See also Dame Christabel Pankhurst, *Unshackled: The Story of How We Won the Vote*, ed. Hon. Lord Pethick-Lawrence of Peaslake (London: Hutchinson, 1959), p. 288. On the maleness of Germany see, for example, Pankhurst quoted in Andrew Rosen, *Rise Up Women! The Militant Campaign of the Women's Social and Political Union, 1903–1914* (London: Routledge and Kegan Paul, 1974), p. 251.

15 *The Suffragette* (19 June 1914), p. 163. On women's resistance to

war and, more generally, militarism (both during and before the 1914–18 conflict) see also, for example: Margaret Kamester and Jo Vellacott (eds), *Militarism Versus Feminism: Writings on Women and War* (London: Virago, 1987); Brown, *'The Truest Form of Patriotism'*; Jill Liddington, *The Long Road to Greenham: Feminism and Anti-Militarism in Britain since 1820* (London: Virago, 1989) pp. 1–129; Anne Wiltshire, *Most Dangerous Women: Feminist Peace Campaigners of the Great War* (London: Pandora, 1985); Sandra Gilbert, 'Maleness Run Riot: the Great War and Women's Resistance to Militarism', *Women's Studies International Forum*, 11:3 (1988), 199–210; Gertrude Bussey and Margaret Tims, *Pioneers for Peace: Women's International League for Peace and Freedom 1915–1965* (London: WILPF, British Section, 1980), chs 1 and 2; Jo Vellacott, 'Women and war in England: the case of Catherine E. Marshall and World War I', *Peace and Change*, 4:3 (1977), 13–17; Sybil Oldfield, *Women Against the Iron Fist: Alternatives to Militarism 1900–1989* (Oxford: Basil Blackwell, 1989), especially chs 3, 4.

16 See further Jo Vellacott, *From Liberal to Labour With Women's Suffrage: The Story of Catherine Marshall* (London: McGill-Queen's University Press, 1993).

17 Norman Angell, *The Great Illusion: A Study of the Relation of Military Power to National Advantage* (London, William Heinemann, 1913 – first printed 1909), p. 317.

18 Harry E. Stanton, 'Will You March Too? 1916–1919', unpublished account of a CO's experiences (privately owned), volume 1, pp. 1–3.

19 Edward Grubb, 'War resistance', in Julian H. Bell (ed.), *We Did Not Fight 1914–1918: Experiences of War Resisters* (London: Cobden Sanderson, 1935).

20 Stephen Hobhouse, 'Fourteen months service with the colours', in Bell (ed.), *We Did Not Fight*, pp. 157–9.

21 Quoted in Martin Gilbert, *Plough My Own Furrow: The Story of Lord Allen of Hurtwood as Told Through his Writings and Correspondence* (London: Longman, 1965), p. 105. Of course, it was in the N-CF's interests to portray their members as patriots in order to gain sympathy and respect for them and their cause.

22 Graham, *Conscription and Conscience*, dedication page.

23 Letter headed 'A CLASH OF CONSCIENCES', *The Nation* (15 April 1916), p. 76.

24 'THE CONSCIENTIOUS OBJECTOR. WORK IN FRANCE. A CONTENTED FORCE DOING USEFUL WORK', *The Times* (19 May 1916), p. 7.

25 5 HC 95, col. 338, 26 June 1917.

26 There could also, unsurprisingly, be different Welsh and Scottish takes

on what objection and allegiances to their own countries might mean. See, for example, William H. Marwick, 'Conscientious objection in Scotland in the First World War', *Scottish Journal of Science*, 1:3 (1972), 157–64.

27 For example, see Ralph James Q. Adams and Philip P. Poirier, *The Conscription Controversy in Great Britain, 1900–1918* (London: Macmillan, 1987), ch. 2.

28 At the same time, others (including the prominent National Service League) were harking back to the days of enforced service and calling for its return. In these appeals to older precedents military compulsion (in the form of shrieval summonses, commissions of array, mustering statutes, militia ordinances, ballots and impressments) was described as having formed a defining part of the country's culture in centuries past. For example, George Gordon Coulton dismissed the idea of a liberal recruiting tradition: 'for a couple of generations – not from all eternity as most Britons seem to think – our army has been a purely voluntary affair' – *A Strong Army in a Free State: Study of the Old English and Modern Swiss Militias* (London: Simpkin, 1900), p. 5. Similarly, Fossey John Cobb Hearnshaw described voluntarism as a 'recent humiliation' rather than a 'heritage' ('Compulsory military service in England', *Quarterly Review* (April 1916), 416–37). See also John William Fortescue, *The British Army, 1783–1801* (London: Macmillan, 1905) and *The County Lieutenancies and the Army 1803–1814* (London: Macmillan, 1908).

Later in 1918 Coulton set out the historical arguments more pointedly in *The Case for Compulsory Military Service* (London: Macmillan, 1918). In this view voluntarism was at best a very recent and untried departure and at its flimsiest 'a fantasy of nineteenth-century masculinity' (Ilana R. Bet-El, 'Men and soldiers: British conscripts, concepts of masculinity, and the Great War', in Billie Melman (ed.), *Borderlines: Genders and Identities in War and Peace 1870–1930* (London: Routledge, 1998), p. 89). Thus, for pro-conscriptionists the 'Whig interpretation' of the history of recruitment, epitomised by Sir John Simon's castigation of the Military Service Bill (discussed momentarily in the main body of the text in this chapter), was a historical myth that celebrated supposedly longstanding English liberties (For discussion of 'the Whig interpretation of history' see, for example: Kumar, *The Making of English National Identity*, pp. 202–7; Herbert Butterfield, *The Whig Interpretation of History* (G. Bell and Sons: London, 1931, p. v.).

29 Arthur Marwick, *Clifford Allen: The Open Conspirator* (London: Oliver and Boyd, 1964), p. 23.

30 Reproduced in M.H. Hale, *Volunteer Soldiers* (London: Kegan Paul and Co, 1900), title page (this is attributed to *Punch* – although no further information is given and the origins of the poem could not be located).

31 5 HC 77 col. 963, January 5, 1916.

32 5 HC 77 col. 974, January 5, 1916.

33 5 HC 77, January 12, 1916 col. 1657.

34 5 HC 77, cols 1684–1687, 12 January 1916.

35 Baker, *The Soul of a Skunk*, p. 173.

36 Friends Library, London, MS VOL 149, No-Conscription Fellowship: duplicated papers (hereafter 'N-CF duplicated papers'), 1914–1919, N-CF letter to members, 31 January 1919. The recognition of individual conscience was also frequently referred to as an intensely English liberal approach which was beyond the contemplation of Prussians. After all, objectors to the military and, more recently, compulsory smallpox vaccination had been recognised by Parliament before. See further Constance Braithwaite, *Conscientious Objection to Compulsions Under the Law* (York: William Sessions, 1995), chs 1–3.

37 Henry Wood Nevinson, 'The conscientious objector', *Atlantic Monthly* 103:695 (November 1916), 686–94, 693.

38 Campbell, Letter, 1915.

39 *Ibid.*, p. 1.

40 *Ibid.*, p. 7.

41 Clifford Allen, 'Pacifism: then and now', in Bell (ed.), *We Did Not Fight*, p. 25.

42 B.N. Langdon-Davies, 'Alternative service', in Bell (ed.), *We Did Not Fight*, pp. 183, 184.

43 T. Edmund Harvey, 'Foreword' to J. Scott Duckers, *Handed Over: The Prison Experiences of Mr. J. Scott Duckers, Solicitor of Chancery Lane, Under the Military Service Act, Written by himself. With Foreword by T. Edmund Harvey* (London: C.W. Daniel, 1917), p. viii.

44 Bertrand Russell, 'Some psychological difficulties of pacifism', in Bell (ed.), *We Did Not Fight*, pp. 330, 329.

45 Stanley Bloomfield James, *The Men Who Dared: The Story of an Adventure* (London: C.W. Daniel, 1917), pp. 13–14.

46 Allen, 'Pacifism: then and now', p. 25.

47 James Primrose Malcolm Millar, 'A socialist in war time', in Bell (ed.), *We Did Not Fight*, pp. 226–7.

48 For example, see Stanton's account, 'Will You March Too? 1916–1919', pp. 114–37.

49 Langdon-Davies, 'Alternative service', p. 188.

50 James, *The Men Who Dared*, p. 7.

51 *Ibid.*, p. 23.

52 Duckers, *Handed Over*, p. 10.

53 Of course, COs and their supporters' depictions of objectors as heroic, honourable and true formed part of their strategies of resistance and challenge. Here a group that was perceived of as deviant and marginal

appropriated facets of a dominant ideology within their arguments and propaganda. The potential usefulness of such tactics as regards gender has been noted elsewhere. For example, R.W. Connell (via Wendy Chapkis's work on female beauty – *Beauty Secrets: Women and the Politics of Appearance* (Boston: South End Press, 1986)) suggests the subversive possibilities offered by 'playing with the elements of gender' by unpacking gendered concepts. By way of example he suggests that, given heroism is a core concept of hegemonic masculinity, representing gay men as heroic could form part of a project of social justice (*Masculinities* (Cambridge: Polity, 2nd edn, 2005), p. 234). However, this is a strategy with inherent limitations. Thus, COs, in seeking to inhabit the land of heroes, might have encouraged some sympathy for their plight and for their stance but in so doing they were also reinforcing the notion of heroism as a vital component of true manliness. So, by drawing upon existing narratives of manhood, objectors and their supporters were merely seeking to challenge the kinds of behaviour that were perceived of as being courageous, rather than the qualities associated with manhood (or, indeed, those associated with womanhood). Nevertheless, attempting to shift or confuse the meaning of key ideas about gender is a worthy project.

On the manipulation of ideas about objectors see further Cyril Pearce, '"Typical" conscientious objectors – a better class of conscience? No-Conscription Fellowship, image management and the Manchester contribution 1916–18', *Manchester Region History Review*, 17 (2004), 38–50, 46–7.

54 Marwick, *Clifford Allen*, p. 29.
55 *Ibid.*, p. 49.
56 Gilbert, *Plough My Own Furrow*, p. 62.
57 See Marwick, *Clifford Allen*, p. 36.
58 An objector recalling spending time with him in Winchester Prison hospital, quoted in *ibid.*, p. 88.
59 Julian Bell, Introduction, in Bell (ed.), *We Did Not Fight*, pp. xii, xv
60 *Ibid.*, p. xix.
61 'N-CF duplicated papers', *Agenda*, 1915, p. 6.
62 Marwick, *Clifford Allen*, p. 23.
63 Baker, *The Soul of a Skunk*, p. 187.
64 James, *The Men Who Dared*, pp. 6–7.
65 See, for example, *ibid.*, p. 9.
66 Quoted in *ibid.*, p. 95.
67 A.T. Fitzroy [Rose Allatini], *Despised and Rejected* (The Gay Men Press Publishers Ltd: London, 1988), p. 301. The novel was first published by C.W. Daniel Ltd (London).
68 John Buchan, *Mr Standfast* (London: Hodder & Stoughton, 1919).

The book has been reprinted several times – references here are to the 1994 version (Ware: Wordsworth Classics, 1994).

69 Buchan, *Mr Standfast*, pp. 189, 222.
70 *Ibid.*, p. 281.
71 Janet A. Smith, *John Buchan* (London: Rupert Hart-Davis, 1965), p. 259. For Smith's discussion of *Mr Standfast* see pp. 257–60.
72 5 HC 77, col. 957–8, 5 January 1916.
73 Letters to Buchan quoted in Smith, *John Buchan*, in Bell (ed.), *We Did Not Fight*, p. 260.
74 5 HC 95, col. 338, 26 June 1917.
75 See Olaf Stapledon, 'Experiences in the Friends Ambulance Unit' in Bell (ed.), *We Did Not Fight*, p. 370.
76 A. Fenner Brockway, 'WALTER ROBERTS', *The Tribunal* (14 September 1916), p. 2.
77 Paul Fussell, *The Great War and Modern Memory* (Oxford: Oxford University Press, 25th anniversary edn, 2000 – first published 1975), pp. 21–3. See Chapter 2 above.
78 James, *The Men Who Dared*, pp. 62–3, 72.
79 Francis McLellan Wilcox, *Seventh Day Adventists in Time of War* (Washington, DC: Review and Herald Pub. Association, 1936 – reprinted Whitefish, MT: Kessinger Publishing, 2006), pp. 290–1.
80 Dr Alfred Salter, September 1914, quoted in Peter Chrisp, *Conscientious Objectors: 1916 to the Present Day* (Brighton: Tressell, 1988), p. 6.
81 Eva Gore-Booth, 'The tribunal' in Graham, *Conscription and Conscience*, pp. 102–9.
82 *Ibid.*, p. 109.
83 James, *The Men Who Dared*, p. 32.
84 Max Plowman (Published under the pseudonym MARK VII), *A Subaltern on the Somme in 1916* (London, Dent & Sons, 1927), p. 29.
85 Baker, *The Soul of a Skunk*, p. 183.
86 John Rae, *Conscience and Politics: The British Government and the Conscientious Objector to Military Service 1916–1919* (London: Oxford University Press, 1970), p. 113.
87 Similar sentiments have been used to describe the tribunal as an initiation for socialist objectors (for example, see Pearce, *Comrades in Conscience*, p. 184).
88 James, *The Men Who Dared*, pp. 20–1.
89 Quoted in *ibid.*, p. 5.
90 John Rodker, 'Twenty years after', in Bell (ed.), *We Did Not Fight*, p. 285.
91 *To the Young Men of Ayrshire*, 12 July 1915, IWM K44699, quoted in William Joseph Reader, *'At Duty's Call': A Study in Obsolete Patriotism* (Manchester: Manchester University Press, 1988), p. 126. This was a

Scottish flyer but it neatly encapsulates the tone and sentiment of many of the materials which were circulating in Britain at this time.

92 Bet-El, 'Men and soldiers', p. 89.

93 Ibid., pp. 76–7. On the conscript see further Ilana R. Bet-El, *Conscripts: Lost Legions of the Great War* (Stroud: Sutton: 1999).

94 For example, see: James, *The Men Who Dared*, pp. 20–1; Pearce, *Comrades in Conscience*, p. 184.

95 'N-CF duplicated papers', *Why We Object*, n.d, p. 1.

96 The release of the manifesto was noted by the authorities monitoring pacifist and anti-war or anti-conscription activities; see National Archives, London (hereafter NA) HO 45/10786/297549/10, Home Office file on the wartime publications of the Independent Labour Party, 1915–17 (this includes documentation from the N-CF).

97 Quoted in Graham, *Conscription and Conscience*, p. 189.

98 James, *The Men Who Dared*, pp. 68, 67.

99 George Thomas, 'PRISON IMPRESSIONS', *The Worker* (22 September 1917), p. 3.

100 Quoted in Caroline Moorehead, *Troublesome People: Enemies of War: 1916–1986* (London: Hamilton, 1987), p. 78.

101 Quoted in *ibid.*, p. 79.

102 For example, see Joanna Bourke, *Dismembering the Male: Men's Bodies, Britain and the Great War* (London: Reaktion, 1996), pp. 171–2. On unfitness during the war see further Jay Murray Winter, 'Military Unfitness and Civilian Health in Britain During the First World War', *Journal of Contemporary History*, 15: 2 (1980), 211–44. The links made between degeneration and COs were noted in Chapter 3 above.

103 Ministry of National Service, *Report Upon the Physical Examination of Men of Military Age by National Service Medical Boards from November 1st, 1917 – October 31st, 1918*, Cmd. 504, 1919, p. 6.

104 Captain James Churchill Dunn, *The War the Infantry Knew: 1914–1919: A Chronicle of Service in France and Belgium* (London: P.S. King & Son Ltd, 1938), p. 245.

105 For example, see: Winter, 'Military Unfitness', 211–44, 221; 'SERVICE WITHOUT ARMS. NEW CORPS FOR CONSCIENTIOUS OBJECTORS', *The Times* (13 March 1916), p. 9. See further Clement Kinloch-Cooke, 'National Service: The National Register and After', *The Nineteenth Century*, 78:464 (1915), 792–807, 798.

106 Samuel Hynes, *A War Imagined: The First World War and English Culture* (London: Pimlico, 1922), p. 225. Jeffrey Weeks, looking at the history of same-sex relations in the army, notes that such conduct tended only to be addressed when it threatened to disrupt military hierarchies. See especially *Coming Out* (London: Quartet Books,1977), pp. 13, 34.

107 See Bourke, *Dismembering the Male*, pp. 174–5.
108 Sandra M. Gilbert, 'Soldier's heart: literary men, literary women, and the Great War', 8: 3 (1983) *Signs*: 422–50, 447–8, 423. See also, Gilbert and Susan Gubar, *No Man's Land: The Place of the Woman Writer in the Twentieth Century, Volume 2, Sexchanges* (New Haven, CT: Yale University Press, 1989), ch. 7, especially pp. 259–60. The latter is a fuller version of the Gilbert article.
109 See further Winter, 'Military unfitness', 218.
110 See Bourke, *Dismembering the Male*, pp. 174–5.
111 See Martin Stone, 'Shellshock and the psychologists', in W.F. Bynum, Roy Porter and Michael Shepherd (eds), *The Anatomy of Madness: Essays on the History of Psychiatry*, vol. 2 (London: Tavistock, 1985), p. 249.
112 Eric J. Leed, *No Man's Land: Combat and Identity in World War I* (Cambridge: Cambridge University Press, 1979), p. 166; Elaine Showalter, *The Female Malady: Women, Madness and English Culture, 1830–1980* (London: Virago, 1987), p. 170.
113 Leed, *No Man's Land*, p. 168.
114 See Showalter, *The Female Malady*, ch. 7. Showalter also considers shell-shock in the 1914–18 conflict in *Hystories: Hysterical Epidemics and Modern Culture* (London: Picador, 2nd edn. with a new preface, 1998), pp. 72–5.
115 Showalter, *The Female Malady*, p. 173.
116 On shell-shock and the Great War see also, for example: Peter Leese, *Shell Shock: Traumatic Neurosis and the British Soldiers of the First World War* (New York: Palgrave, 2002); Tracey Louise Loughran, 'Shell-shock in First World War Britain: An Intellectual and Medical History' (PhD dissertation, University of London, 2006). For more wide-ranging studies see: Ben Shephard, *A War of Nerves: Soldiers and Psychiatrists in the Twentieth Century* (London: Pimlico, 2002); Anthony Babington, *Shell Shock: A History of the Changing Attitudes to War Neurosis* (London: Leo Cooper, 1997).
117 Bourke, *Dismembering the Male*, pp. 81–6.
118 John William Rowarth quoted in *ibid.*, p. 99.
119 See, for example: Duckers, *Handed Over*, pp. 81–2, 93–4; Julian Putkowski, *British Army Mutineers 1914–1922* (London: Francis Boutle, 1998); Bourke, *Dismembering the Male*, pp. 78–81.
120 See: Bourke, *Dismembering the Male*, pp. 94–100; Anthony Babington, *For the Sake of Example: Capital Courts-Martial 1914–1920* (London: Leo Cooper in association with Secker & Warburg, 1983). However, when it came to the ranks (as opposed to the officer classes) death seems to have been imposed much more liberally. See further Julian Putkowski and Julian Sykes, *Shot at Dawn* (Barnsley: Wharncliffe, 1989).

121 See further 'AN OFFICER AND NERVE SHOCK', *The Times* (31 July 1917), p. 8.

122 See Siegfried Sassoon, *Memoirs of an Infantry Officer* (London: Faber and Faber, 1930), pp. 289–334.

123 Max Plowman, *Bridge Into the Future: Letters of Max Plowman*, ed. Dorothy Lloyd Plowman (London: Andrew Dakers, 1944), p. 772.

124 *The Friend* (10 May 1918), cited in James, *The Men Who Dared*, p. 19.

125 Letter c.16 May 1917, quoted in David Roberts, *Minds at War: The Poetry and Experience of the First World War* (Burgess Hill: Saxon, 1996), p. 147.

126 Tony Ashworth, *Trench Warfare 1914–1918: The Live and Let Live System* (London: Macmillan, 1980).

127 Quoted in Roberts, *Minds at War*, p. 129.

128 See (Percy) Wyndham Lewis's depictions of life even at the front lines *Blasting and Bombadiering* (London: Eyre & Spottiswoode, 1937). This text is discussed by Trudi Tate, *Women, Men and the Great War: An Anthology of Stories* (Manchester: Manchester University Press, 1995), p. 5. On the feminising effects of war see also: Showalter, *The Female Malady*, ch. 7, especially pp. 173–4; Gilbert, 'Soldier's heart', especially pp. 47–8; Bourke, *Dismembering the Male*, p. 133.

129 Bourke, *Dismembering the Male*, ch. 3, especially pp. 151–5.

130 Also, despite the fact that the 'Pals' regiments did at least place men from the same locale or workplace together, this often did not last. See, for example, *ibid.*, pp. 131, 170.

131 David Lloyd George, *War Memoirs of David Lloyd George*, vol. I (London: Odhams, 1938, first issued 1933), p. 434.

132 Robert Graves, *Goodbye To All That* (London: Jonathan Cape, 1929), p. 283.

133 Captain Harry Yoxall, 18th Battalion Kings Royal Rifle Corps quoted in Malcolm Brown, *Tommy Goes to War* (London: Dent, 1978), p. 128.

134 Rose Macaulay, *Non-Combatants and Others* (London: Methuen, 1986 – originally published London: Hodder and Stoughton, 1916).

135 *Ibid.*, p. 99.

136 For example, see Tate, *Women, Men*, p. 5 and Bourke, *Dismembering the Male*, p. 21. More generally on the harsh and mundane realities of soldiering see Lewis, *Blasting and Bombadiering*.

Part III

More about *Telling Tales*

Conclusion: of tales and constructions

Telling Tales About Men has sought to proffer neither *the history* nor *a history* of objectors during the First World War. Instead the text presents a series of *histories* of these men, with each chapter configured around particular constructions of objectors. Although the different narratives are linked by the reappearance of recurrent ideas, themes and dichotomies – such as (un)manliness, patriotism, deviance, danger, bravery and cowardice, the majority of the population versus the objector and the soldier versus the conscientious objector – they are also separate accounts. Thus, the text eschews both a single unitary narrative and a conventional closure. Given this unusual approach, it seems appropriate at this point briefly to focus upon some of the thinking that has shaped *Telling Tales* (whilst the Introduction also includes some consideration of this issue, a full discussion of influences and the choice of methods is a task for another day).

As noted in the Introduction, a number of fields of study have informed this book. This is evidenced by the range of sources referenced within its pages, but is also foundational in terms of the book's structure and approach. Not insignificant amongst the various influences upon *Telling Tales* is the author's 'home' discipline, law. Legal studies suggest the device of presenting research through the medium of a number of different narratives about the same people and events. In the paradigmatic legal institution, the criminal jury trial, various people – the suspect, alleged victim, witnesses, including expert witnesses – all tell their versions of the same events and give their accounts of the same characters (insofar as the rules of evidence will allow). Barristers and solicitor advocates, in presenting their case and in their closing speeches, construct and propound their own version of what happened and depict the various players

– in particular, the defendant, the victim and any key witnesses. Judges in summing up adopt a similar approach, although they should effectively be presenting two versions of the same tale – that of the prosecution and defence. Similarly, in explaining their decisions in appeal cases, judges often present versions of events and a portrayal of the key players. In the legal sphere this is known as 'fact construction' and there are techniques involved in practising this skill. Thus, in presenting a particular version of a case lawyers will look to create a coherent story. In this they will include representations of the different people involved and will deploy various devices to reinforce the narrative, such as familiar conceptions of, or stereotypes about, types of people (not least gendered stereotypes). Consequently, different constructions of events and people that run concurrently are central to the practice of law.[1]

The thematic, multi-narrative approach in *Telling Tales* is also informed by an understanding that in representing what happened, there can be no single way of describing the past – whether the research and writing be humanities or social sciences based. To put it another way, 'things happen' and then they 'get told' and these are two ontologically separate things 'which narrative only *seems* to collapse into a voraciously all-encompassing discourse'. Consequently, there is a need to acknowledge 'the role of the . . . narrator', be they historian or social scientist, 'in bringing us the facts'.[2] This means that no one definitive representation of events is possible, although '"competing narratives" can be assessed, criticised and ranked on the basis of their fidelity to the factual record'.[3]

Thus, for historians and others, the representations of the same events and characters can take very different forms.[4] The structure of this book responds to these ideas by presenting a series of interlinked but sometimes contradictory *histories* rather than one unified *history*; *Telling Tales* has consciously fashioned constructions of and told tales about objectors.[5]

Notes

1 On fact construction in law see, for example, Donald Nicolson, 'Truth, reason and justice: epistemology and politics in evidence discourse', *Modern Law Review*, 57:5 (1994), 726–44, 737–9. For examinations of fact construction (and gender) in cases see, for example: Donald Nicolson, 'Telling tales: gender discrimination, gender construction and

battered women who kill', *Feminist Legal Studies* 3:2 (1995), 185–206; Josephine Winter, 'The truth will out? The role of judicial advocacy and gender in verdict construction', *Social and Legal Studies*, 11:3 (2002), 343–67. The inspiration for *Telling Tale*'s title is, in part, taken from Nicolson.

2 James E. Young, 'Towards a received history of the Holocaust', History and Theory, 36:4 (1997), 21–43, 34.

3 *Ibid.*, pp. 24, 23–5 and see generally Hayden White, 'Historical emplotment and the problem of truth', in Saul Friedlander (ed.), *Probing the Limits of Representation: Nazism and the 'Final Solution'* (London: Harvard University Press, 1992).

4 See further, in particular, the work of Hayden White on history writing, tropes and narrative. For example: 'Historical emplotment'; *The Content of Form: Narrative Discourse and Historical Representation* (London: Johns Hopkins University Press, 1987); *Metahistory: The Historical Imagination in Nineteenth-Century Europe* (Baltimore, MA: Johns Hopkins University Press, 1973).

5 Thus, as this very short discussion might suggest, *Telling Tales About Men* takes a broadly postmodern turn via literary studies and, thus, falls into the deconstructionist genre of (history) writing. However, as indicated above, this does not entail that *Telling Tales* adopts an antirealist approach. Nor does the author accept other related stereotypical and erroneous depictions/criticisms of postmodern history, such as the ideas that postmodern approaches are (wholly) relativistic, nihilistic and that there is only representation (the misinterpretation of Jacques Derrida's oft recited idea that 'there is nothing outside of the text': Derrida, *Of Grammatology*, trans. Gayatri Chakravorty Spivak (Baltimore, MD: Johns Hopkins University Press, 1976 – first published in French in 1967), p. 158). On the contrary, to reiterate the perspective adopted in the present text: 'things' really do 'happen' but they can be portrayed in, as James E. Young puts it, 'any number' of narratives' ('Towards a received history', p. 34). Or, to be clear, we need to draw a: 'distinction between the brute *events* of the past and the historical *facts* we construct out of them. Facts are events to which we have given meaning. Different historical perspectives therefore derive different facts from the same events.' Linda Hutcheon, *The Politics of Postmodernism* (London: Routledge, 1989), p. 57. On such criticisms of postmodernism and postmodern histories see, in particular, Keith Jenkins, 'A postmodern reply to Perez Zagorin', *History and Theory* 39:2 (2000), 181–200 (this focuses upon the work of Derrida). Jenkins also suggests that postmodern histories might take very different forms from the types of histories which the likes of Zagorin defend.

Epilogue: on origins and autobiography

I have chosen to include one final tale-telling in this volume and, in doing so, to highlight some of the less academic influences upon *Telling Tales About Men*. The book's beginnings lie not only in the theoretical concerns (discussed to some degree in the Introduction and Conclusion) but also in the stories I remember hearing from a young age; indeed, autobiography as well as theory led to the structure and approach adopted within these pages. Some of these anecdotes about the past related to the Great War, the Second World War and National Service. As family histories would have it, these reminiscences recounted tales of men and women who adopted diametrically opposed stances and took very different courses when it came to war and the military. The following narrative draws primarily upon my own recollections but is also constructed from family papers along with conversations and interviews with my parents conducted during the writing of this book.[1]

My mother, Suzanne, came from a family with military connections. Her paternal grandfather, James Welsh, was a Royal Marine. Her father, Charles Edward, along with his brothers went to the Royal Marine School in Stonehouse Barracks, Plymouth. Charles volunteered for the Royal Navy at the beginning of the First World War, joining his brother, James, who had already chosen the Navy as his career. They served together on HMS Valiant at the Battle of Jutland (31 May–1 June 1916). Their brother William also volunteered, serving in the army. By the end of the war Charles had reached the rank of Second Lieutenant and had transferred to the Royal Naval Air Service Fleet. He subsequently left the military but remained a reservist throughout the inter-war years. On Sunday 3 September 1939 war broke out, he received a recall notice and set out immediately for the Royal Air

Force Cadet College at Cranwell in Lincolnshire. He remained there for the early months of the war and then moved back to Plymouth, becoming Captain of a battalion of the Home Guard. James was still in the military in 1939 and served in the Navy throughout the conflict. He remained in the Navy until he retired. William was seriously ill in 1939 so did not serve and, in fact, died during the war. Suzanne's mother, Gladys Jane, supported her husband and the family, taking a fuller role in running the family business. In addition, she willingly contributed to the war effort through civil defence work, undertaking fire-watching.[2]

According to the story he told in his later years, it was much to his regret that my paternal grandfather, John, was too young to serve in the First World War. In the Second World War he was engaged on the land in food production and, thus, he was exempt from service but subsequently expressed some jealousy of his siblings who saw active service in Africa, Italy, France and Germany. He did, however, join the Home Guard and told tall tales about his escapades. Two of his younger brothers, George and Frank, served in the army. Both were at El Alamein, took part in the recapture of Monte Cassino and arrived in France shortly after D-Day, ending the war in Germany. After the conflict both brothers went back to civilian life. George, in particular, was deeply affected by his experiences. He did not like to talk about the war and vowed that none of his children would ever be soldiers. His uniform and medals were boxed up and whenever the British Legion called asking him to march in Poppy Day parades he firmly refused.

My father, Graham, was called for National Service in 1948. He and his mother, Lottie, were Christian pacifists and felt that he should register a conscientious objection and become a conscientious objector (CO).[3] Years later Lottie recalled her sense of injustice and oppression when recounting stories of women handing out white feathers to men without a military uniform and the illtreatment of such men during the First World War. In addition, it seemed that Lottie's socialism entailed scepticism of wars started by the ruling classes. In her eyes they resulted in the suffering of the workers both during a conflict and beyond when wounded men and the men, women and children left bereft from loss, far from being fully provided for, tended to be discarded and forgotten. However, my grandfather was strongly opposed to the idea of his son refusing to serve. Graham recalls that when the issue of objection was

15 Photographs of the author's family: (clockwise from top left) Charles Welsh during the First World War; James Welsh during the First World War; William Welsh during the First World War; Suzanne Welsh on a boat to Holland, 1937; Frank Bibbings, Second World War; George Bibbings, Second World War; Graham (left) and Stewart Bibbings, mid-1940s; Gladys Jane Welsh, circa 1930; John Bibbings, late 1930s; centre image – Lottie Luxton (subsequently Bibbings), circa 1920.

raised John 'was just agin it', as the idea of refusing to serve was outside his comprehension and his son imagines that he thought it both undignified and unmanly. The difference of opinion continued and was raised again when Graham's younger brother (Stewart) received his papers, although there was no major family split. Once Graham's stance became more widely known he experienced negative reactions from colleagues, his boss, his trade union representative, his community, his church and his (Methodist) minister. Allegations of cowardice were common and his minister found his behaviour 'disgraceful' and 'condemned COs'. However, he found support from the Plymouth (Open) Brethren and became one of their number.

In January 1949, aged 18 and working for the Great Western Railway, Graham appeared before a tribunal and obtained exemption from military service conditional upon his obtaining suitable alternative work. Graham remembers his hearing at the Bristol Appeal Tribunal and his preparation for this daunting event. His and his mother's preparatory notes illustrate that he framed his stance in terms of Christian pacifism and his words resonate with those of Willie Campbell writing in 1915 (see Chapters 1, 4 and 5 above), although he rejects love of his country, seeing himself as having only 'one citizenship to hold and to maintain and it is not earthly and national for my citizenship is in Heaven'. His papers and recollections show that he revered those men who had gone before; they were pacifist heroes and had been COs in Christ's name. In particular, Brethren Pastor Allen, who had been an absolutist in the First World War, scared but also inspired Graham with his stories of ill-treatment and imprisonment.

Once conditionally exempted he was helped by Quaker Gilbert Wride, who put him in contact with a fellow Friend, who had also been a CO. Francis Lawson owned a large market garden business and Graham recalls his 'great kindness' in employing him along with another CO (a British Broadcasting Corporation newsreader). Graham recalls spending twenty months at the market garden[4] and that he was extremely well treated, although non-Quaker workers did not tend to be friendly. However, there was sympathy for his situation. Thanks to a supportive manager, at the end of his alternative service his former employer, the Great Western Railway, re-employed him despite the fact that he, unlike men in the military, had no right to reinstatement.[5] Also, he was allowed to make up the missing payments towards his pension. A little later his younger brother, Stewart, also a railway employee, claimed conscience but was exempted because of his job.

This history, or rather this version of a part of my familial history, might suggest a tension between militarism and pacifism. One of the aims of this text has been to reflect this through the presentation of different dichotomous narratives about the CO (and the soldier along with other women and men), thus maintaining a sense of provisionality. Or, to put it another way, returning to the idea of the CO/soldier binary, in this text both the military man and the objector are represented as heroes as well as cowards, patriots as well as traitors . . . manly as well as unmen. Consequently (for me) autobiographical stories are weaved throughout *Telling Tales About Men*.

Notes

1 Semi-structured interviews were conducted with Graham Bibbings on 16 June 2002 and 12 July 2005, and with Suzanne Bibbings 12 July 2005.

2 During this conflict such civil work, along with industrial labour and military service became subject to compulsion and this applied to (some) women as well as men. However, there was no provision for conscientious objection in the context of civil defence work or industrial conscription. See further Lois Bibbings, 'State reaction to conscientious objection', in Ian Loveland (ed.), *The Frontiers of Criminality* (London: Sweet and Maxwell, 1995), pp. 73–5. On female objectors during this conflict see Hazel Nicholson, 'A disputed identity: women conscientious objectors in the Second World War', *Twentieth Century British History* 18:4 (2007), 409–28.

3 Conscientious objectors were accorded recognition under National Service (s.173(2) National Service Act 1948). The 1948 Act, which took effect from 1 January 1949, fixed the period of National Service for young men to eighteen months with four years in the reserves. In 1950, in response to the war in Korea, the term was altered to two years' service, with three and a half years in the reserves. The call-up finally ended on 31 December 1960 and the very last National Servicemen left the army in 1963. It seems that for most young men service was viewed as 'a fact of life' and accepted, although a small number objected – for example, see further: Trevor Royle, *The Best Years of Their Lives: The National Service Experience 1945–63* (London: Michael Joseph, 1986), p. 24; Bryan Stanley Johnson (ed.), *All Bull: The National Servicemen* (London: Quartet, 1973), p. 15.

4 Precisely why he 'served' twenty months (assuming this period is correct) is now unclear but it may have had something to do with the change of the periods of service in 1950 or may have reflected difficulties in securing re-employment on the railways.

5 See Reinstatement in Civil Employment Act 1944.

Select bibliography

Unpublished sources

Privately owned

Campbell, William (Willie), Letter to his parents, dated November 1915.
Stanton, Harry E., 'Will You March Too? 1916–1919', unpublished
account of a CO's experiences, 2 volumes.

Friends Library, London

Harvey, T. Edmund: Correspondence with COs from 1916–1920, Temp
MSS 835/8/1.
Arnold Rowntree papers, MSS 977/1/2
No-Conscription Fellowship: duplicated papers, 1914–1919, MS VOL
149. (A set of Fellowship publications is also available in the British
Library – 'No-Conscription Fellowship, Miscellaneous publications,
London [1915–1918]'.)
Pelham Committee Papers, in T. Edmund Harvey: Correspondence with
COs from 1916–1920, Temp MSS 835/8/1.
Tait, Fred 'Diary of a Conscientious Objector' (unpublished, 1992), Temp
MSS 907.

Imperial War Museum: Department of Sound Records

Bing, Dorothy, 555/9, Reel 1 ('British civilian pacifist in Croydon and
London, GB, 1914–1945').
Bing, Harold Frederick, 358/11 ('British civilian absolutist conscientious
objector imprisoned in Kingston Barracks, Wormwood Scrubs and
Winchester Prisons, GB, 1916–1919').
Littleboy, Wilfred Ernest, 485/6 ('British civilian absolutist conscientious
objector imprisoned in Warwick Barracks, Wormwood Scrubs and
Dorchester Prisons, GB, 1917–1919').

National Archive, London

Cabinet Papers (CAB).
Central Tribunal Minute Books, Papers and Reports, MH 47/1–3.
Home Office Papers (HO/45).
Kitchener Papers, 30/57.
Local Government Board Circulars, 1914–1919, MH 10/79–84.
Ministry of National Service Papers (NATS).
National Registration and Tribunal Papers, RG.
War Office Papers (WO/32).

Published sources

Government reports

Home Office, 'The Home Office and Conscientious Objectors: A Report Prepared for the Committee of Imperial Defence 1919: Part I, The Brace Committee'.

Home Office, 'The Home Office and Conscientious Objectors: A Report Prepared for the Committee of Imperial Defence 1919: Part II, Conscientious Objectors in Prison'.

Parliament, Report of Select Committee on the Civil Service, 'Employment of Objectors', 1922.

War Office, 'Registration and Recruiting', August 1916.

War Office, 'Statistics of the Military Effort of the British Empire in the Great War 1914–1920', 1922.

Command papers

Report of the Inter-Departmental Committee on Physical Deterioration, Cd. 2175, 1904.

Report of the Commissioners of Prisons and Directors of Convict Prisons, Cd. 6406, 1912.

Earl of Derby, KG, Director-General of Recruiting, *Report on Recruiting*, Cd. 8149, 1916.

Committee on Employment of Conscientious Objectors: Rules, Cds 8627, 8550, 8884, 1917.

Ministry of National Service, *Report Upon the Physical Examination of Men of Military Age by National Service Medical Boards from November 1st, 1917–October 31st, 1918*, Cmd. 504, 1919.

Inquiry Held into the Allegations Made Against the Acting Governor of Wandsworth Prison, Cmd. 131, 1919 (Richardson Report).

General Annual Reports of the British Army for the period from 1 October 1913 to 30 September 1919, Cmd 1193, 1921.

Statutes

Defence of the Realm Act, 1914.
National Registration Act, 1915.
Military Service Act, 1916.
Military Service (No. 2) Act, 1916.
Military Service (Review of Exceptions) Act, 1917.
Military Service Act, 1918.
Military Service (No. 2) Act, 1918.

Cases

R v Lincolnshire Appeal Tribunal; Ex parte Stubbins [1917] 115 Law
Times 513.

Newspapers and periodicals

C.O.'s Hansard
Daily Mail
Daily Sketch
The Friend
John Bull
Punch
The Times
The Tribunal

Articles and books

Adams, Ralph James Q. and Philip P. Poirier, *The Conscription Controversy in Great Britain, 1900–1918* (London: Macmillan, 1987).

Allatini, Rose (published under the pseudonym A.T. Fitzroy), *Despised and Rejected* (London: C.W. Daniel Ltd, 1918; London: The Gay Men's Press, 1988).

Ashworth, Tony, *Trench Warfare 1914–1918: The Live and Let Live System* (London: Macmillan, 1980).

Aubert, Vilhelm, 'Some social functions of legislation', *Acta Sociologica*, 10:1–2 (1966), 98–120.

Babington, Anthony, *For the Sake of Example: Capital Courts-Martial 1914–1920* (London: Leo Cooper in association with Secker & Warburg, 1983).

——, *Shell Shock: A History of the Changing Attitudes to War Neurosis* (London: Leo Cooper, 1997).

Baden-Powell, Robert Stephenson Smyth, *Scouting for Boys: A Handbook for Instruction in Good Citizenship* (London: C. Arthur Pearson, complete edition, revised and illustrated, 1908; reissued as a centenary print London: Scout Association, 2007).

Baker, George, *The Soul of a Skunk: The Autobiography of a Conscientious Objector* (London: Eric Partridge at the Scholartis Press, 1930).

Bell, Julian H. (ed.), *We Did Not Fight: 1914–18 Experiences of War Resisters* (London: Cobden-Saunderson, 1935).

Berger, Peter L. and Thomas Luckmann, *The Social Construction of Reality: A Treatise in the Sociology of Knowledge* (Garden City, NY: Anchor Books, 1966).

Best, Geoffrey, 'Militarism and the Victorian public school', in Brian Simon and Ian Bradley (eds), *The Victorian Public School: Studies in the Development of an Institution: A Symposium* (London: Gill and Macmillan, 1975).

Bet-El, Ilana R., 'Men and Soldiers: British Conscripts, Concepts of Masculinity, and the Great War', in Billie Melman (ed.), *Borderlines: Genders and Identities in War and Peace 1870–1930* (London: Routledge, 1998).

——, *Conscripts: Lost Legions of the Great War* (Stroud: Sutton, 1999).

Bibbings, Lois, 'State reaction to conscientious objection', in Ian Loveland (ed.), *The Frontiers of Criminality* (London: Sweet and Maxwell, 1995).

——, 'Images of manliness: the portrayal of soldiers and conscientious objectors in the Great War', *Social and Legal Studies*, 12:3 (2003), 335–58.

——, 'Conscientious objectors in the Great War: the consequences of rejecting military masculinities', in Paul R. Higate (ed.), *Military Masculinities: Identity and the State* (Westport, CT: Greenwood, 2003).

——, 'Heterosexuality as harm: fitting in', in Paddy Hillyard, Christina Pantazis, Steve Tombs and Dave Gordon (eds), *Beyond Criminology: Taking Harm Seriously* (London: Pluto Press, 2005).

Boulton, David, *Objection Overruled* (London: MacGibbon and Kee, 1967).

Bourke, Joanna, *Dismembering the Male: Men's Bodies, Britain and the Great War* (London: Reaktion, 1996).

Braithwaite, Constance, 'Legal problems of conscientious objection to various compulsions under British law', *Journal of the Friends Historic Society*, 52:1 (1968) 3–18.

Brittain, Vera, *The Rebel Passion: A Short History of Some Pioneer Peacemakers* (London: Allen and Unwin, 1964).

Brock, Peter and Nigel Young, *Pacifism in the Twentieth Century* (Toronto: Toronto University Press, 1999).

Brockway, Archibald Fenner, *Inside the Left: Thirty Years of Platform, Press, Prison and Parliament* (London: Allen and Unwin, 1942; reissued in 1947).

Brown, Heloise, *'The Truest Form of Patriotism' Pacifist Feminism in Britain, 1870–1902* (Manchester: Manchester University Press, 2003).

Buchan, John, *Mr Standfast* (Ware: Wordsworth Classics, 1994; first published London: Hodder & Stoughton, 1919).

Bussey, Gertrude and Margaret Tims, *Pioneers for Peace: Women's International League for Peace and Freedom 1915–1965* (London: WILPF, British Section, 1980).

Butler, Judith, *Gender Trouble: Feminism and the Subversion of Identity* (New York: Routledge, 1990).

Clarke, Ignatius Frederick, *Voices Prophesying War: Future Wars, 1763–3749* (Oxford: Oxford University Press, 2nd edn, 1992; first edition, 1966).

Clarke, Michael J., 'Morbid introspection', in William F. Bynum, Roy Porter and Michael Shepherd (eds), *The Anatomy of Madness; Essays in the History of Psychiatry*, vol. 3, *The Asylum and its Psychiatry* (London: Tavistock Publications, 1988).

Conan Doyle, Arthur, *The Parasite* (London: A. Constable, 1894).

Connell, R.W., *Masculinities* (Cambridge: Polity, 2nd edn, 2005).

Cooper, Sandi E., *Patriotic Pacifism: Waging War on War in Europe, 1815–1914* (Oxford: Oxford University Press, 1991).

Dawson, Graham, *Soldier Heroes: British Adventure, Empire and the Imagining of Masculinities* (London: Routledge, 1994).

Dicey, Albert Venn, 'The conscientious objector', *Nineteenth Century*, 83:492 (1918), 357–73.

Duckers, James Scott, *Handed Over: The Prison Experiences of Mr. J. Scott Duckers, Solicitor of Chancery Lane, Under the Military Service Act, Written by himself. With Foreword by T. Edmund Harvey* (London: C.W. Daniel, 1917).

Ferguson, Niall, *The Pity of War* (London: Allen Lane, 1998).

Friends Service Committee, *The Absolutists' Objection: A Statement and an Appeal to the Conscience of the Nation* (London: Pelican, May 1917).

Fussell, Paul, *The Great War and Modern Memory* (Oxford: Oxford University Press, 25th anniversary edn, 2000; first published 1975).

Garland, David, *Punishment and Welfare: A History of Penal Strategies* (Aldershot: Gower House, 1985).

Gilbert, Martin, *Plough My Own Furrow: The Story of Lord Allen of Hurtwood as Told Through his Writings and Correspondence* (London: Longman, 1965).

Gilbert, Sandra M., 'Soldier's heart: literary men, literary women, and the Great War', *Signs*, 8:3 (1983), 422–50.

——, 'Maleness run riot: the Great War and women's resistance to militarism', *Women's Studies International Forum*, 11:3 (1988), 199–210.

Girard, René, *The Scapegoat*, trans. Yvonne Freccero (London: Athlone, 1986).

Girouard, Mark, *The Return to Camelot: Chivalry and the English Gentleman* (New Haven, CT: Yale University Press, 1981).

Gould, Jenny, 'Women's military services in First World War Britain', in Margaret Randolf Higonnet et al. (eds), *Behind the Lines: Gender and the Two World Wars* (New Haven, CT: Yale University Press, 1987).

Graham, John W., *Conscription and Conscience: A History 1916–1919* (London: George Allen and Unwin, 1971 reprint; first published 1922).

Greenslade, William, *Degeneracy, Culture and the Novel 1880–1940* (Cambridge: Cambridge University Press, 1994).

Gullace, Nicoletta F., 'White feathers and wounded men: female patriotism and the memory of the Great War', *Journal of British Studies*, 36:2 (1997), 178–206.

Hale, M.H., *Volunteer Soldiers* (London: Kegan Paul and Co, 1900).

Hall, Donald E. (ed.), *Muscular Christianity: Embodying the Victorian Age* (Cambridge: Cambridge University Press, 1994).

Haste, Cate, *Keep The Home Fires Burning: Propaganda in the First World War* (London: Allen Lane, 1977).

Hayes, Denis, *Conscription Conflict: The Conflict of Ideas in the Struggle For and Against Military Conscription Between 1901 and 1939* (London: Sheppard Press, 1949).

Hearnshaw, Fossey John Cobb, 'Compulsory military service in England', *Quarterly Review* (April, 1916), 416–37.

Higate, Paul R. (ed.), *Military Masculinities: Identity and the State* (Westport, CT: Greenwood, 2003).

Hoare, Philip, *Wilde's Last Stand: Decadence, Conspiracy and the First World War* (London: Duckworth, 1997).

Hobhouse, Stephen, 'The silence system in British prisons', *Friends Quarterly Examiner*, 52 (July 1918), 249–63.

——, and Archibald Fenner Brockway (eds), *English Prisons To-Day: The Report of the Prison System Committee* (London: Longmans, 1922).

Hynes, Samuel, *A War Imagined: The First World War and English Culture* (London: Pimlico, 1922).

Jackson, Holbrook, *The 1890s* (London: Cresset Library, 1988; first published 1913).

James, Stanley Bloomfield, *The Men Who Dared: The Story of an Adventure* (London: C.W. Daniel, 1917).

Jenkins, Keith, 'A postmodern reply to Perez Zagorin', *History and Theory* 39:2 (2000), 181–200.

Kamester, Margaret and Jo Vellacott (ed.), *Militarism Versus Feminism: Writings on Women and War* (London: Virago, 1987).

Kennedy, Thomas C., 'Public opinion and the conscientious objector, 1915–1919', *The Journal of British Studies*, 12:2 (1973), 105–19.

——, *The Hound of Conscience: A History of the No-Conscription Fellowship* (Fayetteville: University of Arkansas Press, 1981).

Leed, Eric J., *No Man's Land: Combat and Identity in World War I* (Cambridge: Cambridge University Press, 1979).

Leese, Peter, *Shell Shock: Traumatic Neurosis and the British Soldiers of the First World War* (Basingstoke: Palgrave, 2002).

Liddington, Jill, *The Long Road to Greenham: Feminism and Anti-Militarism in Britain since 1820* (London: Virago, 1989).

Macaulay, Rose, *Non-Combatants and Others* (London: Methuen, 1986; originally published London: Hodder and Stoughton, 1916).

MacDonald, Robert H., 'Reproducing the middle-class boy: from purity to patriotism in the boy's magazines, 1892–1914', *Journal of Contemporary History*, 24:3 (1989), 519–39.

Machen, Arthur, *The Angel of Mons: the Bowmen and Other Legends of the War* (London: Simpkin, Marshall and Co., 1915).

Mangan, James Antony, '"Muscular, militaristic and manly": the British middle-class hero as moral messenger', *International Journal of the History of Sport*, 13:1 (1996), 28–47.

Marwick, Arthur, *Clifford Allen: The Open Conspirator* (London: Oliver and Boyd, 1964).

Millman, Brock, *Managing Domestic Dissent in First World War Britain* (London: Frank Cass, 2000).

Mitchell, David John, *Women on the Warpath: The Story of the Women of the First World War* (London: Jonathan Cape, 1966).

Moorehead, Caroline, *Troublesome People: Enemies of War: 1916–1986* (London: Hamilton, 1987).

Morgan, David, 'Theatre of war: combat, the military and maculinities', in Harry Brod and Michael Kaufman (eds), *Theorising Masculinities* (Thousand Oaks, CA: Sage, 1994).

Nevinson, Henry Wood, 'The conscientious objector', *Atlantic Monthly*, 103:695 (November 1916), 686–94.

No-Conscription Fellowship, *The No-Conscription Fellowship: A Souvenir of its Work During the Years 1914–1919* (London: No-Conscription Fellowship, 1920).

Nordau, Max, *Degeneration* (Lincoln, NE: University of Nebraska Press, 1993; this translation originally published 1895).

Oldfield, Sybil, *Women Against the Iron Fist: Alternatives to Militarism 1900–1989* (Oxford: Basil Blackwell, 1989).

Osborne, John Morton, *The Voluntary Recruiting Movement in Britain, 1914–1916* (New York: Garland, 1982).

Pearce, Cyril, *Comrades in Conscience: The Story of an English Community's Opposition to the Great War* (London: Francis Boutle, 2001).

Playne, Caroline, *Britain Holds On, 1917–1918* (London: George Allen & Unwin, 1933).

Price, Theodore, *Crucifiers and Crucified* (Alvechurch: The Author, 1917).

Putkowski, Julian and Julian Sykes, *Shot at Dawn* (Barnsley: Wharncliffe, 1989).

Rae, John, *Conscience and Politics: The British Government and the Conscientious Objector to Military Service 1916–1919* (London: Oxford University Press, 1970).

Reader, William Joseph, *'At Duty's Call': A Study in Obsolete Patriotism* (Manchester: Manchester University Press, 1988).

Robbins, Keith, *The Abolition of War: The 'Peace Movement' in Britain, 1914–1919* (Cardiff: University of Wales Press, 1976).

Robert, Krisztina, 'Gender, class and patriotism: women's paramilitary units in First World War Britain', *International History Review*, 19 (1997), 52–65.

Roberts, David, *Minds at War: The Poetry and Experience of the First World War* (Burgess Hill: Saxon, 1996).

Roper, Michael, 'Re-remembering the soldier hero: the psychic and social construction of memory in personal narratives of the Great War', *History Workshop Journal*, 50:2 (2000), 181–204.

—— and John Tosh, *Manful Assertions: Masculinities in Britain since 1800* (London: Routledge, 1991).

Rosenthal, Michael, 'Knights and retainers: the earliest version of Baden-Powell's Boy Scout scheme', *Journal of Contemporary History*, 15:4 (1980), 603–17, 607–9.

——, *The Character Factory: Baden-Powell and the Origins of the Boy Scout Movement* (London: Collins, 1986).

Rowbotham, Sheila, *Friends of Alice Wheeldon* (London: Pluto, 1986).

Shaw, George Bernard, 'Conscientious objection versus general strike', in *Everybody's Political What's What?* (London: Constable, 2nd edn, 1945).

Shee, George Richard Francis, *The Briton's First Duty: The Case For Conscription* (London: Grant Richards, 1901).

——, 'The deterioration of the national physique', *The Nineteenth Century and After*, 53 (1903), 797–805.

Shephard, Ben, *A War of Nerves: Soldiers and Psychiatrists in the Twentieth Century* (London: Pimlico, 2002).

Showalter, Elaine, *The Female Malady: Women, Madness and English Culture, 1830–1980* (London: Virago, 1987).

Sinfield, Alan, *The Wilde Century: Effeminacy, Oscar Wilde and the Queer Moment* (London: Cassell, 1994).

Smith, Janet A., *John Buchan* (London: Rupert Hart-Davis, 1965).

Snowden, Philip, *British Prussianism: The Scandal of the Tribunals* (Manchester: National Labour Press, 1916).

Soloway, Richard, 'Counting the degenerates: the statistics of race deterioration in Edwardian England', *Journal of Contemporary History*, 17:1 (1982), 137–64.

Springhall, John, 'The Boy Scouts, class, and militarism in relation to British youth movements, 1908–1930', *International Review of Social History*, 16:1 (1971), 125–58.

Stepan, Nancy, 'Biology and degeneration: races and proper places', in J. Edward Chamberlain and Sander L. Gilman (eds), *Degeneration: the Dark Side of Progress* (New York: Columbia University Press, 1985).

Tate, Trudi, *Women, Men and the Great War: An Anthology of Stories* (Manchester: Manchester University Press, 1995).

Tatham, Meaburn and James Edward Miles, *The Friends Ambulance Unit 1914–1919* (London: Swarthmore Press, 1920).

Terraine, John, *The Smoke and the Fire: Myths and Anti-Myths of War, 1861–1945* (London: Sidgwick & Jackson, 1980).

Tosh, John, 'What should historians do with manliness? Reflections on nineteenth-century Britain', *History Workshop Journal*, 38:1 (1994), 179–202.

Tylee, Claire M., *The Great War and Women's Consciousness: Images of Militarism and Womenhood in Women's Writings, 1914–64* (London: Macmillan, 1990).

Vance, Norman, *The Sinews of the Spirit: The Ideal of Christian Manliness in Victorian Literature and Religious Thought* (Cambridge: Cambridge University Press, 1985).

Veitch, Colin, '"Play up! Play up! And win the War!" Football, the nation and the First World War 1914–15', *Journal of Contemporary History*, 20:3 (1985), 363–78.

Vellacott, Jo, 'Women and War in England: The case of Catherine E. Marshall and World War I', *Peace and Change*, 4:3 (1977), 13–17.

Weller, Ken, *'Don't be a Soldier!': The Radical Anti-War Movement in North London, 1914–1918* (London: Journeyman Press, 1985).

Whishaw, Frederick J., *The Degenerate* (London: Everett & Co., 1909).

White, Hayden, *Metahistory: The Historical Imagination in Nineteenth-Century Europe* (Baltimore, MD: Johns Hopkins University Press, 1973).

Wilkinson, Glenn R., '"The Blessings of War": The depiction of military force in Edwardian newspapers', *Journal of Contemporary History*, 33:1 (1998), 97–115.

Wilkinson, Paul, 'English youth movements, 1908–30', *Journal of Contemporary History*, 4:2 (1969), 3–23.

Williams, Basil, *Raising and Training the New Armies* (London: Constable, 1918).

Wilson, Albert, *Unfinished Man: A Scientific Analysis of the Psychopath or Human Degenerate* (London: Greening & Co, 1910).

Wiltshire, Anne, *Most Dangerous Women: Feminist Peace Campaigners of the Great War* (London: Pandora, 1985).

Winter, Jay Murray, 'Military unfitness and civilian health in Britain during the First World War', *Journal of Contemporary History*, 15: 2 (1980), 211–44.

Young, James E., 'Towards a received history of the Holocaust', *History and Theory*, 36:4 (1997), 21–43.

Index

Note: page numbers in *italic* refer to illustrations